Jews and Christians?

Tobias Nicklas

Jews and Christians?

Second Century 'Christian' Perspectives
on the 'Parting of the Ways'

(Annual Deichmann Lectures 2013)

Mohr Siebeck

Tobias Nicklas, Dr. theol., born 1967, is Professor of New Testament at the University of Regensburg, Germany. In addition, he is research associate at the departments of New Testament Studies at the Universities of the Free State, Bloemfontein, and Pretoria, both South Africa.

ISBN 978-3-16-153268-9

Die Deutsche Nationalbibliothek lists this publication in the Deutsche Nationalbibliographie; detailed bibligraphic data is available in the Internet at *http://dnb.dnb.de*.

The book was typeset and printed by Gulde-Druck in Tübingen on non-aging paper and bound by Buchbinderei Nädele in Nehren.

Printed in Germany.

Preface

This book finds its background in the 2013 *Deichmann Lectures* which took place as part of the *Deichmann Programme for Jewish and Christian Literature of the Hellenistic Era* on 9th–10th April 2013 at Ben Gurion University, Beersheva, Israel. Based on a series of lectures, this book is not a comprehensive treatment of sources and questions relevant to the problem of "Jewish – Christian" relations in antiquity. Instead, it offers four essays that aim to nuance our perspective on what we usually call "Parting of the Ways". In each of these essays I have focused upon specific ancient sources that complicate and thus expand and enrich our understanding of the web of relationships at play here. Due to limits of time (and, certainly, also due to the limits of my own expertise) I concentrated on a few second century "Christian" sources, but hope that even this limited perspective shows how our usual categories "Jewish", "Christian" (and "pagan") had different meaning at different places, different historical situations, and even for a single person in different contexts of his or her life.

I am especially grateful to the founder and benefactor of the above lecture series, Dr. Heinz-Horst Deichmann, who, unfortunately, because of health reasons could not participate personally; at the same time I want to say my thanks to Heinrich, Susanne and Samuel Deichmann not only for their great interest in my work, but also for a series of open, intense and good talks. A warm "thank you" goes to Roland Deines (and his amiable family) for the invitation to and organisation of this event (plus his helpful criticism of some of my ideas). Among the colleagues in Beersheva I want to mention Cana Werman and her team who helped a lot to make my stay unforgettable; in addition, I am especially grateful for the astute and helpful questions coming from Michal Bar Asher Siegal, Rivka Nir and the many students and guests present at my lectures. The language of the following manuscript has been corrected by Jeremy Barrier without whom my English would have certainly been unintelligible; and, of course, I owe thanks to many critical readers like Jan Bremmer, Harald Buchinger, Andreas Merkt, Michael Sommer and Michael Tilly (with his Tübingen Oberseminar).

Working together with Mohr Siebeck publishers is always a pleasure and a honor – thanks to Henning Ziebritzki and his fantastic team.

I dedicate this book to my family – and especially to my daughter Veronika, who travelled with me to Israel.

Regensburg, April 2014   Tobias Nicklas

Contents

Introduction

If we believe the account presented by Eusebius of Cae-
sarea's *Ecclesiastical History* (*h.e.* 3.36.1), it must have
been in the last years of the Emperor Trajan (53 – august
117 CE) when Ignatius, bishop of the Syrian metropolis
Antioch, had to enter a ship which would bring him as a
captive to Rome, where a martyrdom among wild beasts
awaited him (Ign., *Rom.* 4 and 5.2; Eusebius, *h.e.* 3.36.2–
4).[1] But surprisingly, Ignatius seems to have been less sor-
rowful concerning his own fate than of the communities
he had to leave behind. So he took the opportunity of
making two stops on his way to dictate seven letters
which, in a certain sense, can be seen as his literary testament: letters to the communities of Ephesus, Magnesia,
Tralles and Rome (written in Smyrna) and letters to the
communities of Philadelphia, Smyrna and to his fel-
low-bishop Polycarp (written in the Troas).[2] Especially

---

[1] For a discussion of reasons and historical backgrounds of this
situation see A. BRENT, *Ignatius of Antioch: A Martyr Bishop and
the Origin of Episcopacy* (London – New York: Continuum, 2007)
14–43.

[2] Actually, we know of even more letters written under Ignatius' name. The question concerning whether or not this "middle"
collection of Ignatius' writings (also mentioned by Eusebius, *h.e.*
3.36.50) was really written by the bishop of Antioch himself has
become a matter of dispute again. At least some authors argue that

in his *Letter to the Magnesians*, Ignatius is concerned with a problem which today might seem somewhat strange.[3] He writes:

we have to consider it as later pseudepigrapha (middle of the second century CE?), i. e. writings authored by another person, but under Ignatius' name. For more information see on the one hand R.M. Hübner, Thesen zur Echtheit und Datierung der sieben Briefe des Ignatius von Antiochien, *ZAC* 1 (1997) 44–72 and T. Lechner, *Ignatius adversus Valentinanos? Chronologische und theologiegeschichtliche Studien zu den Briefen des Ignatius* (VigChr.S 47; Leiden – Boston: Brill, 1999) – both voting for the pseudonymity of the letters – and on the other hand A. Lindemann, Eine Antwort auf die ,Thesen zur Echtheit und Datierung der sieben Briefe des Ignatius von Antiochien', *ZAC* 1 (1997) 185–94; G. Schöllgen, Die Ignatianen als pseudepigraphisches Briefcorpus. Anmerkungen zu den Thesen von Reinhard M. Hübner, *ZAC* 2 (1998) 16–25; M. Edwards, Ignatius and the Second Century: An Answer to R. Hübner, *ZAC* 2 (1998) 214–26, A. Brent, *Ignatius of Antioch*, 95–143 and idem, *Ignatius of Antioch and the Second Sophistic: A Study of Early Christian Transformation of Pagan Culture* (STAC 36; Tübingen: Mohr, 2006) 18–40. While these authors vote for a late date of Ignatius' letters in the middle of the second century, J. Rius-Camps, Indicios de una redacción muy temprana de las cartas auténticas de Ignacio (ca. 70–90 d.C), in: *Studi sul cristianesimo antico e moderno in onore di Maria Grazia Mara* (ed. by M. Simonetti & P. Siniscalco; Aug. 25 ([1995]) 199–214, and idem, *The Four Authentic Letters of Ignatius, the Martyr* (OCA 213; Roma: Pontificium Institutum Orientalium Studiorum, 1980) argues for an extremely early date of at least parts of Ignatius' writings. The question of the exact date of Ignatius' writings, however, is not a primary issue here. I still follow the classical date which is confirmed by the new arguments of P.A. Harland, Christ-Bearers and Fellow-Initiates: Local Cultural Life and Christian Identity in Ignatius' Letters, *JECS* 11 (2003) 481–99, and A. Brent, *Ignatius of Antioch*.

[3] According to W.R. Schoedel, *Die Briefe des Ignatius von Antiochien. Ein Kommentar* (Munich: Chr. Kaiser, 1990) 203, and M. Murray, *Playing a Jewish Game: Gentile Christian Judaizing*

"8 Do not be deceived by strange doctrines or *antiquated myths, since they are worthless. For if we continue to live in accordance with 'Judaism', we admit that we have not received grace. For the most godly prophets lived in accordance with Christ Jesus. This is why they were persecuted*, being inspired as they were by his grace in order that those who are disobedient might be fully convinced that there is one God who revealed himself through Jesus Christ his Son who is his Word that came forth from silence, who in every respect pleased the one who sent him.

9 If then, those who had *lived according to ancient practices* came to the newness of hope, *no longer keeping the Sabbath but living in accordance with the Lord's day*, on which our life also arose through him and his death (which some deny), the mystery though which we came to believe, and because of which we patiently endure, in order that we may be found to be disciples of Jesus Christ, our only teacher, how can we possibly live without him, whom even the prophets who were his disciples in the Spirit, were expecting as their teacher? This is why the one for whom they rightly waited raised them from the dead when he came.

10 Therefore let us not be unaware of his goodness. For if he were to imitate the way we act, we are lost. Therefore, having become his disciples, *let us learn to live in accordance with 'Christianity'*. For whoever is called by any other name than this one does not belong to God. *Throw out, therefore, the bad yeast, which has become stale and sour, and reach for the new*

---

in the First and Second Centuries CE (Studies in Christianity and Judaism 13; Waterloo, Ont.: Wilfried Laurier, 2004) 84, chapters 8–10 form the core of *Magn*. I will not be able to discuss the question, whether Ignatius was concerned with one, two or even three groups of opponents in his letters. If we assume, however, that at least the groups of opponents in the Letters to the *Magnesians* and *Philadelphians* are very similar, we will be on the safe side. – For an overview of the discussion see P. FOSTER, The Epistles of Ignatius of Antioch, in: *The Writings of the Apostolic Fathers* (ed. by P. Foster; London – New York: Continuum, 2007) 81–108, esp. 89–93.

yeast, which is Jesus Christ. Be salted with him, so that none of
you become rotten, for by your odour you will be convicted. *It
is utterly absurd to profess Jesus Christ and to practice 'Judaism'.
For 'Christianity' did not believe in 'Judaism', but 'Judaism' in
'Christianity', in which every tongue believed and as brought
together with God"* (Ignatius, *Magn.* 8–10, translation Michael
Holmes, 105 f.; my italics).[4]

Let us look a little bit closer into a few details: Ignatius
makes a distinction – obviously there are people in the
Magnesian community of Christ-followers who "still ad-
here to worthless ancient fables" – very probably Ignatius
means the Hebrew Bible (perhaps in its Greek translation) or at least parts of it here –, there are people celebrat-
ing the Sabbath and not the "Day of the Lord" (i. e., Sunday),[5] and who still prefer the ancient "documents" –
again Israel's Scriptures (or parts of them) – to the
"Gospel" (see also *Phil.* 8.2)[6]. Even if it seems like these
people did not want to impose their life-style on every

---

[4] Translations from the Apostolic Fathers follow, where not
marked differently, the collection by M. W. HOLMES (ed.), *The Apostolic Fathers in English* (Grand Rapids, Mich.: Baker, [3]2006).
Quotes from the Greek text from A. LINDEMANN – H. PAULSEN
(ed.s), *Die Apostolischen Väter: Griechisch-deutsche Parallelaus-
gabe* (Tübingen: Mohr, 1992).

[5] The impact of holding the "Day of the Lord" is enforced by the
connection Ignatius makes between Sunday and resurrection – this
is the reason not observing "Sunday" indirectly means that one
does not really believe in Jesus' resurrection nor live according to
"grace" and "salvation". For a more detailed argument see W. R.
SCHOEDEL, *Briefe*, 212–3.

[6] Regarding Ignatius' use of the term "Gospel" see C. E. HILL,
Ignatius, 'the Gospel,' and the Gospels, in *Trajectories through the
New Testament and the Apostolic Fathers* (ed. by A. Gregory &
C. M. Tuckett; Oxford: Oxford University Press, 2005) 267–85.

member of the "Christian communities" in Magnesia (and Philadelphia where the situation was comparable),[7] this was obviously an enormous problem for the bishop of Antioch. Did these people create a schism and had they disassociated themselves from the common eucharist as Ignatius, *Phil.* 3–4, wants us to believe?[8] Or does Ignatius, to the contrary, want to bring different groups of Christ-followers together and unite them under the emerging episcopal hierarchy into "the one body of the Church" (*Smyrn.* 1.2)?[9]

Perhaps it is already apparent that (in my own text) I have tried to avoid terms like "Christian" or "Christianity" until now, and perhaps the reason is already evident. I did this because Ignatius' text shows us that at least for some followers of Jesus Christ in the beginning of the second century it was not totally obvious what it meant to behave as "Christians". Clearly some followers of Christ did not feel like members of a "Christian" community distinct from "the Jews".[10] Though we do not

---

[7] The only exception could have been the observation of the Sabbath. See also O. SKARSAUNE, Evidence for Jewish Believers in Greek and Latin Patristic Literature, in: *Jewish Believers in Jesus* (ed. by O. Skarsaune & R. Hvalvik; Peabody, Mass.: Hendrickson, 2007) 505–67, esp. 506.

[8] So O. SKARSAUNE, Evidence, 506.

[9] I think that a text like the first chapter of Ignatius' letter to the community of *Smyrna* could point to the second possibility: Ignatius speaks about two groups here – Jews and Christians – , but also about their "unshakable faith, having been nailed … to the cross of the Lord Jesus Christ", and in addition, he uses the image of "one body of the church" (translation HOLMES, 121).

[10] I also do not like the term "Judaizers" (at least for a pre-Constantinian period), that is Gentile Christians who live like Jews,

know whether they (still?) attended the service at the
synagogue they seemed to be able to integrate their identities as followers of Christ with, according to Ignatius, a

---

very much, because the use of this term presupposes that a clear
distinction already existed between the categories "Gentile",
"Christian" and "Jewish"; distinctions which obviously for the
groups addressed did not play the decisive role. For a description of
the Magnesian "Judaizers" in such a classical manner, which (unin-
tentionally) shows clearly what kind of mix the word "Judaizers"
creates, see, e. g., S. G. WILSON, *Related Strangers: Jews and Christians 70–170 CE* (Minneapolis: Fortress, 1995) 165: Ignatius "could
refer to earlier generations of Christians who had been closely tied
to Judaism, but it seems to refer to Judaizers of Ignatius's day, that
is, Gentiles, who formerly (and presently) lived like Jews and ex-
pounded Judaism ... Most obviously they would have been former
God-fearers or sympathizers, who had been attached to the synagogue, who had now joined the church, and had brought with them
the predilections of their former existence." – Regarding the question whether the Magnesian "Judaizers" were gentile believers in
Christ or "Jewish Christians" see also M. ZETTERHOLM, *The Formation of Christianity in Antioch: A Social-Scientific Approach to
the Separation Between Judaism and Christianity* (London – New
York: Routledge, 2005) 205: "I suggest that Ignatius in Philadelphia
encountered an ordinary community of Jesus-believing Jews with
some Gentile Jesus-believers cloaked as Jews. ... From Ignatius'
point of view, the uncircumcised Gentile adherent to the Jesus-believing Jewish community interpreted 'Judaism,' since there did
not exist a specific term for 'Jewish Christianity.' ... Even though
Ignatius and those following him, in Antioch as well as in other
places, intended to separate from Judaism, *not every Gentile adherent to the Jesus movement found this to be the only solution.* It is
likely that many Gentiles chose to remain in close connection to a
Jesus-believing Jewish community, as their motivation for having
associated themselves with the Jews in the first place was a pro-
found interest in Judaism. Consequently, they had no intention of
leaving messianic Judaism for a Gentile religion stripped of almost
every Jewish influence ..."

life in "Jewish ways". This group of Christ-followers seems to have been strong enough to make Ignatius feel so distressed that he insisted on a strict distinction between "Jews" and "Christians": perhaps one could even go so far as to say that Ignatius "created" a distinction (which seemingly did not exist for at least some members of the Magnesian community):[11] for the first time in ancient Greek literature Ignatius uses the Greek term *Christianismos* (Χριστιανισμός; see also *Rom.* 10.3 and *Phil.* 6.1).[12] This term may first remind us of the word *Hellenismos*, that is, the "Greek way" of life, which after the wars of Alexander the Great had gradually been established all over the Eastern Mediterranean region and which even in Israel began to play a heavily debated role.[13] Ignatius, however, uses it as a counterpart to the much rarer word *Ioudaismos* (see also *Phil.* 6.1). For him, *Christianismos* and *Ioudaismos* are two different ways of

[11] For a comparable idea in relation to Justin Martyr see D. BO-YARIN, *Border Lines: The Partition of Judaeo-Christianity* (Philadelphia: University of Pennsylvania, 2007) 37–73.

[12] In the New Testament we have only two texts where at least the adjective Χριστιανός is used: the book of Acts (11.26 and 26.28) and 1 Peter (4.16), both writings probably from the end of the 1st century CE.

[13] See, for example, the witness of the books of 1–2 Maccabees. Especially 2 Macc is concerned with the distinction between Jewish and Greek way of life. On the development of the term "Judaism" see also Sh. COHEN, *The Beginning of Jewishness: Boundaries, Varieties, Uncertainties* (Berkeley – London: University of California Press, 1999). – For the overall question of the relation between "Judaism" and "Hellenism" in antiquity still see the magisterial volume by M. HENGEL, *Judentum und Hellenismus* (WUNT 10; Tübingen: Mohr, ³1988).

life which in no way may be intermingled.[14] According to Ignatius, *Christianismos* can be distinguished from *Ioudaismos* in several ways. It is characterized by a different use of scripture – in Ignatius' eyes the only proper use of scripture. According to Ignatius, this can be seen by the fact that already the "most godly prophets" had not only been living "according to Jesus Christ" (*Magn.* 8.2), but had announced him (*Phil.* 9.2) and were persecuted because of him (*Magn.* 8.2). For Ignatius, *Christianismos* also has to do with a different way of life, which shows that a person is already living "in grace" (*Magn.* 8.1), while everybody who still follows the "Jewish way of life", according to Ignatius, does not have this grace. Further, it is characterized by a new identity of being a disciple of Jesus Christ (*Magn* 9.1; 10.1),[15] that involves perse-

---

[14] This is, in comparison to Paul, an important step. W.R. SCHOEDEL, *Briefe*, 204–5 writes: "Es sollte in diesem Zusammenhang beachtet werden, daß Ignatius vom Judentum spricht, wo Paulus vom Gesetz gesprochen hätte. Deshalb stellt Ignatius Gnade und Judentum einander gegenüber und nicht, wie Paulus, Gnade und Gesetz (vgl. Röm 6,14)." – Regarding the relation of Ignatius' and Paul's letters see A. LINDEMANN, *Paulus im ältesten Christentum: Das Bild des Apostels und die Rezeption der paulinischen Theologie in der frühchristlichen Literatur bis Marcion* (BHTh 58; Tübingen: Mohr, 1979), P. FOSTER, The Epistles of Ignatius of Antioch and the Writings that later formed the New Testament, in: *The Reception of the New Testament in the Apostolic Fathers* (ed. by A. Gregory & C.M. Tuckett; Oxford: Oxford University Press, 2005) 159–86, and, more specific, D.M. REIS, Following in Paul's Footsteps: Mimesis and Power in Ignatius of Antioch, in: *Trajectories through the New Testament and the Apostolic Fathers* (ed. by A. Gregory & C.M. Tuckett; Oxford: Oxford University Press, 2005) 288–305.

[15] Already Paul defined the new identity of "followers of Christ"

cution which the prophets were already experiencing (*Magn.* 8.2). And if Ignatius finally calls Christ "the *only* teacher" (*Magn.* 9.1), it is very probable that he also wants to say that neither Moses nor any Jewish scribe of his time are appropriate teachers for followers of Christ.[16] In *Magn.* 10.3 Ignatius concludes that the "Jewish way of life" must be inferior to the "Christian one" because *Ioudaismos* came to believe in *Christianismos* and not vice versa (*Magn.* 10.3).[17] This is certainly an argument with two sides: on the one hand Ignatius says that "Christianity" has replaced "Judaism" in the history of salvation, and on the other hand, he at least indirectly admits that "Judaism" *had* an important place in the history of salvation, but lost it to "Christianity"[18] – an admission that not all authors were willing to concede.

It is very important to recognize that Ignatius' voice is only one of many voices mirroring a new kind of relation between groups of followers of Jesus Christ, who gradually not only became known but started to understand themselves as "Christians", and the different Jewish

---

as an "identity-in-relation"; one of the most important "identity markers" here is living "in Christ". For further discussion see T. NICKLAS – H. SCHLÖGEL, Mission to the Gentiles, Construction of Christian Identity and its Relation to Ethics according to Paul, in: *The Dynamic Relationship between Mission and Ethics in Early Christianity* (ed. by K. Kok, T. Nicklas, D. Roth & C.M. Hays; WUNT II 364; Tübingen: Mohr, 2014) .

[16] For a different, also "Christian" attitude see for example Matt 23.3.

[17] W.R. SCHOEDEL, *Briefe*, 216 formulates even sharper: "Das Schlußargument ist historischer Art: das Judentum unterlag dem Christentum, nicht umgekehrt."

[18] See also W.R. SCHOEDEL, *Briefe*, 216.

groups who tried to re-define their identities after the trauma of the destruction of the Second Temple in the year 70 CE. His voice is only one voice speaking from one perspective – the perspective of a member of the developing hierarchy among the so-called "proto-orthodox" Christian groups in Syria and Asia Minor.[19] Already this voice, however, shows us that there must have been different voices, followers of Christ thinking, behaving and living in other ways, people whose own voices are lost to us today, but who are at least mirrored in Ignatius' polemics.

Already in Ignatius' text some of the main issues regarding second-century Jewish-Christian relations are at stake: we hear about a "Christian" identity which is defined over against "Judaism", we hear about the relation between the scriptures of Israel, its prophets and the new "way of life", we read about Jesus Christ who, according to the "Christians", is of decisive relevance for salvation. Ignatius' letter also shows us that at least for him something had happened which we could call a "Parting of the Ways": for him Jews and Christians had begun to be two different groups going on separate ways which should not be intermingled any more.

I am consciously saying "for him" because, even if he was a bishop, he did not represent "the" Church speaking about "the" Jews. But if we want to understand at least a bit better what really happened we should first discuss a few models of thinking:

---

[19] For more information see A. BRENT, *Ignatius.*

Where Judaism and Christianity are understood as two more or less clearly fixed entities one can try to understand their relation with the help of a very simple model: a tree with two branches which from a certain moment grew into two different directions. I must confess that I grew up with this model, and I must confess that I was taught that only one of these two branches still carries green leaves. If one wants to use this model one just has to look out for the concrete point in history where the two branches started to grow into two different directions. Was it already Jesus who separated himself from "the Jews"? There are at least a few passages in the Gospel of John which could make us think this way (see, e. g., John 8:44). Or did Paul with his mission of "pagans"[20] make the decisive step? Or do we have to wait longer – until after 70 CE, when the Jerusalem Temple was destroyed, and different Jewish groups had to define their identities anew? Or should we still wait for even later times – perhaps the end of the Bar-Kokhba war when Jerusalem was destroyed and developed into a Hellenistic city, Aelia Capitolina, which no Jew was allowed to enter any more?[21]

---

[20] The use of the term "pagan", of course, is an anachronism. For an interesting overview of the development of this term in late antiquity see P. Brown, *Through the Eye of a Needle. Wealth, the Fall of Rome, and the Making of Christianity in the West, 350–550 AD* (Princeton, NJ: Princeton University Press, 2012) 102.

[21] For the discussion of different models see also M. Goodman, Modelling the 'Parting of the Ways', in *The Ways That Never Parted: Jews and Christians in Late Antiquity and the Early Middle Ages* (ed. by A. H. Becker & A. Yoshiko Reed; Minneapolis: Fortress, 2007) 119–30.

But reality has been (and, I am sure, it still is) much more complex than such a model would suggest. Both early Judaism (even after 70 CE) and ancient Christianity must have been very complex phenomena – one is even inclined to speak about "Judaisms" and "Christianities".[22] This can already be seen by our first reading of Ignatius' writings. There is more than one group of Christ-followers. That is why we need different models for our understanding of the development. Has there been a "Fork in the Road" or do we have to describe the "Parting of the Ways" between Jews and Christians as a "Multi-Lane Highway", as Adele Reinhartz asked a few years ago?[23]

Let us first concentrate on one part of the image, "Christianity": a classical model for understanding the development of Christianity would, again, be the model of a tree – a tree with the "trunk" of orthodoxy rooting deeply in the Jesus movement itself and a few branches falling apart from this tree – we could call them "heterodoxies" or "heretics". In such an image there is no space for different religious denominations trying to under-

---

[22] See, for example, the title of the well-known volume J. NEUSNER – W.S. GREEN – E.S. FRERICHS (ed.s), *Judaisms and their Messiahs at the Turn of the Christian Era* (Cambridge et al.: Cambridge University Press, ⁴1996 [1987]).

[23] A. REINHARTZ, A Fork in the Road or a Multi-Lane Highway? New Perspectives on the »Parting of the Ways« Between Judaism and Christianity, in *The Changing Face of Judaism, Christianity, and Other Greco-Roman Religions in Antiquity* (ed. by I.H. Henderson & G.S. Oegema; JSHRZ.Studien 2; Gütersloh: Gütersloher, 2006) 280–95. In this article Reinhartz discusses several models of how to understand Jewish-Christian relations in antiquity.

stand each other and trying to find to each other in their different ways of searching for truth.

Around 80 years ago, Walter Bauer in his influential book *Orthodoxy and Heresy in Earliest Christianity* more or less turned this idea on its head.[24] According to Bauer, there has been no real "orthodoxy" before the Constantinian era of the fourth century. And, even more, at least in many cases, "heretics" came first, and the "orthodox" had to define themselves, their beliefs and their identity against the challenges of "heresy". While Bauer's ideas marked an important development, I would prefer to go a few steps further. Bart Ehrman in his much discussed book *Lost Christianities* uses the drastic metaphor of a battle (or a series of battles) between different Christian groups, a battle, which has been won by "proto-orthodox Christian circles" against many other groups which were branded as "heretics".[25] However, I prefer the somewhat more irenic image of a horse-race used by Philip Rousseau.[26] In his recent volume "The Gnostics: Myth, Ritual, and Diversity in Early Christianity" David Brakke describes this idea in the following way:

"Following his [= Rousseau's] lead, we can think of the varieties-of-early-Christianity model as something like a horse race. In this model, we cannot really see the starting gate, but around

---

[24] German Original: W. Bauer, *Rechtgläubigkeit und Ketzerei im ältesten Christentum* (BHTh 10; Tübingen: Mohr, 1964).

[25] B.D. Ehrman, *Lost Christianities: The Battles for Scripture and the Faiths We Never Knew* (Oxford: Oxford University Press, 2005).

[26] P. Rousseau, *Pachomius: The Making of a Community in Fourth-Century Egypt* (Berkeley: University of California, 1985) 19.

the year 100 CE, numerous independent Christian communities come into view, none with a fully convincing claim to exclusive authority as "true Christianity." They jostle for position and argue with one another about which of them are the true Christians. In hindsight we can identify the 'horse' that will emerge as the dominant orthodoxy by the end of the third century: it is represented by Irenaeus and other early Christians such as Justin Martyr, Clement of Alexandria, Origen, Hippolytus of Rome, Tertullian (before he 'became a Montanist'), and others. We call this form of Christianity 'proto-orthodoxy,' because there is not yet an orthodoxy, but it will grow into it. We watch proto-orthodoxy as it competes with and overcomes its rivals, setting itself up as the horse that Constantine will ride, so to speak."[27]

Brakke, however, goes even further, and immediately destructs parts of this image. I would like to mention only his main point:

"[A]ny conception of the 'varieties of early Christianity' that places a single proto-orthodoxy within a plurality of 'other groups' retains one key aspect of the Irenaean view: that proto-orthodoxy was single and consistent wherever it was found, while other forms of Christianity were multiple and diverse. But, as we shall see, in several important ways such proto-orthodox teachers as Justin Martyr and Clement of Alexandria had much more in common with, say, Valentinus than they did with bishop Irenaeus. There was no single and uniform proto-orthodoxy, but multiple modes of piety, authority, and theology that later orthodoxy represents as its forerunners."[28]

If we consider the fact that Judaism even after the destruction of the Second Temple must have been a compa-

---

[27] D. BRAKKE, *The Gnostics: Myth, Ritual, and Diversity in Early Christianity* (Cambridge, Mass. – London: Harvard University Press, 2010) 7.

[28] D. BRAKKE, *Gnostics*, 10.

rably complex phenomenon it becomes clear why there is no simple answer for the questions when, where, why and how exactly the "parting of the ways" between "Jews" and "Christians" took its decisive starting point and when, where, why and how it was fixed. The images used above want to teach us that the story we should develop must be much more complex than just Ignatius' story and that it should be telling about different people at different places, behaving differently at different occasions, in different contexts and even in different situations of their own lives. However, this does not mean that from quite early times there were outsiders' perspectives which (partly because of very practical reasons) wanted to identify "Christians" as "Christians" and were surely not interested in the differentiated inner dynamics of a complicated network of groups. A simple look into Tacitus' *Annals* 15.44.4 where we read about the persecution of "Christians" under Nero after the burning of Rome 64 CE shows that Roman administration already at a very early stage seems to have been able to identify "Christians"[29] – of course, nobody knows which different groups of "Christians" had to suffer and how far these identifications went wrong. A comparable situation can be seen in Pliny the Younger's letters to Emperor Trajan (*ep.* 10.96–97) written between 109 and 113 CE when Pliny, as an Imperial legate of the Roman province Bithynia, had been confronted with rumours regarding the "Christians" of this region. We cannot go into further

---

[29] For a broader discussion of the issue see P. LAMPE, *From Paul to Valentinus: Christians at Rome in the First Two Centuries* (London: Continuum, 2003) 82–4.

detail here – it should just be clear: our story of the past
has not only to do with different contexts and situations,
but with different perspectives (which, of course, again
are related to contexts and situations). In the following
chapters, I do not want to deal with the phenomenon of
second-century Jewish-Christian relations as a whole.
However, the chapters will deal with one group of perspectives: the perspectives of writings we would call
"Christian" in our day. We will see that even this group of
perspectives is extremely complex – we will be able to discuss only parts of the evidence. In addition, we should
always bear in mind that even the most complex story is
just an image of the past – our image – which has to do
with the sources we use and the ones we cannot use any
more because they have been lost; which has to do with
our methods and questions and which therefore also has
to do with ourselves who ask these questions and tell this
story as historians of the 21st century. All of this means
that we will have to concentrate on a few examples and on
a few questions, while acknowledging there are many
more which would make sense. Here are a few of the
questions I will ask:

1. Which images of "Jews" and "Judaism" do we find in
(mainly) second century "Christian" writings? What do
they tell us about "Jewish-Christian" relations in the
contexts they were written for?

2. How do second-century Christian writings deal
with the relationship between God and Israel? How do
these texts deal with the fact that Christians and Jews ad-
here to the same God?

3. What do second-century "Christian" writings tell us about "Christian" uses of the Hebrew Bible, the "Old Testament" respectively the "Scriptures of Israel"?

4. And, related to question 3, what is the role of the Torah according to second-century "Christian" writings?

This, however, will lead us to another, deeper question:

Is it really adequate to speak about a "parting of the ways" or does this image – again an image! – cause a few of the misunderstandings which are a burden for Jewish-Christian relations even until today?

Chapter 1:

Images of the Chosen People: "The Jews" in Second Century "Christian" Writings

Some time in the winter of 1886/87 at an ancient cemetery in the Upper Egyptian town of Panopolis / Akhmim, a 6th or 7th century codex was found.[1] It has been speculated, whether it possibly came from a monk's grave,[2] but due to the lack of a reliable excavation diary we cannot be sure. This codex, now labelled as Papyrus Cairensis 10759, is usually called the "Akhmim-Codex". It contains fragments of the Greek version of the early Jewish book of *1 Enoch*, of the *Martyrdom of Julian Anazarbus* and of two (pseudo)-Petrine apocrypha.[3] The first of

---

[1] For more information see T. J. KRAUS – T. NICKLAS (ed.s), *Das Petrusevangelium und die Petrusapokalypse: Die griechischen Fragmente mit deutscher und englischer Übersetzung* (GCS Neue Folge 11; Neutestamentliche Apokryphen 1; Berlin – New York, De Gruyter, 2004) 25–31. 101–3, and P. FOSTER, The Discovery and Initial Reaction to the So-Called Gospel of Peter, in *Das Evangelium nach Petrus: Text, Kontexte, Intertexte* (ed. by T. J. Kraus & T. Nicklas; TU 158; Berlin – New York: De Gruyter, 2007) 9–30, esp. 9–14.

[2] Until today this information is given in many introductions to the *Gospel of Peter*. It, however, relies on mere speculation.

[3] I have several times argued that these two Petrine apocrypha are literary related or perhaps even part of the same text. This question is, however, not of great importance for the moment. For further information see T. NICKLAS, Das apokryphe *Petrusevangeli-*

these two apocryphal texts gives an account of the passion and resurrection of Jesus, who is mainly called "the
Lord" here. In the last remaining verse of the text it becomes clear that the whole story claims to be told by the
apostle Peter himself. That's why the text is usually identified with the apocryphal *Gospel of Peter* which was
condemned by the late second-century Antiochian bishop Serapion (cf. Eusebius, *h.e.* 6.12.1–6) because of its use
by the so-called "docetists", a group of people who
thought that Christ only seemingly had taken on a human body.[4] The question whether the passion account of
the *Gospel of Peter* is "docetic" or not should not bother
us too much here – I personally think that the text, to the
contrary, wants to depict Jesus "the Lord" as an ideal
martyr.[5] The *Gospel of Peter*, a text likely dating back to

---

um: Stand und Perspektiven der Erforschung, in *Greeks, Jews, and
Christians. Historical, Religious and Phililogcal Studies in Honor of
Jesús Peláez del Rosal* (ed. by L. Roig Lanzillotta & I. Muñoz Gal-
larte ; Estudios de FilolNT 10; Cordoba: Almendro, 2013) 337–70.

[4] Regarding Serapion's witness and its transmission in Eusebius'
Ecclesiastical History, see É. JUNOD, Eusèbe de Césarée, Sérapion
d'Antioche et l' *Évangile de Pierre, RSLR* 24 (1988) 3–16; for a
short discussion of the text see T.J. KRAUS – T. NICKLAS (ed.s),
Petrusevangelium, 12–16. – For a much more detailed discussion of
the term "docetists" plus an overview of different groups see
N. BROX, 'Doketismus' – Eine Problemanzeige, in *Zeitschrift für
Kirchengeschichte* 95 (1984) 301–14.

[5] For a detailed argument see T. NICKLAS, Die Leiblichkeit der
Gepeinigten: Das *Evangelium nach Petrus* und frühchristliche
Märtyrerakten, in *Martyrdom and Persecution in Late Antique
Christianity: Festschrift Boudewijn Dehandschutter* (ed. by J. Lee-
mans; BETL 241; Leuven: Peeters, 2010) 195–219. – For a different
opinion about the text's Christology see M. MYLLYKOSKI, Die
Kraft des Herrn: Erwägungen zur Christologie des Petrusevan-

the middle of the second century, however, depicts his martyrdom – the passion of Jesus – in a different way than what we find in the New Testament accounts:

1. According to *GosPet* 1–5, it is not Pilate, but Herod, who is the judge who decides Jesus' fate. This does by no means mean that Pilate is depicted in a positive manner here,[6] but it shifts the responsibility for Jesus' death clearly to the Jewish side. The text is not interested in questions of historical probabilities – or better: possibilities. Interestingly, the *Gospel of Peter* is not alone in this idea. While in the New Testament Herod (Antipas), the tetrarch of Galilee, appears only in the Lukan passion playing a minor role (see Luke 23.6–12), several second- and third century Christian writings depict him as Jesus' judge.[7]

2. Nowhere in the extant of the *Gospel of Peter* do we get the idea that the things told here happened at concrete places in Israel or Jerusalem. While, for example, the Gospel of John tells us about places like the Kidron valley

---

geliums, in: *Das Evangelium nach Petrus: Text, Kontexte, Intertexte* (ed. by T. J. Kraus & T. Nicklas; TU 158; Berlin – New York: de Gruyter, 2007) 301–25.

[6] For a discussion of the *GosPet's* description of Pontius Pilate see H. OMERZU, Die Pilatusgestalt im Petrusevangelium: Eine erzählanalytische Annäherung, in *Das Evangelium nach Petrus: Text, Kontexte, Intertexte* (ed. by T. J. Kraus & T. Nicklas; TU 158; Berlin – New York: de Gruyter, 2007) 327–47.

[7] The *Ascension of Isaiah*, most likely an early second century apocalypse, for example, speaks about the people of Israel delivering Jesus to "the king" (*AscIsa* 11.17–20). Other texts – mainly from Syria – are even clearer and depict Herod as the person who has given the command to crucify Jesus (see, e. g., the Syrian *Didascalia* 21 or the pseudo-Origenian *Dialogue of Adamantius*).

(John 18.1), the high-priestly palace (John 18.15) or Pilate's *praetorium* (John 18.28) and mentions Jewish customs connected to the celebration of Passover, the *Gospel of Peter* seems to be uninterested in any of these details. Instead, in its V. 60 it speaks about Peter and Andrew going to τὴν θάλασσαν ("the Sea"): one is under the impression that this does not mean the Sea of Galilee, but perhaps the Mediterranean Sea. Of course, we should not be too quick in making far reaching conclusions because we only have a fragment of this text. It is, however, clear that at least the extant fragment disrobes the story about Jesus' passion of its historical concretion as having happened in a "real" first-century Jerusalem.

3. But what counts even more, is the image the *Gospel of Peter* develops of the Jews participating in Jesus' passion.[8] The crucial verse is V. 5:

"And he (= Herod) delivered him *to the people* (λαός!) before the first day of the unleavened bread, *their* feast."

To say it briefly: it is not only clear that the Passover feast is not a feast relevant for the "Christian" group addressed by the *Gospel of Peter* any more. Moreover, and much more important: all tortures done to the Lord from now on are, according to the *Gospel of Peter*, done by "the" Jewish people and not by Roman soldiers. We are told that "the Jews" mock Jesus, torture him, crucify him

---

[8] For a detailed discussion see T. NICKLAS, Die 'Juden' im Petrus-evangelium (P.Cair. 10759): Ein Testfall, in: *NTS* 47 (2001) 206–21, and – criticizing my approach – J. VERHEYDEN, Some Reflections on Determining the Purpose of the 'Gospel of Peter,' in: *Das Evangelium nach Petrus: Text, Kontexte, Intertexte* (ed. by T.J. Kraus & T. Nicklas; TU 158; Berlin – New York: de Gruyter, 2007) 281–99.

and do anything possible to make his death as cruel as possible. To give just one example: according to V. 14 they "commanded that (his) legs should not be broken, so that he might die in torment." The motif of breaking (or not breaking) Jesus' legs is well-known from the Johannine Passion account. While, however, according to John 19.31–36, the Roman soldiers do not break Jesus' bones because he already had died, and while the Gospel of John interprets this as fulfilment of Scripture (John 19.36), a sign which shows that Jesus has been the true Passover Lamb, the *Gospel of Peter* does not know about this function of the motif any more: according to the apocryphal text, the only reason for not breaking Jesus' bones is to torture him as long as possible – the *Gospel of Peter* depicts the "Jews" as executioners who are as brutal as possible.[9] One could go further – according to *GosPet* 48 the leaders of the people after having recognized that Jesus is the Son of God (*GosPet* 45) prefer to make themselves "guilty of the greatest sin before God than to fall into the hands of the people of the Jews and be stoned".

The "Jews" in the *Gospel of Peter* (and even more their leaders) thus are not depicted as fully-fledged characters, but as stereotypes, grotesque faces ..., not really human any more. Even if it is possible to debate that the text at

---

[9] For a more detailed discussion see T. NICKLAS, Rezeption und Entwicklung johanneischer Motive im *Petrusevangelium*, in: *Studien zu Matthäus und Johannes. Études sur Matthieu et Jean. Festschrift für Jean Zumstein zu seinem 65. Geburtstag / Mélanges offerts à Jean Zumstein pour son 65ᵉ anniversaire* (ed. by A. Dettwiler & U. Poplutz; AThANT 97; Zürich: Theologischer Verlag Zürich, 2009) 361–76, esp. 369–70.

least in its second half begins to distinguish between Jewish leaders and the people,[10] the passion story itself develops a purely negative image of the Chosen People.

Today we do not know much about the original purpose of the *Gospel of Peter*: does its presumed interest in motifs of martyrdom suggest that it was written in a situation of persecution? This is perfectly possible, but cannot be proven – and one could even discuss whether Jews played a role in this situation.[11] Or is it mainly an apologetic text trying to show the truth of Christian belief in a resurrection of the body?[12] Or is it just a rewriting, a re-enactment of "the" story of Jesus' passion and resurrection in a context where no copies of other Gospels were extant?[13] Probably, all these suggestions contain at least a piece of truth. At least in the present situation, any answer about the concrete function of the *Gospel of Peter*'s description of the Jews must therefore remain speculation.

The *Gospel of Peter*, however, does not stand alone among second-century Christian writings; one could talk about the early second century *Letter of Barnabas*, surely one of the early Christian writings with the most anti-Jewish potential; or the "Christian" parts of the *Si-*

---

[10] See T. NICKLAS, ‚Juden' im Petrusevangelium.

[11] This is the idea of P. AUGUSTIN who is currently preparing his doctoral thesis on the role of the Jews in the *Gospel of Peter*. I am grateful to Philipp Augustin for sharing his ideas with me.

[12] For this view see (only partly convincing) T.P. HENDERSON, *The Gospel of Peter and Early Christian Apologetics* (WUNT II 30; Tübingen: Mohr, 2011).

[13] For a comparable view see J. VERHEYDEN, Reflections.

bylline Oracles[14]; or finally the so-called *Physiologus*, the earliest "Christian natural history" (at least in part going back to the late second century CE)[15] that tries to show at more than one place that Jews have lost their status as God's Chosen People. I do not want, however, to just put together a series of examples which could shock us; I think instead that it is much more interesting to consider a few writings where we have at least a chance to understand a bit more about the contexts in which they have been written. Some of these texts with comparable stereotypes about "Jews" and "Judaism" can tell us more.

1. Melito of Sardis

During the second century the "Christian communities" in Asia Minor celebrated Easter not on the Sunday of Jesus' resurrection, but on the 14th of Nisan, the first day of Passover. That's why these Christians are called the

---

[14] Regarding the relation between the descriptions of Jesus' passion in the *Gospel of Peter* and the *Sibylline Oracles* see T. NICKLAS, Apokryphe Passionstraditionen im Vergleich: Petrusevangelium und Sibyllinische Orakel (Buch VIII), in: *Das Evangelium nach Petrus: Text, Kontexte, Intertexte* (ed. by T.J. Kraus & T. Nicklas; TU 158; Berlin – New York, 2007) 263–79.

[15] For a discussion see F. SBORDONE (ed.), *Physiologus* (Hildesheim: Olms, 1976); cf. U. TREU, The *Physiologus* and the Early Fathers, *Studia Patristica* 24 (Louvain: Peeters, 1993) 197–200 or R.M. GRANT, *Early Christians and Animals* (London – New York, Routledge, 1999) 52. The text has a rich and diverse transmission history – we must speak of three different recensions going back to 2nd/3rd century CE, Byzantine times (5th/6th cent.) and even the Middle Ages (Basilius recension 10th/11th cent. CE).

"Quartodecimans". The situation led to tensions between the Quartodeciman bishop Polycarp of Smyrna
and Anicetus of Rome (155–166 CE) and later developed
into a conflict with bishop Victor of Rome (189–199 CE)
who wanted to impose the observance of Easter Sunday
on the churches of Asia Minor.[16] It is again Eusebius' *Ecclesiastical History* which preserves parts of a response
letter bishop Polycrates of Ephesus sent to Victor (*h.e.*
5.24.2–8). In this letter, among others, a certain Melito is
mentioned and described as an ascetic, "who always lived
in the Holy Spirit and who lies in Sardis awaiting the vis-
itation from heaven at which he shall rise from the dead"
(*h.e.* 5.24.5). Somewhat later Eusebius even calls Melito
the bishop of Sardis[17] and offers a long list of – now mainly lost – writings of Melito, among them two books *Peri
Pascha* - *On the Passover* (*h.e.* 4.24.1–2).[18] At least regard-

---

[16] On the so-called Quarto-Deciman celebration of Passover see
G. ROUWHORST, The Quartodeciman Passover and Jewish Pesach,
in: *Questions liturgiques* 77 (1996) 152–73; IDEM, Liturgical Time
and Space in Early Christianity in Light of their Jewish Background, in: *Sanctity of Time and Space in Tradition and Modernity*
(ed. by A. Houtman; Jewish and Christian Perspectives 1; Leiden:
Brill, 1998) 265–84, esp. 269–76, and P.F. BRADSHAW, The Origins
of Easter, in: *Passover and Easter: Origin and History to Modern
Times* (ed. by P. Bradshaw and L.A. Hoffman; Notre Dame, Ind.:
University of Notre Dame Press, 1999) 81–97.

[17] The question whether we can trust Eusebius' witness here has
been a matter of dispute. For the different voices see A. STEW-
ART-SYKES, *The Lamb's High Feast: Melito,* Peri Pascha *and The
Quartodeciman Paschal Liturgy at Sardis* (VigChr.S 42; Leiden –
Boston – Cologne: Brill, 1998) 4–5 who argues that Melito has in-
deed been bishop of Sardis.

[18] The whole list consists of more than fifteen different writings.
See for example C. MORESCHINI – E. NORELLI, *Early Christian*

ing some questions, Melito seems to have been highly interested in what we today would call the "Jewish roots"
of "Christianity": it is again Eusebius, who transmits a
letter Melito wrote to a certain Onesimus. According to
this letter, Onesimus was interested in getting excerpts
from the "Laws and the prophets" and wanted to know
the exact number and order of the Old Testament writings. Interestingly, this seems to have been anything but
a usual and simple request: Melito even travelled to Israel
to find out the concrete extent of the Old Testament Canon – and, in this context, must have had contact with Palestinian Jews (or at least Jewish believers in Christ).
While this information seems to show us Melito as still
quite open-minded regarding "Jewish-Christian" relations, his "homily"[19] *Peri Pascha - On the Passover* speaks
another language. This text has first been discovered in a
fourth- or fifth-century papyrus codex from the Ches-
ter-Beatty collection and identified by its editor C. Bonner (1936) as one of the works mentioned by Eusebius.
Bonner's identification could be verified when in 1960 M.
Testuz was able to publish another Greek witness of the
text, this time containing the title. Today we even have a
few more manuscripts containing at least fragments of
ancient Coptic and Georgian versions plus a Latin epito-
me of the text.[20] The homily itself which followed a read-

---

*Greek and Latin Literature: A Literary History 1: From Paul to the
Age of Constantine* (Peabody, Mass.: Hendrickson, 2005) 135–6.

[19] The concrete genre of the text is a matter of discussion. See, for
example, A. STEWART-SYKES, *High Feast*, 55–113.

[20] See C. BONNER (ed.), *The Homily on the Passion by Melito
Bishop of Sardis and Some Fragments of Apocryphal Ezekiel* (StD

ing of Exodus 12 consists of two parts (11–45 // 46–105): while part 1 is mainly concerned with the first Passover of Israel, part 2 is interested in the "Christian" Passover. Interestingly, Melito explains the word "Passover", that is "pascha" by the Greek word πάσχω (= 'to suffer'),[21] of course, a wrong etymology, which, however, allows him to connect Christ's suffering with the feast of Passover.[22] The relation between the two parts of the homily already shows us in which spirit the text is written: while the first Passover is merely understood as prefiguration, the Christian Passover, that is Passion and Easter, is understood as fulfilment. This, again, means that Jewish Passover has lost any significance (or even more: never had any significance).

At least some passages of Melito's text go even further than what we find in the *Gospel of Peter*[23] – the negative (and infamous) highlight surely being *pasch.* 96.714–5:

12; London, 1940). In the meantime a second Greek witness plus several versions have been discovered and edited: M. TESTUZ (ed.), *Papyrus Bodmer XIII, Méliton de Sardes Homélie sur la Pâque* (Geneva: Bodmer, 1960). – For more details see S.G. HALL (ed.), *Melito of Sardis: On Pascha and Fragments* (Oxford: Clarendon, 1979), xvii-xxxix, the most important edition of the text besides O. PERLER (ed.), *Melito de Sardes: Sur la pâque et fragments* (SC 123; Paris: Cerf, 1966).

[21] The text goes: "What is the Pascha? It gets its name from its characteristic: from *suffer (pathein)* comes *suffering (páschein)*" (46, 303–305; translation HALL, 23).

[22] For further discussion see O. SKARSAUNE, Evidence, 526–7.

[23] Since O. PERLER, a literary dependence between Melito and the *Gospel of Peter* has been assumed. The arguments, however, seem not to be strong enough to make this clear. For a detailed discussion see Th. KARMANN, Die Paschahomilie des Melito von Sardes und das Petrusevangelium, in *Das Evangelium nach Petrus:*

"The God has been murdered; the King of Israel has been put to death by an Israelite right hand." This is, however, not an isolated statement, but part of a longer passage (§§ 72–99) where the idea of Israel murdering Christ, the Lord, becomes almost a *Leitmotiv.* For Melito Israel has murdered "the firstborn of God" (*pasch.* 82.593) himself, for him this is the reason of Jerusalem's destruction (*pasch.* 99) and means that Israel now "lies dead" (*pasch.* 100.748) and has no future any more.[24]

Perhaps at least a few passages must be quoted to get an impression of this text:

"72 It is he [the Lord; TN] that has been murdered.
And where has he been murdered? In the middle of Jerusalem.
By whom? By Israel.
Why? Because he healed their lame
And cleaned their lepers
And brought light to their blind
And raised their dead
that is why he died.
Where it is written in law and prophets,
'They repaid me bad things for good,
And childlessness for my soul,
When they devised evil things against me and said,
Let us bind the just one,
Because he is a nuisance to us'" (translation S. G. Hall, 39).

Text, Kontexte, Intertexte (ed. by T. J. Kraus & T. Nicklas; TU 158; Berlin – New York: de Gruyter, 2007), 215–35.

[24] C. MORESCHINI – E. NORELLI, *Early Christian*, 138, conclude: "The work is thus a stage in the disastrous history of Christian antijudaism and anti-Semitism. The influence of Melito is also evident in the *improperia*, the reproaches of Israel as slayer of Christ that were until recently part of the Catholic Good Friday liturgy."

A bit later we read:

"79 ... You prepared for him sharp nails and false witnesses
And ropes and scourges
And vinegar and gall
And sword and forceful restraint as against a murderous robber.
...
And you killed your Lord at the great feast ...

81 O lawless Israel, what is this unprecedented crime you committed,
Thrusting your Lord among unprecedented sufferings,
Your Sovereign,
Who formed you,
Who made you
Who honoured you,
Who called you 'Israel'
82 But you did not turn out to be 'Israel';
You did not 'see God',
You did not recognize the Lord.
You did not know, Israel,
That he is the firstborn of God,
Who was begotten *before the morning star*,
Who tinted the light,
Who lit up the day,
Who divided off the darkness, ..." (translation, S.G. Hall, 45–7).

I will not go further – the following paragraphs recapitulate important steps in the history of salvation trying to show that "the Lord" who, according to Melito, was murdered by Israel has always been with Israel in these steps, but they did not see and recognize him.[25] How is it possible that Melito on the one hand belongs to a group of

---

[25] For the etymology of Israel as "Seeing God" see Philo of Al-

Asian Christians who defend the celebration of Easter on the first day of Passover, but that he on the other hand can formulate such anti-Jewish statements? Claudio Moreschini and Enrico Norelli give the following answer:

"Only in appearance ... are the antijudaism and continuity with the Jewish Passover tradition contradictory. What we see here is an important episode in the 'expropriation' of the Scriptures and the religious tradition of Judaism that was carried on by Christians, especially in the second century, as they claimed for Christianity the authentic understanding of the Bible and continuity with the 'true Israel'. In this perspective, polemical violence against the Jews came naturally in the effort to prove that the Jews had not right to appeal to the revelation that the Christians had inherited from them, but of which the Christians now claim to be the sole possessors."[26]

In addition, Melito develops a model of history of salvation in which the history of Israel is not really history of salvation, but disaster which only has been annihilated by the Christ event. In a certain sense, this draws a borderline quite similar to the one Ignatius created.[27] Judith Lieu is correct when she writes:

"While such a negative remembering, and not-remembering of times of faithfulness and renewal, is a denial of the Jews' own claims to identity, it will also, although as yet hardly explicitly, rule out those of Jewish Christians."[28]

---

exandria, *De mutatione nominum* 81 (already mentioned by S.G. HALL, *Melito*, 45 n. 50).

[26] C. MORESCHINI – E. NORELLI, *Early Christian*, 138.

[27] Interestingly, the relation of "Christianity" and pagan worship does not play a role in this text.

[28] J. LIEU, *Christian Identity in the Jewish and Graeco-Roman World* (Oxford: Oxford University Press, 2004) 82.

Melito is not the sole case for such a text, a lesser known parallel from around the same time is Ps-Hippolytus' homily *In Sanctum Pascha*.[29] In Melito's case, however, it seems easier to say at least a bit more about the setting of this homily – and therefore to formulate at least a few ideas about the concrete function of its description of the "Jews".

For some time scholars tried to explain Melito's alleged anti-Judaism by reconstructing the social context of *Peri Pascha*. The usual argument runs as follows: as we can say late antique Sardis must have been an important centre of Diaspora Judaism. During excavations in the 60s of the last century a huge synagogue building has been found which had been rebuilt several times, but, according to several authors, had been in use from the third century CE until the destruction of Sardis by the Persians in the year 616 CE.[30] In addition to this, several passages in Josephus' *Jewish Antiquities* show that there must have been an important Jewish community in Sardis already in the time of the Seleucid king Antiochus III around 200 BCE (*Ant.* 12.3.4) and that this community enjoyed important privileges (*Ant.* 14.10.14–24). So even if we lack precise sources about the situation of the Jewish community of Sardis at Melito's times, it is usually understood as quite probable that we have to do it with a wealthy and

[29] See G. Visonà, *Pseudo Ippolito. In Sanctum Pascha: studio edizione commento* (Milan: Vita e pensiero, 1988).

[30] For a first overview see L.M. White, *The Social Origins of Christian Architecture II: Texts and Monuments for the Christian Domus Ecclesiae and its Environment* (HTS 42; Valley Forge: Trinity, 1997) 310–23.

very well-accepted group enjoying significant political privileges in the society of Sardis. Ingeborg Angerstorfer for example suggested that the decision to allow the Jewish community to build a monumental synagogue perhaps fell more or less in Melito's times.[31] We do not know much about the situation of the community of Christ-believers in Sardis. Is it possible that parts of Melito's extremely harsh statements against Judaism had to do with the fact that the community of Christ-followers in Sardis must have been quite small and marginal if compared with the Jewish community? Again, Ingeborg Angerstorfer developed the idea that the Sardian group of Christ-followers even felt persecuted and under trial – and that's why parts of Melito's homily are formulated like an attorney's accusation of Israel as persecutor of Christ (and indirectly of his followers).[32] Is it possible that this Jewish community who a few decades later was rich enough to build the biggest ancient synagogue ever discovered, might have been attractive for many Sardian followers of Christ? Is it possible that Melito was interested in holding these people inside the border he defined? And is it possible that the concrete situation of a Easter homily concentrating on the central theme of "Christian" identity enforced Melito's argument even more? And is it possible that Melito, who sometimes is thought to have been born a "Jew" himself,[33] drew this borderline even strong-

---

[31] I. ANGERSTORFER, *Melito und das Judentum* (unpublished diss. Regensburg, 1985) 215.

[32] See I. ANGERSTORFER, *Melito*, 219–27.

[33] See, for example, O. SKARSAUNE, Evidence, 525: "It is precisely the bitterness of the anti-Israel polemic in Melito that makes ex-

er than a "pagan Christian" would have done? We should
be much more cautious than earlier generations of scholars – partly with very good reasons and often with best
will – had been: neither the archaeological evidence is as
unambiguous as one would like to have it,[34] nor do we
know enough about the situation of both "Jewish" and
"Christian" communities in Sardis at Melito's time.[35]
Every answer related to the concrete social context
wherein Melito's *Peri Pascha* was written must remain
speculation:[36] one could even consider the idea that Melito, like the *Improperia* of today's Catholic liturgies of
Good Friday do, addressed his "Christian" audience
when he spoke about Israel's guilt.[37]

---

cellent sense on the assumption that Melito himself was Jewish. It
was the bitterness of a family feud." – See, however, C. LEONHARD,
*The Jewish Pesach and the Origins of the Christian Easter: Open
Questions in Current Research* (SJ 35; Berlin – New York, de
Gruyter, 2006) 46 with clear arguments against this idea.

[34] For recent discussion on the date of the Sardian synagogue
building see, e. g., H. BOTERMANN, Die Synagoge von Sardes: Eine
Synagoge aus dem 4. Jahrhundert? *ZNW* (1990) 103–24, and (even
more radical) J. MAGNESS, The Date of the Sardis Synagogue in
Light of the Numismatic Evidence, *AJA* 109 (2005) 443–75.

[35] See, for example, M. P. BONZ, The Jewish Community of Ancient Sardis: A Reassessment of Its Rise to Prominence, *Harvard
Studies in Classical Philology* 93 (1990) 343–59.

[36] For a critical discussion of the "classical" argument working
with the "social context" of Melito's homily see also D. SATRAN,
Anti-Jewish Polemic in the *Peri Pascha* of Melito of Sardis. The
Problem of Social Context, in *Contra Judaeos. Ancient and Medie-
val Polemics between Christians and Jews* (ed. by O. Limor & G. G.
Stroumsa; TSAJ 10; Tübingen: Mohr, 1996) 49–58.

[37] I am grateful to my colleague Andreas MERKT for this idea.

In any case, it seems that the same person Melito could behave very differently in different situations: when interested in the canon and order of Old Testament books, he must have been in a somewhat solid and even positive contact with Palestinian Jews – believers in Christ or not. When preaching about the Pascha perhaps facing an audience for which their "Christian" identity in relation to the synagogue must have been anything but clear, he could choose words which we can only condemn in our days.[38]

---

[38] Melito is not the only writer who leaves us with the feeling that his attitude to "Jews", "Judaism" and "Israel" could differ in different contexts. Clement of Alexandria (ca. 140/50 – ca. 215 CE) was one of the most erudite Christian thinkers at the turn of the second to the third century CE. At least in his extant writings he seems to be much less anti-Jewish than most of his Christian contemporaries. If we believe Jerome (*Ruf.* 1,13) Clement, when engaged with the discussion of Scripture, used to refer to examples of Jewish exegesis. In addition to this, in his extant writings Clement used Jewish sources and quite regularly quoted Philo of Alexandria as an important authority. This quite "relaxed" attitude perhaps had to do with the fact that Alexandrian Judaism must have been very weak at the turn of the second to the third century CE and with Clement's own ideas of defining Christianity as a "true philosophy" for an educated elite. We know, however, that Clement must have published an otherwise lost work *Against the Judaising Christians* the tone of which was surely much more negative. This text, however, had been requested by the bishop of Jerusalem, that is, it was written for a very different context than Clement's extant writings. In other words: it seems quite sure that even Clement's tone about Jews could differ a lot – and was depending on context and genre of his writings. For more details see: J. CARLETON PA-GET, Clement of Alexandria and the Jews, in his: *Jews, Christians and Jewish Christians in Antiquity* (WUNT 251; Tübingen: Mohr, 2010) 91–102; regarding Clement's use of Philo see A. VAN DEN HOEK, *Clement of Alexandria and his Use of Philo in the* Stro-

2. "Christian" Enemies as "Jews"?

2.1 Papyrus Oxyrhynchus V 840

While we can at least speculate about background and function of Melito's homily, it is much more difficult to interpret another widely disputed early Christian text. *P. Oxy.* V 840 is a fragment of a 4th (or perhaps 5th) century miniature codex containing the remains of an otherwise lost apocryphal Gospel.[39] The exact date of this Gospel text has been a matter of dispute, but it is quite probable that it belongs more or less to the period which is of interest for us.[40] The scene depicted here, however, is quite strange: Jesus, who is called the *Sōtēr* (= the Saviour) here,[41] takes his disciples and leads them to a certain *Hagneuterion*, a rare word, which perhaps means a "place of purification". Then he walks with them "in the Temple". According to the text, one is only allowed to enter this

---

mateis. *An Early Christian Reshaping of a Jewish Model* (VigChr.S 3; Leiden et al.: Brill, 1988).

[39] For a palaeographic introduction see M. Kruger, Papyrus Oxyrhynchus 840, in: T.J. Kraus – M.J. Kruger – T. Nicklas, *Gospel Fragments* (Oxford Early Christian Gospel Texts; Oxford: Oxford University Press, 2009) 121–215, esp. 125–45. For even more details see T.J. Kraus, P.Oxy. 840 – Amulet or Miniature Codex? Principal and Additional Remarks on the Two Terms, in his: *Ad Fontes: Original Manuscripts and Their Significance for Studying Early Christianity. Selected Essays* (TENT 3; Leiden: Brill, 2007) 47–67.

[40] For an introductory overview see T. Nicklas, Das Fragment Oxyrhynchus V 840, in: *Antike christliche Apokryphen in deutscher Übersetzung I: Evangelien und Verwandtes 1* (ed. by C. Markschies & J. Schröter; Tübingen: Mohr Siebeck, 2012) 357–9.

[41] This title is an indication that the text should not be too early.

temple and see the "holy vessels" contained in it with cleaned feet. A bit later, a "pool of David" with two different staircases is mentioned. At the place of purification Jesus and his disciples meet "a certain Pharisee, a chief priest named Levi" who accuses them in the following way:

"Who allowed you to trample this place of purification and to see these holy vessels, when you have not bathed yourself nor have your disciples washed their feet?" (translation: Kruger, 171).

A discussion on matters of purification through water arises – and, as usual in Gospel accounts, Jesus, who argues that natural water cannot clean a person from its sins, ends up with the last (and decisive) word. Immediately after its first publication in 1908 a controversy arose whether this fragment contained material going back to the historical Jesus or whether it described a situation which did not show any signs of historical knowledge about a pre 70 CE situation. One aspect of the discussion had to do with the question of whether there had been any *archiereus*, i. e., a high priest (and in some cases a chief priest), from the Pharisaic party. While scholars who want to find some authentic Jesus material in our text usually interpret the priest only as a "Pharisaic" chief priest and try to find material which shows the plausibility of such a scene,[42] others are more reluctant to interpret

---

[42] The most prominent voice pleading for the authenticity of the scene was J. JEREMIAS, Der Zusammenstoß Jesu auf dem Tempelplatz. Zu Pap.Ox.V 840, in: *Coniectanea Neotestamentica XI in honorem A. Fridrichsen* (Lund – Kopenhagen: Wifstrand, 1947),

the text in this way. My own impression is somewhat different: does not the combination of a Pharisee, a high priest (or chief priest) and a name "Levi" (which is, however, only partly extant on the existing fragment) create something like an artificial "opera figure", something comparable to the Turks in Mozart's "The Abduction from the Seraglio", written around a century after the Turkish siege of Vienna? Like the Turks in Mozart's opera, the "Jew" in this text would be some figure from the past, a figure, however, which still has to do with identity matters, but is nothing more than a stereotype for an "opponent" of Jesus. Different, however, from "the Jews" in the *Gospel of Peter*, we have a figure who is a combined representative of "Jewish elite" here. But does this figure really represent "Judaism"? Recently, several scholars, among them Francois Bovon, raised some serious doubts regarding the question whether Papyrus Oxyrhynchus 840's "Levi" really represents a group which we would call "Judaism" today.[43] According to Bovon, the text does not mirror any conflict between Jesus (and/or an early Christian community) and Judaism, but a controversy between different early Christian groups about matters of purification through water. Bovon first shows that

---

97–108; see also his *Unbekannte Jesusworte* (Gütersloh: Gerd Mohn, ³1965) 50–60.

[43] Besides F. Bovon, *Fragment Oxyrhynchus 840*, Fragment of a Lost Gospel, Witness of an Early Christian Controversy over Purity, in his: *New Testament and Christian Apocrypha* (ed. by G.E. Snyder; Grand Rapids: Baker, 2011) 174–96 (first published in *JBL* 119 [2000]] 705–28), see already D. Tripp, Meanings of Footwashing: John 13 and Oxyrhynchus Papyrus 840, *ExpT* 103 (1992) 237–9.

many elements of our text do not fit the situation we
know from the Jerusalem Temple:[44] although the "pool of
David" could have been a *miqveh*, we do not know of any
miqveh bearing this name, its description would, however, fit very well the structures of early Christian baptis-
teries. In addition, the "holy vessels" in the sanctuary of
the Jerusalem usually could not be seen because a curtain
covered them. While these and related issues had been
discussed since the discovery of our papyrus, Bovon's
key idea is to identify the *Hagneuterion* mentioned in the
text with "the water basin or fountain, located outside an
ancient Christian basilica, often in the middle of the atri-
um preceding the church."[45] Starting with this observation, Bovon is able to relate every important motif of the
text convincingly with aspects of Christian rites of baptism. The text thus can be read very well as part of a controversy between two groups of Christ-followers about
decisive elements of baptism rituals. Bovon concludes:

"The author of the fragment is hostile to any water ritual, and
he or she is probably a member of a Christian community located at the trajectory leading from certain Jesus traditions to
Manichaeism through Gnostic communities. The use of the title Savior and the absence of the name Jesus suggest a location
for the fragment within a Gnostic or Manichaean milieu using
apocryphal traditions. The opposition to water baptism, built
upon a dogmatic dualism between two types of water, water of
putrefaction and water of eternal life, also leads the reader to a
later chronological date. The fragment attacks the sacerdotal
attitude of the priest and the respect for water baptism and lus-
trations. Including references to liturgical clothes and holy ves-

---

[44] F. Bovon, Fragment, 185.
[45] F. Bovon, Fragment, 187.

sels, all the elements are consistent with the life of a Jewish Christian Baptist sect or with the practice of the mainstream Christian church. ... The fragment belongs, therefore, either in the second-century Gnostic opposition to a Jewish Christian Baptist movement or to the mainstream Church, or in the third-century Manichaean polemic against the Elkesaites."[46]

Of course, one could discuss details of Bovon's conclusions[47] – the striking thing, however, is the following: If we agree at least with his main argument, the "Pharisaic high priest Levi" of our fragment is not a stereotype for people we would call "Jews" any more, he is – in the perspective of a (probably) Christian group what we would call "heretic" today – a representative of another Christian group which in the eyes of the author of this text is too Jewish in its conception of baptism. It is even possible that P.Oxy. 840 is a document representing the ideas of a "Christian" group rejecting water baptism, a group which accused "proto-orthodox" Christian circles for being too Jewish. Be it as it may: it should become clearer that in the eyes of different Christian groups the lines between what was seen as "Jewish" and what was seen as "truly Christian" ran on very different tracks ...

---

[46] F. BOVON, Fragment, 196.

[47] M.J. KRUGER, *The Gospel of the Savior : An Analysis of P. Oxy. 840 and its Place in the Gospel Traditions of Early Christianity* (TENT 1; Leiden et al.: Brill, 2005) comes to different, yet more conservative conclusions than BOVON. For a critical evaluation of KRUGER's book see my review in *Apocrypha* 17 (2006) 203–10. – For another interpretation contextualizing P.Oxy. 840 in a Samaritan-Christian controversy see now L. ZELYCK, Recontextualizing Papyrus Oxyrhynchus 840, *Early Christianity* 4 (2013) 1–15.

2.2 Two "Gnostic" examples: The Gospel of Judas (CT 3) and the Coptic Apocalypse of Peter (NHC VII,3)

The Gospel fragment on P.Oxy. 840 is not the only example of such a text. The case is perhaps even clearer with two writings usually labelled as "Gnostic":[48]

2.2.1 Until a few years ago the existence of the second century *Gospel of Judas* has only been known via a few more or less cryptic references from authors like Irenaeus of Lyons, Theodoret of Cyrus and Epiphanius of Salamis.[49] In the year 2006, however, the so-called Codex Tchacos, probably from the 4th century CE, was published. This manuscript contains several apocryphal writings, the third of which is a Coptic version of the otherwise lost *Gospel of Judas*. This text which understands itself as a "secret word of declaration by which Jesus

---

[48] The use of the term "Gnostic" coined by ancient heresiologists like Irenaeus of Lyons, Hippolytus and others has been severely criticized in recent years. See, for example, M. A. WILLIAMS, *Rethinking 'Gnosticism': An Argument for Dismantling a Dubious Category* (Princeton: Princeton University Press, 1996), and K. L. KING, *What is Gnosticism?* (Cambridge, Mass. – London: Harvard University Press, 2003) and the discussion in A. MARJANEN (ed.), *Was There a Gnostic Religion?* (Publications of the Finnish Exegetical Society 87; Helsinki – Göttingen: Vandenhoeck & Ruprecht, 2005).

[49] For an introduction to this text see G. WURST, Das Judasevangelium (CT 3), in: *Antike christliche Apokryphen in deutscher Übersetzung I: Evangelien und Verwandtes 2* (ed. by C. Markschies & J. Schröter; Tübingen: Mohr, 2012) 1220–38. Translations according to R. KASSER – G. WURST (ed.s), *The Gospel of Judas. Together with the Letter of Peter to Philip, James and a Book of Allogenes from Codex Tchacos. Critical Edition* (Washington, D.C.: National Geographic, 2007).

spoke in conversation with Judas Iscariot" (translation Kasser/Wurst, 185) is a kind of a so-called "dialogue Gospel"[50] containing secret revelations of Jesus allegedly given to Judas Iscariot. Because of its creation myth the text is probably going back to a group of so-called "Sethian" Gnostic Christians[51] who understood the creator God as a terrible demonic "demiurge".[52] In several passages of this text Jesus criticizes the disciples of adhering to the wrong – i. e., the Jewish – God. According to p. 38, the disciples tell Jesus about a cruel vision they had:

"38 And they [said: 'We have'] seen a great house [with a] large altar [in it, and] twelve men – they are the priests, we would say; and a name [...]; and a crowd of people s waiting at the alter [until] the priests [presenting] the offerings. We [also] kept waiting.' [Jesus said], 'What are [...] like?' And they [said],

---

[50] Regarding this special type of gospel genre see J. Harten-stein, *Die zweite Lehre: Erscheinungen des Auferstandenen als Rahmenerzählungen frühchristlicher Dialoge* (TU 146; Berlin: Akademie, 2000).

[51] For a definition of "Sethianism" see H.-M. Schenke, Das sethianische System nach Nag-Hammadi-Handschriften, in: *Der Same Seths: Hans-Martin Schenkes Kleine Schriften zu Gnosis, Koptologie und Neuem Testament* (ed. by G. Schenke Robinson, G. Schenke & U.-K. Plisch; NHMS 78; Leiden et al: Brill, 2012) 285–92, esp. 286.

[52] For the *Gospel of Judas'* concrete position in the history of Sethian thinking see J. D. Turner, The Place of the Gospel of Judas in Sethian Tradition, in: *The* Gospel of Judas *in Context: Proceedings of the First International Conference on the* Gospel of Judas (ed. by M. Scopello; NHMS 62; Leiden – Boston: Brill, 2008) 187–237; for its idea of the demiurge see T. Nicklas, Der Demiurg des Judasevangeliums, in: *Judasevangelium und Codex Tchacos: Studien zur religionsgeschichtlichen Verortung einer gnostischen Schriftensammlung* (ed. by E. E. Popkes & G. Wurst; WUNT 297; Tübingen: Mohr, 2012) 99–120.

'Some [... for] two weeks; [others] sacrifice their own children, others their wives, in praise [and] humility with each other; others sleep with men; others are involved in slaugh[ter]; still others commit a multitude of sins and deeds of lawlessness. [And] the men who stand [before] the altar invoke your [name]. 39 And while they are involved in all the deeds of their sacrifice, that [altar] is filled.' ... Jesus said to them: 'It is you who are presenting the offerings on the altar you have seen. That one is the god you serve and you are the twelve men you gave seen. And the cattle that are brought in are the sacrifices you have seen – that is, the many people you lead astray" (translation *Editio Princeps*, 195–197).

The imagery used here is quite clear: the text offers a very polemical description of a sacrifice in a Temple – or better: an extremely polemical description of Jewish sacrifice.[53] Jesus' disciples are not only identified with the priests at the altar of sacrifice, they are accused of worshipping the wrong god and leading people astray. This is illustrated with typical motifs of ancient polemics: the text blames them for sacrifice of children and women, slaughter (of people), homoerotic practices etc. etc. It is a matter of critical debate concerning what stands behind the text: while authors like Karen King and Elaine Pagels understood this and other passages of the *Gospel of Judas* as a criticism of proto-orthodox attitudes of martyrdom,[54] I proposed that the text was mainly concerned

---

[53] The text's reference to Jewish sacrifice has already been seen by J. Van Oort, *Het Evangelie van Judas: Inleiding, Vertaling, Toelichting* (Kampen: Ten Have, 2006) 118.

[54] E. Pagels – K. L. King, *Reading Judas: The Gospel of Judas and the Shaping of Christianity* (New York: Viking, 2007), and K. L. King, Martyrdom and its Discontents in the Tchacos Codex, in: *The Codex Judas Papers: Proceedings of the International Con-*

with developments in sacramental and liturgical practices in the developing second century proto-orthodoxy.[55] Be it as it may – one thing, however, seems clear: although, contrary to P.Oxy. 840, the *Gospel of Judas* does not use the term "Jews", "Jewish" or "Israel" here, it is very clear who is addressed in this passage. Jesus' disciples are identified with a group in the Church who – at least in the eyes of the author of our text – leads people astray by still adhering to the God of Israel – a group which therefore is regarded as too Jewish. This group, however, is certainly not a marginal group of Christ followers still attending the synagogue; this group, which in the eyes of our Sethian Gnostic Christians behind the *Gospel of Judas* is too Jewish, is nothing less than what we could call "proto-orthodoxy" today. Again we see that the borderlines between "Jewish" and "Christian" could be drawn in very different ways.

---

gress on the Tchacos Codex held at Rice University, Houston Texas, March 13–16, 2008 (ed. by A. DeConick; NHMS 71; Leiden – Boston: Brill, 2011) 23–42.

[55] T. NICKLAS, Die andere Seite: Das Judasevangelium und seine Polemik im Kontext altkirchlicher Diskurse, in: *The Apocryphal Gospels within the Context of Early Christianity* (ed. by J. Schröter; BETL 260; Leuven et al.: Peeters, 2013) 127–55. See also H. SCHMID, Was hat der ‚Judasevangelist' eigentlich gegen die Eucharistie? in: *Judasevangelium und Codex Tchacos: Studien zur religionsgeschichtlichen Verortung einer gnostischen Schriftensammlung* (ed. by E.E. Popkes & G. Wurst; WUNT 297; Tübingen: Mohr, 2012) 71–98, and IDEM, Eucharistie und Opfer: Das *Evangelium des Judas* im Kontext der Eucharistiedeutungen des 2. Jahrhunderts, *Early Christianity* 3 (2012) 85–108.

2.2.2 While the *Gospel of Judas* provides us with a very different view of Judas Iscariot,[56] Simon Peter is the sole protagonist of the Coptic *Apocalypse of Peter* (NHC VII,3, p. 70,14–84,14), a text which should not be confused with the Greek / Ethiopic *Apocalypse* or *Revelation of Peter*.[57] In many respects the Coptic *Apocalypse of Peter* belongs to the most mysterious Christian writings we know: it is almost impossible to date it exactly (late second or third century CE?),[58] and its place of origin is unknown: as in many other cases Syria or Egypt are named, but there is no clear evidence in either direction. Even its exact "Gnostic" character could be debated: no traces of a Sophia myth or a description of the *Pleroma* can be found. The main elements which could allow for the label "Gnostic" which can be seen in the text are its reference to Archons, the idea of the souls' return to their origin,

---

[56] The question whether this is (entirely) positive or not is still debated. See, for example, A. MARJANEN, Does the *Gospel of Judas* Rehabilitate Judas Iscariot? in: *Gelitten – Gestorben – Auferstanden. Passions- und Ostertraditionen im antiken Christentum* (ed. by T. Nicklas, A. Merkt & J. Verheyden; WUNT II.273; Tübingen: Mohr, 2010) 209–24.

[57] Parts of 2.2.2 have already been used in T. NICKLAS, "Gnostic" Perspectives on Peter, in *Peter in Early Christianity* (ed. by H. Bond & L. W. Hurtado; Grand Rapids: Eerdmans, 2014); for a comparable overview on "Gnostic" descriptions of Peter see W. PRATSCHER, Die Bedeutung des Petrus in gnostischen Texten, *SNTU.A* 37 (2012) 111–50.

[58] Recently, A. L. MOLINARI, The Apocalypse of Peter and its Dating, in: *Coptica – Gnostica – Manichaica. Mélanges offerts à Wolf-Peter-Funk* (ed. by L. Painchaud & P.-H. Poirier; Bibliothèque Cope de Nag Hammadi. Section Études 7; Québec: Université Laval – Leuven – Paris: Peeters, 2006) 583–605, esp. 605 has even proposed a date between 320 and 340 CE.

the impact of "knowledge" (= Gnosis) for salvation and, finally, the text's "docetism".[59] The text connects two main parts, a revelation of the Saviour in the form of visions and auditions (p. 72,4–81,3) and a vision of his passion which, however, is interpreted in a "docetic" way (p. 81,3–82,17).

In p. 72,4–13 we read:

"And as he [the Saviour who is not identical with the human Jesus; TN] was saying these things, I [Peter; TN] saw the priests and the people (λαός) running toward us with stones, as if (ὡς) they were about to kill us. And (δέ) I was afraid that we were going to die. And he said to me, 'Peter, I have told you many times that they are blind ones who have no leader'" (translation J. Brashler).

The passage thus connects two motifs which are important for the *Apocalypse of Peter*: on the one hand the "we"-group represented by Peter feels persecuted, and these persecutions cause suffering and even danger of death. At least here, in a context which is reminiscent of Jesus' passion, and a bit later, during the vision of Jesus' passion (p. 81,3–82,17) and its interpretation (p. 82,17–84,13), they seem to be identified with the "people" who are involved in the passion of Jesus (and the disciples' al-

---

[59] For an introduction to the text see M. DESJARDINS, NHC VII,3: *Apocalypse of Peter* (with a presentation of text, translation and notes by J. Brashler), in: *Nag Hammadi Codex CII* (ed. by B.A. Pearson; NHMS 30; Leiden – New York – Cologne: Brill, 1996) 201–49, esp. 201–14, and H. HAVELAAR, Die Apokalypse des Petrus (NHC VII,3), in *Nag Hammadi Deutsch 2: NHC V,2 XIII,1, BG 1 und 4* (ed. by : G. Schenke Robinson, G. Schenke & U.-K. Plisch; GCS 12; Koptisch-Gnostische Schriften III; Berlin – New York: De Gruyter, 2003) 591–600, esp. 592–5.

leged persecution). Throughout the *Apocalypse of Peter*, however, we encounter the motif of the opponents' being blind and deaf (which is perhaps taken from Matt 23). Only Peter sees what is truly happening. The text distinguishes between a "living Jesus" (p. 81,18) who is "above the cross, glad and laughing" (p. 81,16–7) and who later is identified with the "Saviour" (p. 82,9.28), while the one crucified is only "his physical part, which is the substitute" (p. 81,21–2). The others standing around (and identified implicitly with the text's opponents) are called "born blind" (p. 83,3). They are looking only at the substitute, the suffering one, while Peter is the "one to whom these mysteries have been given, to know through revelation that he whom they crucified is the first-born, and the home of demons, and the clay vessel in which they dwell, belonging to *Elohim*, and belonging to the cross that is under the law" (p. 82,18–26).

The last sentences mentioned are revealing and they connect the passion scene with the text's polemics against allegedly "blind" "proto-orthodox" followers of Christ (p. p. 73,10–81,3): according to the *Apocalypse of Peter* (NHC VII,3) everybody who believes in a Jesus suffering at the cross belongs to the ones born blind, he is connected to *Elohim* who is understood as a demonic demiurge. These persons cannot see the real Saviour who "stands joyfully looking at those who persecuted him", but are "divided upon themselves" (p. 82,31–33) – and thus they are like the Jewish people under the cross and persecuting the text's "we"-group. Peter, the representative of the "we-group", however, has to be "strong" (p. 82,18 and 84,10) but should not fear his enemies because the Saviour will be "with him" (p. 84,8–9; cf. Matt 28.20?). On the level of the story these enemies are the "priests and the people" (p. 72,5–6), it is, however, clear that the real enemies in the background of our text are the representatives of "proto-orthodoxy" seen as dangerous enemies of the group of "Gnostics" behind our text.

We cannot be sure whether there has been a "real" we-group behind the Coptic *Apocalypse of Peter* – without the witness in Nag Hammadi Codex VII we would not even know about the existence of this text which, at least to my knowledge, did not leave any traces in later literature. But even if it was nothing more than an exercise in a "docetic" Christology it, again, represents a thinking where "Jews" or "the people" did not always represent persons we would call "Jews" today, but stood for a group of (in our view "proto-orthodox") opponents who were, in the eyes of a second or third-century "Christian" author, too much on the wrong side of the "borderline"[60] to be part of "us".

2.3 The Other Way Round: The Pseudo-Clementines

Perhaps it is necessary to add at least one example of a group of Christ-believers whose polemics was going in exactly the opposite direction – a group which understood "proto-orthodoxy" obviously as not Jewish enough! The *Pseudo-Clementines* which today are transmitted in two different recensions – the so-called Greek

---

[60] The word "borderline" in this context is, of course, taken from D. Boyarin's monograph *Borderlines*.

"Homilies" and the Latin / Syriac "Recognitions" – can be seen as an early attempt to adapt the ancient idea of a romance for "Christian" purposes.[61] It is not necessary to retell its complicated (and sometimes a bit boring) story here; the text, the *Grundschrift* of which goes back to the first decades of the third century CE (probably between 220 and 230 CE),[62] is of high interest partly because of the very old traditions it contains. Some of these traditions preserve forms of "Christian" thinking with perspectives very different from what we find in "proto-orthodox" writings. Already a close reading of the authentic Pauline letters reveals that there must have been a strong opposition against Paul's interpretation of the Christ-event and,

---

[61] Other early examples can be seen in the *Apocryphal Acts of the Apostles*, like the *Acts of John, Peter* and others. For more information see: J. N. BREMMER, The Apocryphal Acts of the Apostles: Authors, Place, Time and Readership, in: *The Apocryphal Acts of Thomas* (ed. by J. N. Bremmer; Studies on Early Christian Apocrypha 6; Leuven: Peeters, 2001) 149–70. – The complicated relation between both recensions is still a matter of dispute – perhaps the question cannot be solved adequately. For an overview of recent research see F. AMSLER, État de la recherché récente sur le roman pseudo-clémentin, in: *Nouvelles intrigues pseudo-clementines: Plots in the Pseudo-Clementine Romance. Actes du deuxième colloque international sur la literature apocryphe chrétenne, Lausanne – Genève, 30 août – 2 septembre 2006* (ed. by F. Amsler, A. Frey, C. Touati & R. Girardet; PIRSB 6 ; Prahins, CH : Éditions du Zèbre, 2008) 25–45, esp. 30–8, and J. N. BREMMER, Pseudo-Clementines : Texts, Dates, Places, Authors, and Magic, in: *The Pseudo-Clementines* (ed. by J. N. Bremmer; Studies on Early Christian Apocrypha 10; Leuven: Peeters, 2010) 1–23, esp. 1–9.

[62] See, for example, the introduction by J. N. BREMMER, Pseudo-Clementines: Texts, Dates, Places, Authors and Magic, in: *The Pseudo-Clementines* (Studies on Early Christian Apocrypha 10; Leuven: Peeters, 2010) 1–23, esp. 6–9.

connected to it, his mission to the Gentiles. At least in some passages, the *Pseudo-Clementines* offer us an insight into the perspective of anti-Pauline followers of Christ – and even if these texts do not go back to the first century CE, they show us that at least in some "Christian" circles opposition to Pauline Christianity continued for quite a long time.[63]

Let me give just a few examples:[64]

1. The *Pseudo-Clementines* develop a dualistic idea of the so-called "syzygies" (or "pairs"): according to the text there have been, starting with Cain and Abel and fin-

---

[63] For an overview of the history of research on the topic see J. VERHEYDEN, The Demonization of the Opponent in Early Christian Literature: The Case of the Pseudo-Clementines, in: *Religious Polemics in Context. Papers Presented to the Second International Conference of the Leiden Institute for the Study of Religions (LISOR) held at Leiden, 27–28 April 2000* (ed. by T. L. Hettema & A. van der Kooij; Studies in Theology and Religion 11; Assen: Van Gorcum, 2004) 330–59; for an extensive recent discussion of the Pseudo-Clementines' anti-Paulinism see P. PIOVANELLI, « L' enemi est parmi nous ». Présences rhétoriques et narratives de Paul dans les *Pseudo-clémentines* et autres écrits apparentés, in: *Nouvelles intrigues pseudo-clementines: Plots in the Pseudo-Clementine Romance. Actes du deuxième colloque international sur la literature apocryphe chrétenne, Lausanne – Genève, 30 août – 2 septembre 2006* (ed. by F. Amsler, A. Frey, C. Touati & R. Girardet; PIRSB 6; Prahins, CH : Éditions du Zèbre, 2008) 241–8 ; G. STANTON, Jewish-Chistian Elements in the Pseudo-Clementine Writings, in his : *Studies in Matthew and Early Christianity* (WUNT 309; Tübingen: Mohr, 2013) 419–39, esp. 429–32, and J. WEHNERT, Antipaulinismus in den Pseudoklementinen, in: *Ancient Perspectives on Paul* (ed. by T. Nicklas, A. Merkt & J. Verheyden ; NTOA 102; Göttingen: Vandenhoeck & Ruprecht, 2013) 170–90.

[64] For a more detailed discussion see J. WEHNERT, Antipaulinismus, 177–87.

ishing with Antichrist and Christ, six pairs of false and
true prophets. According to this idea, a false prophet
must always come first to preach a deceptive gospel
which, afterwards, has to be destroyed by a true prophet.
As an example, Pseudo-Clementine *Homilies* 2.17.3–4
binds together two Christian missions to pagans. Even if
the text does not mention Paul by name, but uses the "cipher" of the arch-heretic Simon Magus, who is nowhere
else called a missionary to pagans, it is quite clear that it
understands Paul as a false prophet preaching a false Gospel. Peter, according to the *Pseudo-Clementines* the ideal
apostle and preacher, must destroy it and put it into right
order. *Homilies* 2.18.1 goes even further and describes
Paul as a death bringing "enemy"; a virtually "satanic"
character.

2. Other parts of the *Pseudo-Clementines* go into more
detail. Pseudo-Clementine *Homilies* 17.13–20, for example, recounts a dispute between Peter and Simon Magus,
where Simon is depicted in a way that the reader is almost
forced to identify him with Paul. Simon describes himself
as an apostle of Jesus who was called by a vision of the
Lord (*Hom.* 17.13.1–2; cf. 17.19.7). Contrary to the rest of
the *Pseudo-Clementines*, the text is full of allusions to
Pauline Letters and the book of Acts. Interestingly, one
text focuses upon the Antiochian conflict between Paul
and Peter in Gal 2.11–14.

3. But even in the Pseudo-Clementine *Recognitions*, today preserved in a Latin and a Syriac version, a text which
is much more polished in an "orthodox" way, shows traces of anti-Paulinism. The *Recognitions* contain a Jewish-Christian source (*Rec.* 1.27–71), according to which

James, the Brother of the Lord, is murdered by a *homo inimicus* (*Rec.* 1.70). A bit later we read that the High Priest Caiaphas has ordered this "enemy" to persecute all followers of Christ and, equipped with letters of recommendation, the "enemy" leaves for Damascus to kill all followers of Christ – after this, it is not necessary to give a name to this character.

We could go on with further examples from the *Pseudo-Clementines*. It is, however, perhaps even more interesting that the *Pseudo-Clementines* are no isolated case[65] – traces of "Christian" anti-Pauline tendencies can be found among several Christian writers: this is perhaps already the case in the canonical Letter of James,[66] it can be seen in the extant fragments of Hegesippus (2nd half of the second century CE) or in the *Anabathmoi Jakobou*, an apocryphal text going back to a Jewish Christian group called Ebionites (summarized by Epiphanius, *haer.* 30.16.6–9)[67] and goes on into late texts like the re-

---

[65] For more information see G. LÜDEMANN, *Paulus der Heidenapostel II: Antipaulinismus im frühen Christentum* (FRLANT 130; Göttingen: Vandenhoeck & Ruprecht, 1983) who concludes that the different anti-Pauline traditions must be seen as traditionally connected with each other.

[66] The question, however, whether James has to be read as a response to Pauline ideas or even an emerging corpus of Pauline texts is still a matter of dispute. For a discussion of the state of research see D.C. ALLISON, James 2:14–26: Polemic against Paul, Apology for James, in: *Ancient Perspectives on Paul* (ed. by T. Nicklas, A. Merkt & J. Verheyden; NTOA 102; Göttingen: Vandenhoeck & Ruprecht, 2013) 123–49.

[67] See R.E. VAN VOORST, *The Ascents of James: History and Theology of a Jewish-Christian Community* (SBL.DS 112; Atlanta: Scholars, 1989).

cently edited Ethiopian apocryphal passion narrative called the *Book of the Cock* (second half of the 5th century CE) which presents Paul even as a persecutor of Jesus himself.[68]

Again, these texts offer us another perspective: the borderlines between "Jewish", "Christian" or "not Jewish" enough could be drawn in very different ways.

3. The *Martyrdom of Polycarp* and the Situation in ancient Smyrna

While the *Gospel of Peter* offers an account of Jesus' passion and resurrection probably from the mid-second century, some of the earliest martyrdom accounts depicted the Christian martyrs in roles comparable to Christ.[69] This is already an issue in the story of Stephen's martyrdom according to the canonical book of Acts[70] where

---

[68] See P. PIOVANELLI, Enemi, 244–5; and IDEM, The *Book of the Cock* and the Rediscovery of Ancient Jewish-Christian Traditions in Fifth-Century Palestine, in: *The Changing Face of Judaism, Christanity, and Other Greco-Roman Religions in Antiquity* (ed. by I.H. Henderson & G.S. Oegema; JSHRZ.Studien 2; Gütersloh: Gütersloher, 2006) 308–22, esp. 311–3. – For some more information on this almost totally neglected writing see P. PIOVANELLI, Livre du Coq, in: *Écrits apocryphes chrétiens* II (ed. by P. Geoltrain & J.-D. Kaestli; Bibliothèque de la Pléiade; Paris: Gallimard, 2005) 137–52 (introduction) and 153–203 (French translation).

[69] For a full treatment of this issue see C.R. Moss, *The Other Christs: Imitating Jesus in Ancient Christian Ideologies of Martyrdom* (Oxford et al.: Oxford University Press, 2010).

[70] For a detailed interpretation of this text see H. BRAUN, *Geschichte des Gottesvolkes und christliche Identität. Eine kanon-*

many motifs depict Stephen as dying in the way Jesus did (see, for example the parallels between Luke 23.34,46 and Acts 7.59–60). In a comparable manner, the *Martyrdom of Polycarp* narrates Polycarp's death as a kind of an ideal martyrdom where the old bishop Polycarp of Smyrna is described as a Christ-like hero and a sacrifice for the powerful creator God (*Mart.Pol.* 14.1).[71]

Interestingly, even the "Jews" play their role in this account. Contrary to the stories about Jesus' passion they are not depicted as Polycarp's murderers, they play, however, a somewhat strange role. They appear for the first time in chapter 12 where they are mentioned together with the crowd responding to Polycarp's confession that he is a "Christian":

When Polycarp's confession "was proclaimed by the herald, the entire crowd, *Gentiles as well as Jews living in Smyrna*, cried out with uncontrollable anger and with a

isch-intertextuelle Auslegung der Stephanusepisode Apg 6,1–8,3 (WUNT II.279; Tübingen: Mohr, 2010).

[71] The date of this text has been a matter of renewed dispute during the last years. For a discussion of different views see B. DE-HANDSCHUTTER, The Martyrium Polycarpi: A Century of Research, in his: *Polycarpiana: Studies on Martyrdom and Persecution in Early Christianity* (BETL 205; Leuven et al.: Peeters, 2007) 43–83, esp. 56–62. – In even more recent literature see the differing views of S. PARVIS, The Martyrdom of Polycarp, in: *The Writings of the Apostolic Fathers* (ed. by P. Foster; London – New York: Continuum, 2007), 126–46, esp. 145, who votes for a conservative date around the middle of the second century CE, and C.R. Moss, On the Dating of Polycarp: Rethinking the place of the Martyrdom of Polycarp in the History of Christianity, *Early Christianity* 1 (2010) 539–74; EADEM, *Ancient Christian Martyrdom: Diverse Practices, Theologies, and Traditions* (New Haven – London: Yale University Press, 2012) 62–72.

loud shout: 'This is the teacher of Asia, the father of the Christians, *the destroyer of our gods*, who teaches not to sacrifice or worship" (*Mart.Pol.* 12.2; translation Holmes, 151). Is it possible that this account is based on memory or historical events? The sentence that Polycarp is "the destroyer of our gods" is not believable in the mouth of Jews. That's why the words "Gentiles as well as Jews living in Smyrna" look like a later insertion not concerned with the inner logic of the text.

A little bit later we find a comparable case: according to *Mart.Pol.* 13.1 the crowd is collecting wood for the pyre – the text adds: "the Jews being especially eager to assist in this, as is their custom" (translation Holmes, 152). Again, the words quoted above are at least unnecessary for the flow of the story because we do not hear about Jews in the immediate context again. Especially striking, however, is the fact that the whole scene is taking place on a "Great Sabbath" (21).[72] Even if we do not know the exact Sabbath practices of the second-century Smyrnean Jews, cutting and carrying wood was not one of them, as this belongs to the works which the Hebrew Bible forbids doing on a Sabbath. Again, it seems that we are dealing with an insertion into a text which is not interested in the

---

[72] On the problem of the "Great Sabbath" see mainly W. ROR-DORF, Zum Problem des grossen Sabbats im Polykarp- und Pioni-usmartyrium, in: *Pietas: Festschrift für Bernhard Kötting* (ed. by E. Dassmann & K.S. Frank; JAC.E 8; Münster: Aschendorff, 1980) 246–51. – See, however, R. CACITTI, *Grande Sabato: Il contesto pasquale quartodecimano nella formazione della teologia del martirio* (Studia Patristica Mediolanensia 19; Milan, 1994) who wants to interpret the motif of the "Great Sabbath" as a theological cipher and not an indication of time.

logic of the story, but wants to throw a very bad light on the Jews of Smyrna.

Finally, chapters 17–18 are even more problematic. According to the text, the "evil one" – that is, the devil – after having seen that Polycarp's martyrdom has won him "the crown of immortality" (17.1), wants to prevent the Christians from taking away his dead body. The text goes on: "So he incited Nicetes, the father of Herod and brother of Alce, to appeal to the magistrate not to hand over his body, 'or else,' he said, 'they may abandon the crucified one and begin to worship this man.' All this was done at the instigation and insistence of the Jews, who even watched when we were about to take the body from the fire" (17.2) ... and a little later the text goes on: "The centurion, therefore, seeing the opposition raised by the Jews, set Polycarp's body in the middle and cremated it, as is their custom" (18.1; translations Holmes, 153–4). Both passages evoke several questions:

Who is speaking to the magistrate? It seems like the "evil one" himself is addressing them, but obviously the text wants us to believe, it is the devil speaking through Nicetes. In any case, it is absolutely unthinkable that a Roman official argues in the way Nicetes does. Why should he be interested in the proper worship of Jesus? And why does the text additionally mention the Jews who, according to 17.2 and 18.1, insist on not releasing Polycarp's dead body?[73]

---

[73] One could, in addition to this, discuss the meaning of the words ὡς ἔθος αὐτοῖς ("as is their custom") in 18.1. Does the text refer to a Jewish custom of burning dead bodies? This would not be totally impossible, but at least somewhat strange. Perhaps, howev-

Even if we cannot be absolutely sure whether the name Herod wants to create a link to Jesus' passion according to Luke, the text, again, establishes a connection between the Jews of Smyrna and Polycarp's death.[74] Obviously, the *Mart.Pol.* is interested in describing the Jews of Smyrna as at least sharing in the responsibility for Polycarp's death.

What is the reason for this description of the "Jews"? Scholars have traditionally given two kinds of responses (which can, however, be combined).[75] I think, it has become clear that at least most of the passages where *Mart. Pol.* refers to Jews must be literary creations because they more or less contradict everything we know about Jewish beliefs and customs. At least, that is the reason why a purely "historical" interpretation of the passages does not seem to be plausible. Of course, this does not exclude the possibility that the text refers to memories about Jewish influence and hostility in second-century Smyrna.[76]

---

er, the text just refers to Gentile customs – and then does not create any problems at all. For this interpretation see G. BUSCHMANN, *Martyrium des Polykarp* (KAV 6; Göttingen: Vandenhoeck & Ruprecht, 1998) 338.

[74] See also G. BUSCHMANN, *Martyrium*, 147: "Mit dem jüdischen Namen Herodes ist nicht nur die Parallele zum Evangelium erzeugt (Lk 13,31; Lk 23,6–12; Act 4,27 ...), der jüdische Name Herodes, der als Eirenarch zu den einflußreichen Kreisen gehört, nimmt zugleich die später als Drahtzieher genannten ‚Juden' vorweg, vgl. MartPol 12,2 f., 1,1; 17. Die jüdische Lokalgewalt wird zur eigentlichen Verfolgungsinstanz."

[75] Also, see the overview of G. BUSCHMANN, *Martyrium*, 209.

[76] See the important data brought together by G. BUSCHMANN, *Martyrium*, 210–2 who himself leans toward a "historical interpretation".

Be this as it may, I think the role of the Jews in the *Martyrdom of Polycarp* is not only part of a reflection of (somewhat strange) memories about past events (and thus directed backwards), but must be understood as part of the text's literary strategy. At least in some cases one can read that it is trying diligently to harmonize Polycarp's death as much as possible with Jesus' passion.[77] This, however, would mean that the idea of "the Jews'" responsibility for Jesus' (and his followers') death must have been established already as a literary "topos" which (at least for the author of the *Martyrdom of Polycarp*) belonged to and was expected in any real "passion account". I am not sure whether this is really the case. If it were, then I would expect some clearer literary links between the passages about Jews in the *Martyrdom of Polycarp* and the canonical passion accounts.

A few years ago, an alternative solution for the problem was offered. According to E. Leigh Gibson, the description of "Jews" in the *Martyrdom of Polycarp* must be read alongside two other texts which only seemingly are witnesses to Jewish-Christian polemics in late ancient Smyrna: the New Testament Book of Revelation and the third-century *Martyrdom of Pionius*.[78] In accordance

---

[77] See, for example, W.R. SCHOEDEL, *The Apostolic Fathers: A New Translation and Commentary* 5 (Camden, N.Y. – Toronto, 1967) 67.

[78] For more details see E. Leigh GIBSON, The Jews and Christians in the *Martyrdom of Polycarp*, in: *The Ways That Never Parted: Jews and Christians in Late Antiquity and the Early Middle Ages* (ed. by A.H. Becker & A. Yoshiko Reed; Minneapolis: Fortress, 2007) 145–58 who is developing ideas of J.M. LIEU, *Image*

with recent studies on Revelation[79] Leigh Gibson gives a new interpretation of the infamous passage Rev 2.9–10 (addressed to the community of Smyrna: "I know the slander on the part of those who say they are Jews and are not, but are a synagogue of Satan. Do not fear what you are about to suffer."): according to Gibson, this text does not refer to Jews, but to members of the "Christian" community who still participated in the community life of the Jewish synagogue. The same issue seems to have been at stake in the third century *Martyrdom of Pionius* also located in Smyrna.[80] Gibson concludes: "Long misread as polemics against outsiders, these texts address communities of Jesus-followers who do not agree on the status of their Jewish inheritance."[81]

Gibson's own solution of the problem, however, seems to draw the parallel to the other witnesses too far.

He suggests "that the insertion of Jews into the passage regarding Polycarp's remains reflects a practice Christians employed in other contexts: 'thinking with Jews' about Judaizers. Although the best known example of this is John Chrysostom's fourth-century sermons (long called *Against the Jews* even though it was the synagogue, attending members of his Antiochene Christian congregation who precipitated his attacks),

---

and Reality: The Jews in the World of the Christians in the Second Century (Edinburgh: T & T Clark, 1996).

[79] J.W. MARSHALL, *Parables of War: Reading John's Jewish Apocalypse* (Studies in Christianity and Judaism / Études sur le christianisme et le judaïsme 19; Waterloo, Ont.: Wilfrid Laurier University Press, 2001), and D. FRANKFURTER, Jews or Not? Reconstructing the 'Other' in Rev 2:9 and 3:9, *HTR* 94 (2001) 403–25.

[80] E. Leigh GIBSON, Jewish Antagonism or Christian Polemic: The Case of the *Martyrdom of Pionius*, *JECS* 9 (2001) 339–58.

[81] E. Leigh GIBSON, Jews, 151.

the technique is also employed in the other Smyrnean martyrdom text, the third-century *Martyrdom of Pionius.* ... [A] contributor to *MPoly*, wanting to claim Polycarp's legacy for his
brand of Christianity, uses a hostile depiction of Jews as a sur-
rogate for criticizing Judaizing Christians. In this contributor's
avoidance of a more direct attack, the original target, the Judaizers, recedes as the original context of the polemics shifts
over time. Eventually, tensions over the place of the Jewish law
within the Christian community diminish and are replaced by
those between Jews and Christians, producing the vexing inter-
pretative challenge we have just examined."[82]

I agree with part of Gibson's analysis. Although the situation is even less clear than in Sardis mentioned above,
there is indeed some evidence for at least one community
of non-Christian Jews in ancient Smyrna. At least some
inscriptions tell us about the existence of a synagogue,
and at least in a few places we find grave inscriptions
mentioning Jewish names.[83] Perhaps at least parts of this
community must have been quite liberal; the most interesting Jewish inscription of Smyrna (IJO II 43; 2nd or 3rd
century CE) mentions that a certain Rufina held the office of an *Archisynagogos*, the head of a synagogue.[84] In

---

[82] E. Leigh GIBSON, Jews, 158.

[83] For more information see E. Leigh GIBSON, Jews in the Inscriptions of Smyrna, *JJS* 56 (2005) 66–79; and A. ANGERSTORFER,
Antike jüdische Grabinschriften aus christlicher Zeit (ca. 100–500
n.Chr.): Spuren von Hoffnung auf eine Auferstehung der Toten
und die 'kommende Welt', in: J. DRESKEN-WEILAND – A. AN-
GERSTORFER – A. MERKT, *Himmel – Paradies – Schalom: Tod und
Jenseits in antiken christlichen und jüdischen Grabinschriften*
(Handbuch zur Geschichte des Todes im frühen Christentum und
seiner Umwelt 1; Regensburg: Schnell & Steiner, 2012) 277–386,
esp. 304–8.

[84] For the text see A. ANGERSTORFER, Grabinschriften, 305. –

addition to this, like Gibson I think that, if put together
with Revelation and the *Martyrdom of Pionius* (and perhaps even Ignatius, *Smyrn.*), the *Martyrdom of Polycarp*
can be read as a witness of a conflict between followers
of Christ who were struggling for their identity in relation to the synagogue. I would, however, not agree that
the text – where speaking about "Jews" – speaks about
"Judaizers" (surely another anachronism …), that is
Christ-followers, who are still associated with the synagogue. Why, then, would he speak about them as putting
together wood for Polycarp's pyre? And why would they
not be interested in handing over Polycarp's body to the
"we-group" writing the text? I would, while taking Gibson's interpretation of Revelation and *Martyrdom of Pionius* in account, therefore, propose a somewhat different
solution. In fact, the groups of "Christ-followers" in
Smyrna have an identity problem. At least some of them
still feel connected with the synagogue, probably follow
the Torah (or at least have developed a certain Torah-observance), while others have ceased their relations with
"Jews". This is, not only in times of persecution, where
the confession of being a Christian matters, seen as a real
problem. The *Martyrdom of Polycarp*, that's why, does
not depict "Judaizers" as Jews, but develops a stereotype
of "Jews" comparable to the one we find in passion accounts like the *Gospel of Peter.* The function of this stere-

---

For the office of an *archisynagogos* see: T. RAJAK – D. NOY, Ar-
chisynagogoi: Office, Title and Social Status in Greco-Roman Synagogue, in: *The Jewish Dialogue with Greece and Rome. Studies in
Cultural and Social Interaction* (ed. by T. Rajak; AGAJU 48; Leiden – Boston – Cologne: Brill, 2001) 393–429.

otype in the Smyrnean context is quite clear. It "creates" boundaries by describing two groups with two distinct roles in the story: while there is a "we-group" standing on the side of Polycarp, the martyr, the "Jews" are among the persecutors[85] – and there is surely no bridge between persecutors and martyrs. That's why, Christ-followers, according to our text, are forced to decide whether they still want to be related with the persecutors or with their victims. At least indirectly (and read together with other witnesses about Jewish-Christian relations in Smyrna) the *Martyrdom of Polycarp* thus can be understood as a text witnessing struggles within different groups of "Christ-followers" in second-century Smyrna, a text which created borderlines which – at least for some "Christians" who (still?) felt as a part of the synagogue – did not exist.

4. Conclusion

Even after only a few examples it already becomes clear: speaking about the relation of "Judaism" and "Christianity" in the second century CE is somewhat difficult, or even more: it is in danger of taking over a simplifying anachronism. We have to be aware of a few problems: first, we should not simply read today's images of "Juda-

---

[85] The question whether and how far "Jews" participated in the persecution of Christ-followers is heavily debated. Texts like the *Martyrdom of Polycarp*, Justin, *apol.* 1.31.6; Tertullian, *scorp.* 10 or Eusebius, *h.e.* 5.16, however, mean that we should not exclude this possibility too quickly.

ism" and "Christianity" into the ancient texts, and second – deeply connected to it – we should avoid taking over simplifying images created by a few Christian fathers who tried to create "orthodoxy" and called it "Christianity". Third, we should take into account that even authors like Ignatius or Irenaeus – in a certain sense, powerful figures – did not have the power to establish their ideas through anything else but the power of writing and speaking. At least from what we can imagine about ancient perspectives they were only part of a much broader debate of very different groups and voices. They created and/or took over categories like "Judaism" and "Christianity" but these categories only mirrored parts of past realities: in fact what we can see until today is a multifaceted mosaïque of groups struggling for truth and trying to define their identities against others. Perhaps a few more conclusions can be added:

1. Our second century sources should never be read as theological tractates written at the desk of professional theologians for publication in the modern world of books, they are instead writings written for very concrete contexts and situations which we – at least in some cases – can partially (re-)construct. This means:

2. The introduction of categories like "Judaism" or "Christianity" has to do with burning questions of developing and defining identities in challenging situations within a complex world. The less complex these categories are the more they can easily be taken over – this has been true, in some cases, even until our times – and, as a consequence, they lead with greater ease to stereotypes of the "other(s)", the "opponents" which, in the case of

many second-century Christian writings, are simply called "the Jews".

3. As far as we have seen, however, the different stereotypes we have discovered are by no means stereotype, but have very different functions, denote very different groups and draw very different borderlines between these different groups.

4. And, finally, our second century "Christian" sources represent only a very small spectrum of "reality". In other words, even if we take everything that we have into account, we still lack the biggest part of real "ancient perspectives" on the topic: how did the many uneducated followers of Christ who were not able to write and to read, think about the situation? In fact, their voices, which probably represent something of a majority, will remain silent forever. In line with this, to what degree are basic, fundamental statements from elite members within the different groups of what came to be considered "Christian churches" made in situations of challenge and crisis that we may consider representative for the manifold situations of everyday life for common people?

We can only imagine that their reality was much more complex, and also more fascinating than what history can tell us.

Chapter 2:

The Chosen People, its God
and the Covenant

How did early "Christian" writers deal with the fact that "Jews" and "Christians" worship the same God? Or perhaps better: how did followers of Jesus Christ perceive the relationship between "Jews" and their God? We will see that at least a few "Christian" groups claimed that the "Jews" adhered to an erroneous, perhaps evil, perhaps just (but not merciful) God, while only they worshipped a good deity. In our eyes this might seem strange: how is it possible to discuss the question whether the God of Jesus, the Jew, could be anyone other than the God of Israel? What, in our eyes, may seem incredible, however, has bothered followers of Jesus Christ until today. While our problem today has to do with the fact that Christians, on the one hand, speak about a Trinitarian God and, on the other hand, identify this God with the One God of Israel, in the first and second centuries – that is, more than a hundred years before the Ecumenical Councils of Nicaea (325 CE) and Constantinople (381 CE) – the problem has been posed in different ways:

While Paul in his letter to the Romans, chapters 9–11, argued that, if God's life-giving word is trustworthy, His Covenant with Israel must be eternal, and, finally, the

whole of Israel will be saved (Rom 11.26),[1] many second-century "Christian" authors thought differently: at
least according to some, if not many "Christian" writings, Israel had, with its refusal of Christ, lost its status as
a Chosen People. Several writers went even further – according to them, there had never been anything like a
valid covenant between God and His People. Finally,
others tried to solve the question in a different manner:
for them, the God of Israel was only a minor, evil deity
who had to be distinguished from the "Christian" God.

Again, I would like to show this by a few examples:

Quite a few ancient "Christian" authors were mainly
interested to show that "Christian" worship and, in addition to this, perhaps also "Christian" understandings of
God were superior to Jewish ideas. A context which was
especially suitable for comparisons between different
kinds of worship was the apologetic discourse where
"Christians" tried to defend their way of life against accusation and criticism from the side of pagans.[2] Many of
the extant written apologies were comparing different

---

[1] For extensive discussions on the role and interpretation of
Rom 9–11 see the articles collected in F. WILK – J. ROSS WAGNER
(ed.s), *Between Gospel and Election* (WUNT 257; Tübingen: Mohr
2010). For my own view of the text see T. NICKLAS, Paulus und die
Errettung Israels: Röm 11,25–36 in der exegetischen Diskussion
und im jüdisch-christlichen Dialog, *Early Christianity* 2 (2011)
173–97.

[2] For more information on the genre see: A.-C. JACOBSEN, Apologetics and Apologies – Some Definitions, in *Continuity and Dis-
continuity in Early Christian Apologetics* (ed. by J. Ulrich, A.-J.
Jacobsen & M. Kahlos; Early Christianity in the Context of Antiquity 5; Frankfurt am Main et al: Peter Lang, 2009) 5–21.

categories of worship – "pagan" forms of worship[3] were compared to "Jewish" and, finally, "Christian" worship. Thus, these texts reused and/or created categories we tend to use even today. At least the writers mentioned in the following paragraph thus distinguished between the categories of "Judaism" and "Christianity" – and they understood "Christianity" more or less as a single, unified entity distinct from "Judaism". Even if their arguments were not only directed outwards, but intended to grant and strengthen inward certainty for the groups they represented,[4] they depicted "Christianity" as a uniform movement as it had been seen and attacked from many outsiders.

---

[3] I deliberately choose the word "worship" instead of "religion". Regarding the problems of this category if used for ancient forms of "worship" see for example B. NONGBRI, *Before Religion: A History of a Modern Concept* (New Haven – London: Yale University Press, 2012).

[4] See for example the discussion in L.S. NASRALLAH, *Christian Responses to Roman Art and Architecture: The Second-Century Church Amid the Spaces of Empire* (Cambridge et al.: Cambridge University Press, 2010) 23–8. – For an argument working with concrete texts see C. SCHUBERT, Heiden oder Christen? Das Zielpublikum von Minucius Felix' *Octavius*, in: *Ad veram religionem reformare. Frühchristliche Apologetik zwischen Anspruch und Wirklichkeit* (ed. by C. Schubert & A. von Stockhausen; Erlanger Forschungen A. Geisteswissenschaften 109; Erlangen: Universitätsverlag Erlangen-Nürnberg, 2006) 123–48, and T.P. HENDERSON, *The Gospel of Peter and Early Christian Apologetics. Rewriting the Story of Jesus' Death, Burial, and Resurrection* (WUNT II.301; Tübingen: Mohr, 2011).

1. Covenant Refused …

A first group of texts concentrate mainly on the idea of *God's Covenant with Israel*. They develop the idea that at least after the rejection of the Messiah, God refused his Chosen People.

1.1 The Epistle of Barnabas

Let me start with an extreme example: *Barn.* 16.3–4 seems to refer to Emperor Hadrian's order to rebuild Jerusalem as a Hellenistic city called *Aelia Capitolina* and to build a Jupiter Temple at the place of the former Second Temple, (mentioned also by Cassius Dio 69.12.1–2), which lead to the Bar Kohkba War of 132–135 CE.[5] That's why the *Letter of Barnabas* can probably be dated to the time between spring 130 and the outbreak of the war early 132 CE. While the text's provenance is insecure, there is, however, a certain probability that it originated in the Egyptian metropolis Alexandria[6] and goes back to an

---

[5] For a detailed discussion see for example R. Hvalvik, *The Struggle for Scripture and Covenant: The Purpose of the Epistle of Barnabas and Jewish-Christian Competition in the Second Century* (WUNT II 82; Tübingen: Mohr, 1996) 18–23, and F.R. Prostmeier, *Der Barnabasbrief* (KAV 8; Göttingen: Vandenhoeck & Ruprecht, 1999) 119–30.

[6] Regarding introductory issues see the detailed analysis F.R. Prostmeier, *Barnabasbrief* (1999), 11–134, and idem, Der Barnabasbrief, in: *Die Apostolischen Väter: Eine Einleitung* (ed. by W. Pratscher; UTB; Göttingen: Vandenhoeck & Ruprecht, 2009) 39–58, esp. 45–6. The main arguments for an Alexandrian provenance are: the author's use of an allegorical method of Scriptural interpretation and its early use by authors like Clement and Origen. – This

early "Christian" teacher with a good knowledge of Israel's Scriptures.[7] Although the author's pseudonym refers to "Barnabas", Paul's "Jewish" companion,[8] the text belongs to the early "Christian" writings with the deepest anti-Jewish potential.[9] The most interesting point to us, here, is the fact that *Barnabas* does not just develop the idea that Israel has lost its status as a chosen people after the rejection of Jesus. According to *Barnabas*, this happened much earlier, immediately after the covenant was given:

---

solution is, however, quite insecure. A full overview and critical discussion of proposals (Egypt / Syria / Palestine / Asia Minor) is offered by R. HVALVIK, *Struggle*, 35–42, who finally remains hesitating about a firm conclusion. Different ideas about the provenance of the text sometimes also lead to different dating. See, e. g., P. PRIGENT, *Épitre de Barnabé* (SC 172; Paris: Cerf, 1971) 26–7, who cautiously discusses the broader time window between the two Jewish wars of 115/16 and 132–135 CE as relevant, while P. RICHARDSON and M. SHUKSTER, Barnabas, Nerva, and the Yavnean Rabbis, *JTS* 34 (1983) 31–55, argue for an earlier date during the reign of Nerva. This, however, is dependent on ideas about the early Rabbinic movement which seem not to be acceptable any more.

[7] For more details regarding the author of *Barn.* as a teacher see U. NEYMEYR, *Die christlichen Lehrer im zweiten Jahrhundert: Ihre Lehrtätigkeit, ihr Selbstverständnis und ihre Geschichte* (VigChr.S 4; Leiden et al: Brill, 1989) 169–80.

[8] For a full discussion of the figure of Barnabas in life and literature see M. ÖHLER, *Barnabas: Die historische Person und ihre Rezeption in der Apostelgeschichte* (WUNT 156; Tübingen: Mohr, 2003).

[9] For further information and a much more detailed discussion than the one I can provide here, see the important study by F. R. PROSTMEIER, Antijüdische Polemik im Rahmen christlicher Hermeneutik. Zum Streit über christliche Identität in der Alten Kirche, *ZAC* 6 (2002) 38–58.

Two passages are especially interesting:

(1) "[D]o not be like certain people; that is do not continue to pile up your sins while claiming, 'Our covenant remains valid.' In fact, those people lost it completely in the following way, when Moses had just received it. For the scripture says: 'And Moses was on the mountain fasting for forty days and forty nights, and he received the covenant from the Lord, stone tablets inscribed by the finger of the hand of the Lord.' But by turning to idols they lost it. For thus says the Lord: 'Moses, Moses, go down quickly, because your people, whom you led out of Egypt, have broken the law.' And Moses understood and hurled the two tablets from his hands, and their covenant was shattered, in order that the covenant of the beloved Jesus might be sealed in our heart, in hope inspired by faith in him" (*Barn.* 4.6c-8; translation Holmes, 180).

Somewhat later we read:

(2) "But let us see if he has actually given the covenant that he swore to the fathers he would give to the people. He has indeed given it; but they were not worthy to receive it because of their sins. For the prophet says: 'And Moses was fasting on Mount Sinai forty days and forty nights in order to receive the Lord's covenant with the people. And Moses received from the Lord the two tablets that were inscribed by the finger of the hand of the Lord in the spirit.' And when Moses received them he began to carry them down to give them to the people. And the Lord said to Moses: 'Moses, Moses, go down quickly, because your people, whom you led out of the land of Egypt, has broken the law.' And Moses understood that once again they had made cast images for themselves, and he hurled the tablets from his hands, and the tablets of the Lord's covenant were shattered. So Moses received it, but they were not worthy" (*Barn.* 14.1b-4a; translation Holmes, 192).

The question whether God's covenant with Israel[10] was
still valid and of impact for followers of Christ seems to
have been not only a theoretical problem for *Barn.*'s community, but a burning issue (see also *Barn.* 13). From
Barn. 4.6 it becomes clear that our author had "certain
people" in mind who obviously thought that the covenant
between God and his people "remains valid"[11] – and that's
why they behaved "like Jews".[12] These believers in Christ
seemingly still observed the Sabbath. This behaviour led
Barn. to sharp polemics (see *Barn.* 15 with a quote of Isa
1.13 in 15.8; cf. also *Barn.* 2.5); another issue probably had
to do with questions of proper fasting and the Mosaic
food laws, as *Barn.* 3 and 10 suggest.[13] Chapter 9, in addition, utters sharp polemics against circumcision – *Barn.*
9.4 even goes so far to interpret this practice as due to the

---

[10] On *Barn.*'s idea of "covenant" see F.R. Prostmeier, *Barnabasbrief*, 208–11.

[11] We have, however, to admit that the textual transmission of
Barn. 4.6 causes some troubles. For more information see F.R.
Prostmeier, *Barnabasbrief*, 191–2, and P. Prigent – R.A. Kraft,
Épître de Barnabé (SC 172; Paris: Cerf, 1971) 96–7.

[12] The question whether these people are pagan "Judaizers"
(e.g., M. Murray, *Playing a Jewish Game. Gentile Christian Judaizing in the First and Second Centuries CE* [Studies in Christianity and Judaism/Études sur le christianisme et le judaïsme 13; Waterloo, Ont.: Wilfried Laurier, 2004]) or "Jewish Christians" (e.g.,
S.C. Mimouni, *Early Judaeo-Christianity. Historical Essays* [In-
terdisciplinary Studies in Ancient Culture and Religion 13]; Leuven: Peeters, 2012], 205–8) is still a matter of debate. For my own
analysis it is most important to deal with "Christian" believers for
whom the covenant between God and Israel remained valid even
after the Christ event.

[13] For more details see S.G. Wilson, *Related Strangers: Jews
and Christians 70–170 C.E.* (Minneapolis: Fortress, 1995) 129–31.

lead of an "evil angel".[14] *Barn.*'s main argument, as we see it in both the quotes above, however, goes deeper: according to him, there has never been a successful covenant between God and Israel.[15] God made an attempt according to both *Barn.* 4 and 14, but because of its worship of the Golden Calf (a scene which is, however, only indirectly alluded to) Israel immediately lost its status as a chosen people. The author of *Barn.* bases his argument on a mixture of quotes from Exod 31.18; 34.28, 32.7 and 19 (*Barn.* 4), respectively on quotes from and allusions to Exod

---

[14] For a detailed analysis of this passage and its backgrounds see J. CARLETON PAGET, *Barnabas 9.4, a peculiar verse on circumcision*, in his: *Jews, Christians and Jewish Christians in Antiquity* (WUNT 251; Tübingen: Mohr, 2010) 77–89 who calls this argument "unique" (87).

[15] J.N. RHODES, *The Epistle of Barnabas and the Deuteronomic Tradition: Polemics, Paraenesis, and the Legacy of the Golden Calf Incident* (WUNT II.188; Tübingen: Mohr, 2004) 175, however, would criticize this view. He argues: "On the one hand, Barnabas asserts that because of its worship of the golden calf, Israel lost its covenant once and for all at Sinai. On the other hand, various data in the epistle suggest that Israel's covenant relationship with God remains intact until the coming of Jesus. These data include (1) the citation of prophetic authorities from the later history of Israel; (2) appeal to the prophetic/typological significance of a few subsequent events or rituals; (3) hints of a gospel mission to Israel; (4) declarations that the rejection of Jesus was what brought Israel's sins to completion. Barnabas thus identifies not one but two climactic thresholds in the history of Israel: the debacle at Sinai and the rejection of Jesus." While I would agree with the last sentence, I would not agree with the arguments before: If – like in Ignatius – the prophets are already seen as "hidden" followers of Christ, (1) and (2) do not count, (3) a gospel mission to Israel does not contradict the idea that there is no valid covenant between God and Israel and (4) just shows that Israel, according to *Barn*, has always sinned.

31.18; 32.7–19; Deut 9.12–17 (*Barn.* 14), most of them
more or less related to the crisis of the events around the
worship of the Golden Calf. With these passages, the Torah indeed describes a deep crisis in the relation between
God and his People[16] – however, the argument can work
only if the author of *Barn.* consciously avoids any hint
that the same Torah tells us that by Moses' initiative and
through God's mercy this crisis was overcome.

If our text really was written in Alexandria around 130
CE, its violent abuse of scripture to prove a point can perhaps not be excused, but contextualized and thus be understood somewhat better: Alexandria had just survived
the cruel Diaspora War of the years 115–117 CE which
must have been a catastrophe for the formerly proud and
glorious Jewish community/ies of the city (but also of the
Egyptian land).[17] But the situation was perhaps even
more dangerous with another catastrophe, a new "Jewish" War – the Bar Kokhba War – on the horizon.[18] In this

---

[16] For a detailed and sensitive analysis of the stories around the
Golden Calf event see M. MARK, *'Mein Angesicht geht' (Ex 33,14):
Gottes Zusage personaler Führung* (HBS 66; Freiburg et al.: Herder,
2011).

[17] See, for example, the interesting analysis of E. J. EPP, Jews and
the Jewish Community in Oxyrhynchus: Socio-Religious Context
for the New Testament Papyri, in: *New Testament Manuscripts.
Their Texts and Their World* (ed. by T. J. Kraus & T. Nicklas; TENT
2; Leiden – Boston: Brill, 2006) 13–52 about the presence of "Jews"
in papyri from Upper Egypt.

[18] The main parts of my interpretation thus also hold when
Barn., as S. C. MIMOUNI, *Judaeo-Christianty*, 204–5, suggests, has
been written in a Syro-Palestinian context where the future war
must have meant an even more dangerous threat for ancient Christians.

context,[19] it could have been especially dangerous for the Christian community to be associated too closely with "Jews".[20] The author of *Barn.*'s purpose was two-fold: on the one hand, the anti-Jewish "propaganda" text[21] serves to convince as many members of his community[22] as possible not to follow "Christ believers" who behaved like Jews. On the other hand, the author did not want to abandon Scripture[23] – that's why it was claimed for the "Christians" – or better: for his group of "Christians" – alone.

---

[19] One has to add: in the context of a city like Alexandria which was infamous for its history of anti-Judaism. For more information see for example J.J. COLLINS, Anti-Semitism in Antiquity? The Case of Alexandria, in his: *Jewish Cult and Hellenistic Culture: Essays on the Jewish Encounter with Hellenism and Roman Rule* (JSJ.S 100; Leiden – Boston: Brill, 2005) 181–201, and J. CARLETON PAGET, Jews and Christians in ancient Alexandria – from the Ptolemies to Caracalla, in his: *Jews, Christians and Jewish Christians in Antiquity* (WUNT 251; Tübingen: Mohr, 2010) 123–47, esp. 126–37.

[20] This must, however, remain a bit of speculation. For a different interpretation reading *Barn.* in a Syrian context see, e.g., M. MURRAY, *Playing*, 50–9; for a different interpretation in the context of Alexandria, see J. CARLETON PAGET, *Barnabas* 9.4, 87 who interprets the text as an answer to proselytizing activities "on the part of Jews whose confidence had been revitalized by the prospect of a rebuilt temple", or R.S. MACLENNAN, *Early Christian Texts on Jews and Judaism* (BJS 194; Atlanta: Scholars, 1990) who dates *Barn.* to 115–117 and interprets the text as a "moderating voice in the crisis" (43) of this time around the Diaspora War.

[21] So K. WENGST, *Didache (Apostellehre), Barnabasbrief, Zweiter Klemensbrief, Schrift an Diognet* (Darmstadt: WBG, 1984) 113: "ein in Brieform gekleidetes Propagandaschreiben".

[22] Of course, we can only assume whether the author of *Barn.* was a male.

[23] Regarding the role of Scripture in *Barn.* see R. HVALVIK, *Struggle*, 102–36.

What does this mean for our main question? *Barn.* does
not deny that the God of the "Christians" is identical
with the God worshipped by the Jews. He would, however, hesitate to call this God the God of Israel any more,
because Israel had been lead astray already long ago: for
Barn., the idea that there never had been a valid covenant
between God and Israel leads to the conclusion that there
cannot be any salvation through "Jewish" worship and
"Judaism". The "Christianity" proclaimed by *Barn.* thus
cuts all connections to "lived" "Judaism" while claiming
the God of Israel and its Scriptures solely for itself.

1.2 Justin, First Apology

In his *First Apology*,[24] addressed to Emperor Antoninus
Pius (138–161 CE),[25] Justin Martyr wants to show
through many examples the importance of belief in
Christ, but also important aspects of the present situation
of Israel and the Church that have already been prophe-
sied in the Scriptures of Israel. In this context, he is not
only concerned with the relationship of a Church mainly
consisting of pagan "Christians" and "the Jews," but he
even roots this relation in Israel's scriptures. *Apol.* 1.47
addresses the destruction of Jerusalem during the wars of

---

[24] The text is usually dated to the years around 153 or 154/55
CE. See short overview in S. PARVIS – P. FOSTER (ed.s), *Justin Martyr and His Worlds* (Minneapolis: Fortress, 2007) xiii and the detailed discussion of Ch. MUNIER, *Justin: Apologie pour des Chrétiens* (SC 507; Paris: Cerf, 2006) 24–8.

[25] For more details on the politics of Antoninus Pius and the
situation of the Christians at this time see C. MUNIER, *Justin: Apologie*, 43–56.

66–70 CE and 132–135 CE and the fact that after 135 Jews were not allowed to enter the former Jerusalem any more. According to Justin, this bitter fate must be seen as a fulfilment of Isa 64.9–11; 1.7 and Jer 27.3 LXX. *Apol.* 1.49 treats similar issues. We read:

And again, how it was said by the same Isaiah: the Gentile nations who were not looking for Him should worship Him, but the Jews who always expected Him should not recognize Him when He came. And the words are spoken as from the person of Christ; and they are these *"I was manifest to them that asked not for Me; I was found of them that sought Me not: I said, Behold Me, to a nation that called not on My name. I spread out My hands to a disobedient and gainsaying people, to those who walked in a way that is not good, but follow after their own sins; a people that provoked Me to anger to My face"* (Isa 65.1–3 LXX). For the Jews having the prophecies, and being always in expectation of the Christ to come, did not recognize Him; and not only so, but even treated Him shamefully. But the Gentiles, who had never heard anything about Christ, until the apostles set out from Jerusalem, preached concerning Him and gave them the prophecies, were filled with joy and faith, cast away their idols, and dedicated themselves to the Unbegotten God through Christ. And that it was foreknown that these infamous things should be uttered against those who confessed Christ, and that those who slandered Him, and said that it was well to preserve the ancient customs, should be miserable, hear what was briefly said by Isaiah; it is this: *"Woe unto them that call sweet bitter, and bitter sweet"* (Isa 5.20) (adapted from *Ante-Nicene Fathers* I).

The key of Justin's argument is a quote of Isa 65.1–3 LXX (cf. also Rom 10.20–21) which he understands as Christ's own word. According to this, two kinds of humans have to be distinguished: one group who has not known about Christ before, and one who knew about the coming of

Christ, but did not recognize him when he came, did not walk in the way of truth and even scorned him. Justin identifies both with the "Church of the pagans" and with "the Jews". Groups which do not fit into this scheme – like "Jewish" followers of Christ – are not even mentioned here. The crucial point of distinction here is connected to Christology. For Justin, who already understands Jesus Christ as the incarnation of the pre-existent divine Logos who was himself speaking in the words of the prophets (*apol.* 1.38),[26] not understanding Jesus as Christ, means not recognizing that this Christ has spoken to (and through) Moses and the prophets. That's why, even if Justin does not go so far as to say that God has revoked his Covenant with Israel, this conclusion is more or less at hand. The key problem, however, here does not have to do with *halakha*, but with *theo*-logy, a theology which for Justin cannot be understood without Christology any more.

---

[26] For an overview of Justin Martyr's Christology see A. GRILL-MEIER, *Jesus der Christus im Glauben der Kirche 1: Von der Apostolischen Zeit bis zum Konzil von Chalcedon (451)* (Freiburg et al.: ³1990) 202–5 and L. W. HURTADO, 'Jesus' as God's Name, and Jesus and God's Embodied Name in Justin Martyr, in: *Justin Martyr and His Worlds* (ed. by S. Parvis & P. Foster; Minneapolis: Fortress, 2007) 128–36. – On the relation between God's word and Christ, the logos, in Justin's writings, see M. J. EDWARDS, Justin's Logos and the Word of God, *JECS* 3 (1995) 261–80.

1.3 Some more examples:

1.3.1 Justin is only one of many authors one could mention.[27] Among the lesser known examples is the so-called
Physiologus, the first "Christian" semi-popular "natural
history" already mentioned in chapter 1, a text bringing
together alleged characteristics of animals, plants and
stones with aspects of salvation history.[28] According to
the *Physiologus'* idea of salvation history, the covenant
between God and Israel has been renounced when Israel
did not accept Jesus as Christ. What makes the *Physiologus* special is the fact that it relates natural phenomena, an
allegorical interpretation of Scripture and a "Christian"
idea of salvation history according to which God has rejected Israel. A typical example can be seen in chapter 27
speaking about the crow:

"Nicely has Jeremiah spoken to Jerusalem [Jer 3.2]: 'You sat
down like a widowed crow.' The *Physiologus* says about the
crow that she takes only one spouse, and if her husband dies, she

---

[27] For some more examples – perhaps not all of them fully con-
vincing – see for example, H. C. BRENNECKE, Die Kirche als wahres
Israel. Ein apologetischer Topos in der Auseinandersetzung mit
Markion und der Gnosis, in: *Ad veram religionem reformare:
Frühchristliche Apologetik zwischen Anspruch und Wirklichkeit*
(ed. by C. Schubert & A. von Stockhausen; Erlanger Forschungen
Reihe A: Geisteswissenschaften 109; Erlangen: Universitätsbund
Erlangen-Nürnberg, 2006) 47–69, esp. 49–57.

[28] Regarding the *Physiologus'* techniques of educating, enter-
taining and, finally, convincing its readers by introducing them
into its world see T. NICKLAS, Staunen über Natur – Wunder des
Glaubens: Die "Welten" des Physiologus, in *Credible, Incredible:
The Miraculous in the Ancient Mediterranean World* (ed. by J. E.
Spittler & T. Nicklas; WUNT 321; Tübingen: Mohr, 2014) 228–51.

does not take another spouse, like the Raven does not take another wife.

The Jewish synagogue is the earthly Jerusalem that has killed the Lord; Christ will never be her spouse. 'I promised you to one husband, to Christ, so that I might present you as a pure virgin to him.' [2 Cor 11.2]. But they have committed adultery with wood and stone."

Although stated in another genre from Justin, we find aspects of the same argument: even in the times of the *Physiologus*, almost two centuries after Jesus' death, the synagogue, already called "synagogue *of the Jews*", is identified with "Jerusalem who has killed the Lord". Again, the idea that "the synagogue of the Jews" is responsible for the Lord's death, forms the background of the idea that Christ cannot be Israel's bridegroom: this very personal, intimate image of the "covenant" finds its roots already in the Scriptures of Israel and their reception history (see, e. g., Hosea or the reception of the *Song of Songs*). While the Scriptures of Israel, however, understand God as the bridegroom, Christ has taken his place.

1.3.2 The *Kerygma Petri* (= *Preaching of Peter*) has been a pseudepigraphical apologetic writing going back to the first quarter of the second century CE;[29] an Egyptian provenance seems likely, but cannot be proven any more.[30] Today only a few fragments of the original text

---

[29] For more detailed arguments see, e.g., H. PAULSEN, Das Kerygma Petri und die urchristliche Apologetik, *Zeitschrift für Kirchengeschichte* 88 (1977) 1–37, esp. 13.

[30] For a more detailed argument see M. CAMBE, *Kerygma Petri: Textus et Commentarius* (Corpus Christianorum. Series Apocryphorum 15; Turnhout: Brepols, 2003) 15–9 & 44–5.

are extant, mainly quotations in the writings of Clement of Alexandria, a few additional fragments in the writings of Origen, Gregory Nazianzen and John of Damascus and the newly edited "Berlin Coptic Book"[31] have been discussed. Even if we cannot be absolutely sure about its overall structure and character,[32] the text probably claimed to be a kind of a compendium of Peter's proclamation of the Gospel. Fragment 2 quoted by Clement of Alexandria in his *strom.* 6.5.39–41,[33] closely resembles

---

[31] Cf. G. Schenke Robinson (in collab. with H.-M. Schenke & U.K. Plisch), *Das Berliner "Koptische Buch". Eine wiederhergestellte frühchristlich-theologische Abhandlung* (CSCO 610 & 611; Scriptores Coptici 49; Leuven: Peeters, 2004).

[32] A new proposal has recently been given by W. Rutherford, On the Trail of the Scribal Peter: Apostolic Authority and the Production of Jewish/Christian Difference in the *Preaching of Peter*, in: *Peter in Early Christianity* (ed. by H. Bond & L.W. Hurtado; Grand Rapids: Eerdmans, 2014) . I am grateful to Dr. Rutherford who kindly shared his work with me.

[33] The text goes: "And that the men of highest repute among the Greeks knew God, not by positive knowledge, but by indirect expression, Peter says in the *Preaching*: "Know then that there is one God, who made the beginning of all things, and holds the power of the end; and is the Invisible, who sees all things; incapable of being contained, who contains all things; needing nothing, whom all things need, and by whom they are; incomprehensible, everlasting, unmade, who made all things by the 'Word of His power,' that is, according to the gnostic scripture, His Son." Then he adds: "Worship this God not as the Greeks,"– signifying plainly, that the excellent among the Greeks worshipped the same God as we, but that they had not learned by perfect knowledge that which was delivered by the Son. "Do not then worship," he did not say, the God whom the Greeks worship, but "as the Greeks,"– changing the manner of the worship of God, not announcing another God. What, then, the expression "not as the Greeks" means, Peter himself shall explain, as he adds: "Since they are carried away by igno-

parts of arguments on the character of Greek, Jewish and
Christian worship which we later will see in the writings
of the "Christian" philosopher Aristides, who quite plau-

---

rance, and know not God" (as we do, according to the perfect
knowledge); "but giving shape to the things of which He gave them
the power for use–stocks and stones, brass and iron, gold and silver–matter;–and setting up the things which are slaves for use and
possession, worship them. And what God hath given to them for
food–the fowls of the air, and the fish of the sea, and the creeping
things of the earth, and the wild beasts with the four-footed cattle
of the field, weasels and mice, cats and dogs and apes, and their own
proper food–they sacrifice as sacrifices to mortals; and offering
dead things to the dead, as to gods, are unthankful to God, denying
His existence by these things." And that it is said, that we and the
Greeks know the same God, though not in the same way, he will
infer thus: "Neither worship as the Jews; for they, thinking that
they only know God, do not know Him, adoring as they do angels
and archangels, the month and the moon. And if the moon be not
visible, they do not hold the Sabbath, which is called the first; nor
do they hold the new moon, nor the feast of unleavened bread, nor
the feast, nor the great day." Then he gives the finishing stroke to
the question: "So that do ye also, learning holily and righteously
what we deliver to you; keep them, worshipping God in a new way,
by Christ." For we find in the Scriptures, as the Lord says: "Behold,
I make with you a new covenant, not as I made with your fathers in
Mount Horeb." He made a new covenant with us; for what belonged to the Greeks and Jews is old. But we, who worship Him in
a new way, in the third form, are Christians. For clearly, as I think,
he showed that the one and only God was known by the Greeks in
a Gentile way, by the Jews Judaically, and in a new and spiritual way
by us. – And further, that the same God that furnished both the
Covenants was the giver of Greek philosophy to the Greeks, by
which the Almighty is glorified among the Greeks, he shows. And
it is clear from this. Accordingly, then, from the Hellenic training,
and also from that of the law are gathered into the one race of the
saved people those who accept faith: not that the three peoples are
separated by time, so that one might suppose three natures, but
trained in different Covenants of the one Lord, by the word of the

sibly used the *Kerygma* for his own (somewhat later) apology.[34]

As far as we can see here, the *Kerygma Petri* collects arguments for the idea that "the Jews" worship God in an incorrect manner; the "Christians", however, are understood as having a "new kind of worship" corresponding to a new covenant which is different to the one God has given to Israel's forefathers at the mountain of Horeb (cf. Jer 31/38.31–32; Deut 29.1). In conclusion, the text puts Israel and pagans side by side, both are considered old, while the Christians as a "new genos" worship God in a new manner. While at least in the extant fragments the text does not explicitly speak about God's rejection of Israel, this last statement seems to be quite clear. In addition to this, according to fragment 1 (quoted by Clement

---

one Lord. For that, as God wished to save the Jews by giving to them prophets, so also by raising up prophets of their own in their own tongue, as they were able to receive God's beneficence, He distinguished the most excellent of the Greeks from the common herd, in addition to *"Peter's Preaching,"* the Apostle Paul will show, saying: "Take also the Hellenic books, read the Sibyl, how it is shown that God is one, and how the future is indicated. And taking Hystaspes, read, and you will find much more luminously and distinctly the Son of God described, and how many kings shall draw up their forces against Christ, hating Him and those that bear His name, and His faithful ones, and His patience, and His coming." Then in one word he asks us, "Whose is the world, and all that is in the world? Are they not God's?" Wherefore Peter says, that the Lord said to the apostles: "If any one of Israel then, wishes to repent, and by my name to believe in God, his sins shall be forgiven him, after twelve years. Go forth into the world, that no one may say, We have not heard" (translation *Ante-Nicene Fathers* 2).

[34] For more details on the relation between Aristides and the *Kerygma Petri* see M. CAMBE, *Kerygma Petri*, 173–4.

of Alexandria three times, *strom.* 1.29.182; *strom.* 2.15.68 and *ecl. proph.* 58) Christ the Lord is called "Law and Logos" (that is, Word).[35] Even if we cannot know for sure which kind of theology of the covenant the group behind the *Kerygma* developed out of this thought, it is clear that for them belief in Christ and being part of a new covenant must have belonged together.[36] Although fragment 4, finally, quoted in Clement, *strom.* 6.15.128, almost as a matter of course speaks about Jesus' suffering through the Jews, at least the extant fragments of the *Kerygma* do not connect the installation of the new covenant with Israel's rejection of Christ.

1.3.3 The (pseudepigraphic) *Third Letter of Paul to the Corinthians* (*3 Cor*) has been mainly transmitted as part of the apocryphal *Acts of Paul*.[37] This second-century anti-Gnostic writing,[38] which is mainly concerned with the relevance of Jesus' fleshly suffering and his bodily resurrection, also develops an idea of salvation history accord-

---

[35] Regarding the impact of this idea for second century "Christian" authors see A. Grillmeier, *Jesus*, 203.

[36] For a very detailed discussion of this idea (with parallels in the *Pastor Hermae* and Ps-Hippolytus' *Peri Pascha*) see M. Cambe, *Kerygma Petri*, 283–313.

[37] While this pseudepigraphical writing was considered apocryphal in Greek and Latin proto-orthodox churches it formed a part of Armenian Bibles until the Middle Ages. For more information see V. Hovhanessian, *Third Corinthians: Reclaiming Paul for Christian Orthodoxy* (Studies in Biblical Literature 16; Frankfurt am Main et al.: Peter Lang, 2000) 3–10 (Manuscript Evidence) and 10–16 (History of Reception).

[38] According to V. Hovhanessian, *Third Corinthians*, 81–131, the text has been written as a Pauline pseudepigraphon against the use of Pauline texts and ideas by Gnostic authors.

ing to which the Church has replaced Israel as God's people. According to *3 Cor.* 3.10, God had decided to rescue the House of Israel and sent the Spirit of Christ into the prophets. The Jews, however, who rejected Jesus the saviour of "all flesh" (3.16), are now understood as "children of wrath" (3.19, 20) because they have the "accursed belief of the snake" (3.20), that is, the Devil.

1.3.4 Finally, some of the sharpest passages are found in the Christian passages of the *Sibylline Oracles*: the collection of *Sibylline Oracles* extant today consist of 12 books, on the whole more than 4200 verses in hexameters in two different collections (books 1–8 and 11–14) – the extant *Oracles* are of different length and provenance and go back to a period of perhaps 500 years.[39] Put in the mouth of a pagan prophetess, the Sibyl, the Oracles want to prove the truth of "Judaism" or – in the case of the "Christian" parts – "Christianity" against other kinds of worship. While some of the "Jewish" texts show a very sharp anti-pagan attitude, perhaps understood as responses to Alexandrian or more generally Egyptian anti-Judaism, there are at least some highly anti-Jewish passages in the Christian oracles. The closing verses of *Sib. Or.* 1 (approximately second century CE) are a very good

---

[39] Regarding introductory issues see J.J. COLLINS, The Sibylline Oracles, in: *Jewish Writings of the Second Temple Period: Apocrypha, Pseudepigrapha, Qumran Sectarian Writings, Philo, Josephus* (ed. by M.E. Stone; CRINT II.2; Assen – Philadelphia: van Gorcum, 1984) 357–81 (with a focus on Jewish passages) and U. TREU, Christliche Sibyllinen, in: *Neutestamentliche Apokryphen II: Apostolisches, Apokryphen und Verwandtes* (ed. by W. Schneemelcher; Tübingen: Mohr, ⁶1999) 591–619.

example: according to this text, Israel is under the "wrath of God" (1.362–3; see also 1.400) because it has "killed the Son of the heavenly God" (1.364), who now "snatches away their belief from them" (1.363), and the destruction of Jerusalem is the "fruit of Jewish sacrilege" (against Christ) (*Sib.Or.* 1.385; cf. also 1.395–6). In addition, because Israel has fallen, the pagans are collected under the leadership of Christ (1.345–6).

This is only a small selection of relevant second (or possibly third) century "Christian" writings. However, one thing is already clear: the main texts discussed above – *Barn.* writing in the crisis of an upcoming war, Justin defending "Christianity" against pagan polemics[40] – work with very clear categories of "Jews" and "Christians". This is, at least in part, due to the issue of identity formation or defence: where a quasi-parochial group is under pressure from outside, it has to defend itself and, in the process, has to define itself. However, every definition means that they have to draw and at the same time close boundaries more clearly than before. A second point which is already becoming clear is that Justin's *Apology 1* and the *Physiologus* are already working with opposing groups, a "Christian Church of pagans" on the one side and "Judaism" on the other, while *Barnabas* cannot ignore groups with ideas about "Jewish-Christian" relations different from his own. Although groups of

---

[40] The *Physiologus* with its *play* on Christian identity, correct behaviour etc. is surely to be seen on another level. This text does not have to create boundaries; its argument (if we should speak about an "argument") is already relying on quite fixed self-definitions.

people who understand themselves as followers of Christ while not being members of a Church of pagan followers of Christ still existed, they are either simply ignored because they do not fit into the system any more or they are attacked because they are believed to be dangerous. This is, as far as I see, related to the texts' argument which is connected closely to matters of Christology: if Israel's rejection of Christ affects its relationship to God, or – even clearer – means that God's covenant with Israel does not count or even exist any more, then the communities behind these texts cannot accept followers of Christ *within* Judaism as well. If the category "Judaism" becomes theologically worthless then, if we follow the logic of these texts, Christians must form a group separate and apart from Judaism.

2. Distinguishing "Jewish" and "Christian" Forms of Worship

Other texts seem to go in the same direction, but add a new dimension: they understand parts of Jewish worship as signs of an incorrect understanding of God; meaning that it is against God's will. In this way they are making preparations for the idea of distinguishing between two deities – a Jewish and a Christian one:

2.1 The Apology of Aristides

The first example I would like to introduce is Aristides, who according to Eusebius, *h.e.* 4.3.3 was a philosopher and Christ-follower from Athens. Today his apology, originally written in Greek, is extant in some Armenian fragments, a Syriac version and as part of the later *Life of Barlaam and Josaphat* (a text previously attributed to John of Damascus in the 7th century but now, more probably, attributed to Euthymios of Athos, 11th century CE).[41] This makes a reconstruction of the original text very problematic. According to Eusebius, Aristides wrote in the time of Emperor Hadrian (117–138 CE); according to the Syriac title of his work, the apology was addressed to Hadrian's successor Antoninus Pius (138–161 CE). While the work is anything but a brilliant masterpiece of argumentation, the fact that it is one of the oldest "Christian" apologetic writings extant today makes Aristides' work interesting to us.[42]

The overall structure of Aristides' apology is quite simple: after an introduction, he gives a first overview of the different groups he wants to address. Then he gives detailed criticisms of the worship of Barbarians, Greeks (with sub-paragraphs on Egyptians and Greek philosophers), Jews, and, finally, Christians. Interestingly, he does not use a three-category system, but divides into

---

[41] Regarding the text's very complex history of transmission see B. POUDERON – M.-J. PIERRE (ed.s), *Aristide. Apologie* (SC 470; Paris, Cerf, 2003) 107–72 – the authors vote for the superiority of the Syriac version.

[42] For a positive judgment and a history of research on Aristides and his work see M. LATTKE, War der Apologet Aristides ein Mann von Bildung? Forschungsgeschichtliches Protokoll eines (nicht nur) deutschen Gelehrtenstreits in den ersten 40 Jahren der Aristides-Forschung, in: *Frühchristentum und Kultur* (ed. by F.R. Prostmeier; KfA. Ergänzungsband 2; Freiburg et al.: Herder, 2007) 35–74.

nationalities, thus the only group who does not fit well into these categories are the "Christians." Within this system, the origins of the Jewish identity (i.e., a group from Abraham and his sons) are stressed (*apol.* 2.5). However, Aristides' treatment of the Jews is quite short, and the text differs in its different versions. Although in *apol.* 2.8 we first read that Jesus came from the Jews, the typical idea that the Jews were responsible for Jesus' death follows. Chapter 14 is more interesting for us, because it treats Jewish worship. Compared to his treatment of barbarians and pagans, Aristides is quite positive regarding Judaism. He writes:

Let us come now, O King, to the question of the Jews also, and see what opinion they have as to God. The Jews then say that God is one, the Creator of all, and omnipotent; and that it is not right that any other should be worshipped except this God alone. And herein they appear to approach the truth more than all the nations, especially in that they worship God and not His works. And they imitate God by the philanthropy which prevails among them; for they have compassion on the poor, and they release the captives, and bury the dead, and do such things as these, which are acceptable before God and well-pleasing also to men, – which (customs) they have received from their forefathers. Nevertheless they too erred from true knowledge. And in their imagination they conceive that it is God they serve; whereas by their mode of observance it is to the angels and not to God that their service is rendered: as when they observe the sabbaths and the beginning of the months, and feasts of unleavened bread, and a great fasting[43] and fasting[44] and circumcision and the puri-

---

[43] According to B. Pouderon – M.-J. Pierre, *Aristide*, 235 n. 4, the Yom Kippur is meant here.

[44] B. Pouderon – M.-J. Pierre, *Aristide*, 235 n. 5 regard a dittography possible here.

fication of meats, which things, however, they do not observe
perfectly (translation adapted from *Ante-Nicene Fathers*).

Several points here are interesting: on the one hand, Aristides holds "Jewish" ideas of God in high regard; questions of Jesus' status do not play any role in his argument
– he can agree with "Jewish" monotheism and the main
lines of "Jewish" ideas of God. He also sees important
parts of Jewish ethics as pleasing God and man. The crucial point of his criticism, however, is his idea of aspects
of Jewish *halakha*: observing the Sabbath and important
Jewish feasts, fasting, circumcision and questions of food
purity, according to Aristides, do not have to do with
God's will as expressed in the Torah, but show a Jewish
misunderstanding. By following these laws, Jews worship angels and not God any more,[45] an idea which already finds its backgrounds in the New Testament (perhaps already Col 2.18[46]; Hebr 1.4–5, 14, 2.5–7[47]). Aristides
thus begins to make a distinction. At least here he is not

---

[45] For further examples see S. Krauss – W. Horbury, *The Jewish-Christian Controversy from the Earliest Times to 1789 I: History* (TSAJ 56; Tübingen: Mohr, 1995) 19.

[46] See, however, I. Maisch, *Der Brief an die Gemeinde von Ko-
lossä* (ThKNT 12; Stuttgart: Kohlhammer, 2003) 190, who writes:
"Im Zusammenhang der gegen die Philosophie gerichteten Polemik
ist jedoch – in Analogie zu V. 16 und 23, ... – eher an die Verehrung
der Engel durch die Anhänger der Philosophie ... zu denken."

[47] Regarding the role of angels in Hebrews see G. Gäbel, Rivals
in Heaven. Angels in the Epistle to the Hebrews, in: *Angels: The
Concept of Celestial Beings – Origins, Development and Reception*
(ed. by F. V. Reiterer, T. Nicklas & K. Schöpflin; DCLY 2007; Berlin – New York: de Gruyter, 2007) 357–76 and G. Steyn, Addressing an Angelomorphic Christological Myth in Hebrews? *Hervorm-
de Teologiesche Studies* 59 (2003) 1107–28.

interested in the question pertaining to why Jews do not understand Jesus as their Messiah; he connects important aspects of *halakha* with his "Christian" understanding of proper worship of God: while, according to Aristides, any expression of love for one's neighbour is according to God's will, other aspects of the Torah – like observation of the Sabbath or ritual and purity laws – show that Jews do not solely worship God, but also fulfil the will of (obviously imperfect) angels. This distinction is perhaps the first step that led to an even more dramatic distinction: the distinction between a "Christian" and a "Jewish" Deity – the latter often seen as an imperfect, silly or even evil angel.

As we have seen, apologies trying to defend "the Christian way of life" against outsiders' attacks, serve the function to create and strengthen identity. It is thus quite natural that they work with categories, and that they – under the pressure of outsiders' attacks – draw boundary lines where they – perhaps in real life – did not always exist.

2.2 Ad Diognetum

One of the more mysterious Christian writings of the late second century is the so-called *Epistle Ad Diognetum*[48]

---

[48] For the following passage see the more detailed argument in my article: T. NICKLAS, Identitätsbildung durch Konstruktion der "Anderen": Die Schrift *Ad Diognetum*, in *Christian Communities in the Second Century: Between Ideal and Reality* (ed. by J. Verheyden & M. Grundeken; WUNT; Tübingen: Mohr, 2014). In this article I am also able to give a fuller discussion of secondary literature – mainly H.E. LONA's magisterial commentary to whom I owe many of my thoughts.

– or better: only *Ad Diognetum* – because this writing is
surely not an epistle or a letter, but a so-called *logos protreptikos* with at least some elements of an apology for
Christianity.[49] In other words: *Ad Diognetum* belongs to
an ancient genre of literature which usually promotes the
study of philosophy. For *Ad Diognetum*, however, there
is only one true philosophy, the truth of a "new message"
or "new doctrine," that is "Christianity". In other words,
this text wants to be an invitation or introduction to the
truth of "Christianity", which is understood as a "new
genos", i. e. a "new people" with a new form of worship, as
compared to "Jews" and pagans. It is quite striking that
Ad Diognetum, in a world where the truth of a doctrine
usually had to be connected to its antiquity, insists so
much on the novelty of "Christianity" which is understood as the only proper worship of God. To enforce its
own positive argument for the truth of Christianity, *Ad
Diognetum* first deals with two (other) ways of worship.
First we find a list of arguments against pagan worship:

"See not only with your eyes but also with your intellect what
substance or what form those happen to have whom you call
and regard as gods. Is not one of them stone, like that upon we
walk, and another bronze, not better than the utensils that have
been forged for our use, and another wood, already rotted away,
and another silver, which needs a watchman to guard it lest it be
stolen, and another iron, corroded by rust, and another pottery,
not a bit more attractive than that made for the most unmen-
tionable use? Are not all these made of perishable matter? Are
they not forged by iron and fire? Did the sculptor not make one

---

[49] Regarding introductory questions see H. E. LONA, An Diognet, in: *Die Apostolischen Väter: Eine Einleitung* (ed. by W. Pratscher; UTB; Göttingen: Vandenhoeck & Ruprecht, 2009) 208–25.

of them, and the coppersmith another, the silversmith another, and the potter yet another? Before they were shaped by the skills of these craftsmen into the form they have, was it not possible ... for each of them to have been given a different form? Might not the ordinary utensils now formed out of the same material be made similar to such images as these, if the same craftsmen were available? Again, could not these things that are now worshiped by you be made by human hands into utensils like the rest? Are they not all deaf and blind, without souls, without feelings, without movement? Do they not all rot, do they not all decay? These are the things you call gods; you serve them, you worship them, and in the end you become like them ..." (*Diogn.* 2; translation Holmes, 293–4).

All the points mentioned are everything but original, surely not really engaging the centre of "real" pagan theologies as represented by elite authors such as Porphyrios (ca. 233–301/305 CE) or the Emperor Julian (later called "the Apostate", 331–363 CE).[50] Interestingly, however, *Diogn.*'s arguments correspond quite well with the kind of polemics some pagan authors like Lucian of Samosata (ca. 120–180 CE) and others uttered against the superstitious worship of the uneducated masses.[51] It thus looks very much like the author wants to be part of an intellectual debate regarding the question of true worship. It does, however, not stop with a severe criticism of pagan worship, but in chapters 3–4 concentrates on "Judaism". Although *Diogn.* 3.2 distinguishes between "Pagans" and "Jews" because the latter "rightly claim to worship the one God of the universe and think of him as Master"

---

[50] For more details see the examples given by H. E. LONA, *Diognet*.

[51] Again, see the examples given by H. E. LONA, *Diognet*.

(transl. Holmes), on the whole for the author of *Ad Diognetum* "Judaism" is, in fact, as wrong as "pagan" worship; it is called a "superstition" (*Diogn.* 1), and qualified
as sin (διαμαρτάνουσιν; 3.2). While the author of *Diogn.*
never goes so far as to say that the God of Israel is different from the "Christian" God, it implies that their manner of worship demonstrates that "Jews" have a completely inaccurate understanding of his nature.[52]

The text continues:

> "[W]hereas the Greeks provide an example of their stupidity by
> offering things to senseless and deaf images, the Jews, thinking
> that they are offering these things to God as if he were in need
> of them, could rightly consider it folly rather than worship. ...
> In any case, those who imagine that they are offering sacrifices
> to him by means of blood and fat and whole burnt offerings and
> are honouring him with these tokens of respect do not seem to
> me to be the least bit different from those who show the same
> respect to deaf images: the latter make offerings to things una-
> ble to receive the honour, while the former think they offer
> something to the one who is in need of nothing" (*Diogn.* 3.3 and
> 5; translation Holmes: 294–5).

This is clearly a caricature of ancient "Jewish" ideas of
sacrifices. But the author *Ad Diognetum* is not interested
in giving a correct image, he is neither interested in the
question of (more or less) correct "Jewish" theologies of
sacrifice, nor does he acknowledge the fact that the sacrificial cult in Jerusalem had come to an end after the destruction of the Second Temple in the year 70 CE (or at
least after the Bar Kochba War of 132–135 CE) – he sim-

---

[52] See, e. g., K. SCHNEIDER, Die Stellung der Juden und Christen
in der Welt nach dem Diognetbrief, *JAC* 42 (1999) 20–41, esp. 21–
31, and H. E. LONA, *Diognet*, 141–50.

ply wants to show that Jews, even if they worship the same God as the Christians do, do it in ways which clearly show that they have a totally incorrect perception of this God.[53] This is the reason why he repeats traditional ideas of pagan Anti-Jewish polemics[54] while he, interestingly, does not give typical "Christian" arguments: for example, we do not find anything about the Jewish rejection of Jesus Christ in this text. Neither are there any discussions on an appropriate understanding of the Jewish Scriptures.[55] This different kind of polemics, the repetition of pagan arguments against "Jews" and "Jewish" worship, shows a very special quality: it further disconnects the "new people" of Christians much more from its "Jewish" roots than any discussion pertaining to the true

---

[53] K. Schneider, Stellung, 22: "Während die Propheten gegen die falsche Opfergesinnung Israels polemisieren, richtet sich in 'Ad Diognetum' der Angriff nicht so sehr gegen die jüdischen Opfer selbst, als vielmehr gegen das aus ihnen abgeleitete Gottesbild, welches der Verfasser den Juden zuschreibt."

[54] The most interesting parallel of thoughts can be shown with the arguments of Apion reflected in Josephus, *Contra Apionem* 2.137.

[55] For further comments on the Old Testament in *Diognet*, see for example R. Brändle, D*ie Ethik der "Schrift an Diognet". Eine Wiederaufnahme paulinischer und johanneischer Theologie am Ausgang des zweiten Jahrhunderts* (AThANT 64; Zürich: Theologischer Verlag, 1975), 61, who writes: Der Autor *ad Diognetum* "kennt zwar das AT …, aber er vermag zwischen ihm und der einen Offenbarung Gottes in seinem Sohn keine Verbindung herzustellen. Er versucht weder mit Hilfe der allegorischen Methode, eine Brücke zu schlagen zwischen Altem und Neuem, noch mittels des Alters- und Weissagungsbeweises den Ursprung des christlichen Glaubens möglichst früh in der Geschichte der Menschheit zu verankern. Zwischen Altem und Neuem Testament klafft für ihn ein Bruch."

Messiah, the quality of God's covenant, or the correct interpretation of Scriptures could ever do.

While *Diogn.*'s polemics have often been understood as
a sign for ongoing factual conflicts between Jews and
Christians and the text's attempt to convince pagan
God-Fearers about the truth of the Christian movement,[56] I would raise some doubts against this idea. My
main point of criticism is: would a God-fearer (i. e., a pagan person who already believes in the God of Israel and
is connected to a synagogal community) really believe
this kind of criticism? Would it not be much wiser to tell
such a person about the basic quality of "Jewish" forms
of belief, but then convince him or her about the superiority of Christian worship? That's why I think it makes

---

[56] H. E. LONA, *Diognet*, 149–50: Der Text "schreibt keine Apologie des Christentums, sondern unternimmt – ganz konsequent
und entschieden – die Demontage des Judentums, indem er dessen
nichtigen religiösen Wert nachweist. Nach dieser Erklärung ist die
Schärfe seiner Polemik durch eine ebenso scharfe Kritik [von jüdis-
cher Seite] mitbedingt. Seine Adressaten wussten nur zu gut, warum sie sich von den Götzen fernzuhalten hatten. Ihr Verhältnis
zum Judentum war nicht so eindeutig. Wenn sie nun mit der Au-
torität des christlichen Lehrers dazu geführt werden, das Judentum
für so wertlos zu halten wie den Götzendienst, dann deswegen weil
es – wie auch immer – für sie eine potentielle Gefährdung wie das
religiöse Angebot des Heidentums darstellte. Ohne diesen po-
lemischen Hintergrund – die jüdische Kritik am christlichen Glauben – bleibt die durchgeführte Widerlegung des Judentums in Diog
3–4 schwer erklärbar. Von der Geschichte der christlichen Mission
her lässt sich auch verstehen, warum das Judentum für diese Heiden
eine solche Gefahr war. Die Adressaten der christlichen Missionare
waren schwerlich ‚Heiden' schlechthin, sondern solche, die schon
mit der hellenistischen Synagoge in Kontakt standen und zu den
Sympathisanten oder gar zu den ‚Gottesfürchtigen' zählten."

much more sense to understand *Diogn.*'s polemics differently. *Diogn.* was probably written in late second century Alexandria, the capital of Egypt.[57] This is interesting to us for two reasons. On the one hand, Alexandria had been home to one of the most prosperous and well-known Jewish communities in the whole diaspora until the catastrophe of the diaspora war of the years 115–117 CE almost totally destroyed it. On the other hand, Alexandria had a long-standing tradition of anti-Judaism which, as we can see in the philosopher Celsus' primarily anti-"Christian" text *Alethes Logos*, survived until the late second century.[58] If we take this context seriously, the special form of *Diogn.*'s polemics makes very good sense:[59] it seems that at least parts of the "Christian" movement in Alexandria from a certain point on did not want to be associated with Jews any more, while at the same time they began to address members of the educated pagan elite. In referring to 'pagan elite', I am referring to people who were former pagan worshippers but were

---

[57] Cf. H. E. LONA, *Diognet*, 67–9 and IDEM, *An Diognet*, 223–4. But see also, for example, C. N. JEFFORD, *The Apostolic Fathers and the New Testament* (Peabody: Hendrickson, 2006) 35–6. 217–9, or M. W. HOLMES, *The Apostolic Fathers. Greek Texts and English Translations* (Grand Rapids: Baker, ³2007) 687 ("In many respects the author anticipates later Alexandrian writers."); see also the cautious judgment by K. WENGST, *Diognet*, 309 ("Als Ort der Abfassung wird oft Alexandrien genannt.").

[58] For more information on the pre-war "tradition" of anti-Judaism in Alexandria see J. G. GAGER, *The Origins of Anti-Semitism: Attitudes Toward Judaism in Pagan and Christian Antiquity* (New York – Oxford: Oxford University Press, 1983), 43–54.

[59] Of course, this means that we have to speculate here – a decisive proof is not possible any more.

looking for a new "religious" identity, but who also were
usually full of biases against Judaism. In such a context –
anti-Jewish on the one hand and looking for a new way of
truth besides traditional ways of worship – a form of
"Christianity" like the one described in *Diogn.* could
evolve: a *new genos* which more or less tried to cut off all
connections to a diaspora Judaism which was, on the one
hand extremely weakened after the war, and on the other
hand, still under the pressures of anti-Judaism.

3. Distinguishing Two Deities:
Marcion of Sinope

Some decades before *Diogn.* had been completed, the rich
ship-owner Marcion went even further than the writings
above.[60] Probably born in Sinope in the Pontus region
some time at the beginning of the second century CE, he
seems to have been raised in a circle of Christ-followers
for whom the Scriptures of Israel played an important
role. Some time around the middle of the second century
CE – our sources differ, but the years around 140 CE are
quite probable – he arrived at Rome where he supposedly
gave a donation of 200,000 sesterces, an asset half the
amount expected of a person belonging to equestrian
ranks, to the "Christian" community in Rome. However,
further clarification is necessary, when mentioning "the"
Christian community of middle second-century Rome.

---

[60] For a reconstruction of the few data we can know about Marcion's life see S. MOLL, *The Arch-Heretic Marcion* (WUNT 250;
Tübingen: Mohr, 2010) 25–46.

There was surely no single "Christian" community in Rome at this very time, but several communities with quite different doctrines, meeting in different "House-Churches" and only loosely connected. Peter Lampe writes:

"In Rome of the second century we find evidence of breath-taking theological diversity. Besides the representatives of orthodox Christianity, we saw in their own circles Marcionites with their independently ... developed school circles, Valentinians, Carpocratians, dynamistic monarchians (= Theodotians), modalistic monarchians under Praxeas, Montanists ..., Quartodecimans, Jewish Christians with Torah observance, Cerdo with his Gnosis ..."[61]

Interestingly, these diverse groups showed a high degree of mutual tolerance – Lampe goes on:

"Before the end of the second century, specifically before the episcopacy of Victor (189–99 C.E.), hardly any Roman Christian group excluded another group in the city from the communion of the faithful."[62]

Marcion and his followers, however, very soon became an exception to his rule: probably around 144/145 a decisive break must have occurred – the Roman "church(es)" even gave Marcion his money back! From this moment on, Marcion started his own movement which seems to have been quite successful – we hear about Marcionite Churches until the fifth century C.E. (see Theodoret of Cyrus, *ep.* 81). What led to this new situation?

---

[61] P. Lampe, *From Paul to Valentinus: Christians at Rome in the First Two Centuries* (London: Continuum, 2003) 381–2.

[62] P. Lampe, *From Paul*, 385.

Although Marcion's own works are lost today, we can reconstruct the main lines of his teaching via some of the later authors who criticized him. Until a few years ago, our modern image of Marcion was very much affected by Adolf von Harnack's influential monograph *Marcion: Das Evangelium vom fremden Gott*.[63] According to von Harnack, Marcion developed a dualism, distinguishing between a *just* God and a good God. This interpretation of Marcion's thinking, however, seems to be an anachronism at least partly reading Lutheran theology into Marcion's thinking.[64] In his recent monograph on Marcion, Sebastian Moll has criticized Harnack's view. According to Moll, Marcion did distinguished between two Gods, but he was not so much interested in the opposition of good and *just*, but good and evil.[65] This evil God, howev-

---

[63] A von HARNACK, *Marcion: Das Evangelium vom fremden Gott* (Darmstadt: WBG, ³1996). For a critical discussion of Harnack's image of Marcion and his views on Judaism see W. KINZIG, *Harnack, Marcion und das Judentum: Nebst einer kommentierten Edition des Briefwechsels Adolf von Harnacks mit Houston Stewart Chamberlain* (Arbeiten zur Kirchen- und Theologiegeschichte 13; Leipzig: Evangelische Verlagsanstalt, 2004).

[64] For a critical analysis of this view see W. LÖHR, Did Marcion distinguish between a just god and a good god?, in: *Marcion und seine kirchengeschichtliche Wirkung. Marcion and His Impact on Church History. Vorträge der Internationalen Fachkonferenz zu Marcion, gehalten vom 15.–18. August 2001 in Mainz* (ed. by G. May, K. Greschat & M. Meiser; TU 150; Berlin – New York: de Gruyter, 2002) 131–46.

[65] S. MOLL, *Arch-Heretic*, 47–76. – According to Moll, "it would be false to claim that there was no evidence in the sources to support his [Harnack's; TN] view of a just and a good god within Marcion's system. As so often, the sources do not provide a coherent picture of Marcion's doctrine in this matter; however, an extensive chrono-

er, is identified with the God of the Old Testament, while Jesus proclaimed another, good deity which he established primarily from the Gospel of Luke.

Let us first have a look into two of the oldest sources:

The earliest witness about Marcion's doctrine we have is Ptolemy's *Letter to Flora* written about 150 C.E. The identity of "Flora" is debated; R.M. Grant has suggested that it is a "hieratic" name of the city of Rome, where Ptolemy was preaching.[66] Ptolemy himself, as a disciple of Valentinus, would be called a "heretic" today, but this should not concern us too much here.[67] Ptolemy writes:

"Many do not understand the Law ordained through Moses, my good sister Flora, since they know neither the one who ordained it nor its exact commandments, but I think it will readi-

---

logical overview of the sources' testimony will show that Marcion's original distinction was in fact between an evil and a good God, whereas the figure of the just God was only introduced by later generations of his followers" (p. 47).

[66] The exact dates of Ptolemy's life are in the dark. For a first-hand account see W.A. Löhr, Ptolemäus, Gnostiker, *LACL* (1998) 527–8.

[67] Valentinus, one of the most influential "Christian" teachers in the middle-of-the second century Rome, and his school are usually labelled among the most important "Gnostic" Christian movements. This idea, however, has recently been challenged with good arguments. See mainly C. Markschies, *Valentinus Gnosticus? Untersuchungen zur valentinianischen Gnosis mit einem Kommentar zu den Fragmenten Valentins* (WUNT 65; Tübingen: Mohr, 1992); E. Thomassen, *The Spiritual Seed: The Church of the 'Valentinians'* (NHMS 60; Leiden – Boston: Brill, 2006) and (even more radical) I. Dunderberg, *Beyond Gnosticism: Myth, Lifestyle, and Society in the School of Valentinus* (New York: Columbia University Press, 2008).

ly become clear to you if you learn the varying opinions about it" (translation Grant, 63).

After this introductory sentence, he quotes two of these opinions – the common one and another one which probably reflects Marcion's ideas – Ptolemy himself disagrees with both of them. He goes on:

"There are those who say it was decreed by God the Father; others, on the contrary, assert that it was ordained by the hostile and corrupting Devil, to whom they attribute the creation of the world, calling him the father and creator of this universe. But those who recite this to one another are quite wrong, and in both ways they go astray from the evident truth. For it is clear that the Law, which is secondary, was not ordained by the perfect God and Father, since it is imperfect, lacks completion [by Christ], and contains commandments alien to the nature and purpose of such a God. Again, the Law cannot be attributed to the injustice of the Adversary, for it is opposition to injustice" (translation Grant, 63).

In other words, even if Ptolemy himself does not agree with the idea that the Torah is perfect and has been given by God the Father himself, he also disagrees with Marcion's alleged view that it has been given by the Devil who also created the world. Sebastian Moll concludes:

"[T]he orthodox Christians, Marcion and Ptolemy all agree that the creator of the world is also the Lawgiver. For the orthodox Christians this God is again identical, so to speak, with the good God, the Father of Jesus Christ. This position is absurd to Ptolemy since the imperfect Law could not have been given by the perfect God. For the Marcionites, the Creator forms a second, evil deity who is in opposition to the good God. This position is even more absurd to Ptolemy, as it is obvious that the

unjust Adversary cannot be the author of the Law which elimi-
nates injustice."[68]

While Justin Martyr's *First Apology* 26.5 does not provide new information about the alleged nature of Marcion's two deities, Irenaeus of Lyons, an important "proto-orthodox" author, who at the end of the second century (180/185 CE?) wrote a treatise against all "heresies",[69]
is quite clear:

'The followers of Marcion do directly blaspheme the Creator,
alleging him to be the creator of evils, [and even] holding a more
intolerable[70] theory as to his origin, maintaining that there are
two beings, gods by nature, differing from each other, the one
being good, but the other evil (*haer.* 3.12.12, adapted from *Ante-Nicene Fathers*).

At least in these oldest witnesses we always have a dualistic system which, however, seems to have been developed
into a tripartite one by (some of?) Marcion's followers: a
distinction between evil, just and good Gods.

If we concentrate on Marcion himself, it becomes clear
that he identified this evil God with the God of the Old
Testament, the God of the Jews "and of the Jews only, the
proprius deus Iudaicae gentis"[71], giver of the Torah etc.
This God for Marcion stands in clear opposition to the
God proclaimed by Jesus and Paul – according to Mar-

---

[68] S. MOLL, *Arch-Heretic*, 49.

[69] For an extensive introduction to the life and thought of Irenaeus of Lyons see R.M. GRANT, *Irenaeus of Lyons* (The Early
Church Fathers; London – New York: Routledge, 2005 [1997]).

[70] The text here is insecure – I think, however, that the wording
"intolerable" is better.

[71] S. MOLL, *Arch-Heretic*, 60 – For more details see MOLL,
Arch-Heretic, 58–71.

cion, Christ's teaching must be understood as a "battle
against the Old Testament God" and his Law.[72]

Marcion's teaching did not only cause a break between
"proto-orthodox" Christian circles and his own followers, it is, of course, very clear that he broke off all kinds of
bridges with Jews and Jewish followers of Christ. In addition to this, his distinction between two deities is only
possible if it relates already to previously established
group identities: the identities of groups who *only* read
and follow the Scriptures of Israel, and those who follow
the teachings of Jesus. Here, Marcion seems to presup-
pose a distinction between "Jews" and at least some
"Christians". He, however, is going a decisive step further; according to proto-orthodox Christians, one step
too far.

4. Distinguishing Two Deities: Sethian "Gnostics"

Marcion and his group, however, were not the only
"Christians" who distinguished between different deities. This was also the case with the manifold "Gnostic"
groups we know from ancient times. More than any other
categories that scholars have become accustomed to using
in understanding ancient Christianity, the terms "Gnosis" and "Gnostics" respectively have become extremely
problematic during the last decades. This is the case
mainly because this terminology seems to uncritically

---

[72] S. MOLL, *Arch-Heretic*, 66.

adopt the perspective(s) of ancient "proto-orthodox" heresiologists like Irenaeus of Lyons, Hippolytus of Rome, Tertullian or Epiphanius of Salamis. While we, however, until a few generations ago, were more or less dependent on these authors when we tried to reconstruct the thinking of "Gnostic" circles the 1945 discovery and later edition of the Coptic library of Nag Hammadi provided us with different perspectives: for the first time in modern history researchers had the chance to read a whole library of texts coming from "Gnostic" authors themselves. Thus, the modern term 'Gnosis' which was coined by Henry More (1614–1687) as late as the 17th century, is always in danger of anachronistically understanding "Gnostic" texts from the perspectives of their opponents. Even if the views of some recent authors like Karen King or – perhaps even more – M.A. Williams challenged the use of terms like "Gnosis", "Gnosticism" or "Gnostics" sharply,[73] I would not like to totally abandon them, but use them in a cautious manner. This is the reason I use a somewhat compromise definition made by R. van den Broek:

"It is undeniable that there existed in Antiquity a broad and variegated religious current characterized by a strong emphasis on esoteric knowledge (Gnosis) as the only means of salvation, which implied the return to one's divine origin. This religious current can best be referred to as the 'Gnostic movement' or 'Gnostic religiosity'. The great Gnostic systems of the 2nd and 3rd centuries are integral parts of this broader Gnostic move-

---

[73] See M.A. WILLIAMS, *Rethinking 'Gnosticism': An Argument for Dismantling a Dubious Category* (New Haven: Princeton University Press, 1996), and K. KING, *What is Gnosticism?* (Cambridge, Mass. – London: Harvard University Press, 2003).

ment and should not be isolated from it. The main character of these systems is that their central ideas are expressed in myths, which may vary from one system to another, but as a whole display strong similarities. For that reason, and to maintain the link with the Gnostic current in general, it is preferable to speak here of mythological Gnostic texts or systems. The term 'Gnosticism', if used at all, should be reserved for these more or less coherent expressions of mythological Gnosis."[74]

In addition to this, after the important monographs of Christoph Markschies and (perhaps even more) Ismo Dunderberg I would hesitate to include the second century teacher Valentinus, his school and his followers, under the label of "Gnosis" or "Gnosticism"[75] – so I will, following David Brakke, concentrate on the movement of the so-called Sethian Gnosticism, sometimes also called "classical Gnosticism".[76] The central source for the ideas of "Sethian Gnostics" is the *Apocryphon of John* which today is extant in four Coptic manuscripts and, in parts, in presented in Irenaeus of Lyons, *haer.* 1.29.[77] I will, however, concentrate on another (very probable) witness of Sethian theology: the so-called *Gospel of Judas* which

---

[74] R. Van den Broek, Gnosticism I: Gnostic Religion, in: *Dictionary of Gnosis and Western Esotericism* I (ed. by W.J. Hanegraaff; Leiden – Boston: Brill, 2005) 403–16, esp. 404.

[75] See above note 67.

[76] D. Brakke, *The Gnostics: Myth, Ritual, and Diversity in Early Christianity* (Cambridge, Mass.: Harvard, 2010).

[77] For a definition of "Sethianism" and its ideas, see H.-M. Schenke, Das sethianische System nach den Nag-Hammadi-Handschriften, in: *Der Same Seths: Hans-Martin Schenkes Kleine Schriften zu Gnosis, Koptologie und Neuem Testament* (ed. by G. Schenke Robinson, G. Schenke & U.-K. Plisch; NHMS 78; Leiden et al: Brill, 2012) 285–92, esp. 286.

I mentioned already in chapter 1. According to the *Gospel of Judas* it would be a severe misunderstanding to confess Jesus as the Son of God, that is the Son of the God of Israel (see CT p. 34,12–17) who demands perverse sacrifices (see CT 37,20–43,11) and is identified with a demiurge called Saklas and/or Jaldabaoth/Nebro.[78] The figure of Jaldabaoth is well-known from other Sethian Gnostic literature. According to the *Apocryphon of John* he has the face of a snake and a lion (respectively the figure of a snake with the face of a lion).[79] In the *Gospel of Judas* Jaldabaoth/Nebro has a face "flashed with fire" (CT p. 51,10) and his "appearance [is] defiled with blood" (CT, p. 51,11–2). A bit later the *Gospel of Judas* introduces a second figure named Saklas who, later in the text, seems to replace Jaldabaoth/Nebro more or less.[80] The figure or Saklas, again, is well-known from other "Gnostic" writings like the Coptic *Gospel of the Egyptians* (NHC III,2 and IV,2) and the *Apocalypse of Adam* (NHC V,5) where he is usually described as a demonic power which can be associated or even identified with Satan or Sammael.[81]

---

[78] On the problem of the demiurge's name according to the *Gospel of Judas*, see T. NICKLAS, Der Demiurg des Judasevangeliums, in: *Judasevangelium und Codex Tchacos: Studien zur religionsgeschichtlichen Verortung einer gnostischen Schriftensammlung* (ed. by E.E. Popkes & G. Wurst; WUNT 297; Tübingen: Mohr, 2012) 99–120, esp. 113–4.

[79] Regarding the Platonic background of this idea see H.M. JACKSON, *The Lion That Became Man: The Gnostic Leontomorphic Character and the Platonic Tradition* (Atlanta: Scholars, 1985).

[80] Perhaps due to the corrupt condition of the extant manuscript the relation between the two figures is not clear – it seems that they are more or less representing the same satanic deity.

[81] For more details see for example J. VAN DER VLIET, *Het Evan-*

For the *Gospel of Judas* Saklas is the creator of humanity and the source of all evil – several allusions to the book of Genesis make it clear that the text identifies him with the God of Israel – , he is the one who leads astray the "proto-orthodox" church which does not distinguish between Jesus' God and the God of Israel. The good news of the *Gospel of Judas* is that we are already living at the end of times: Saklas and his corrupt, evil creation will be totally destroyed soon.

Marcion and the *Gospel of Judas* must be seen as extremes: for them following Jesus is incompatible with an adherence to the God of Israel. The emerging second-century "Christian" proto-orthodoxy reacted against these claims very sharply – here, again, a borderline had been crossed, which was not acceptable any more. Both Marcionism and Sethian Gnosticism, however, should not be seen too quickly as a marginal phenomena – H. Räisänen, for example, writes about the history of the Marcionite movement:

"Although Marcion's church already faded in the West before the time of Constantine, it remained strong for centuries in the East. Before Constantine, the Roman state did not distinguish between orthodox and heretic; Catholic and Marcionite Christians died side by side in religious persecutions. Constantine, however, having put an end to these persecutions, soon took action against 'heretical' Christians. In the times of his successors, the state and mainstream church joined forces in order to destroy rival congregations. It was not easy. As late as in the fifth century, a Syrian bishop boasted of converting no less than eight Marcionite villages – thousands of people – to the true

gelie van Judas: Verrader of bevrijder (Utrecht – Antwerpen: Servire, 2006) 107.

faith. In the East, traces of Marcionite groups are found in Arabic sources as late as the 10th century."[82]

5. Transcending Categories: The *Testaments of the XII Patriarchs* and other Pseudepigrapha

It is quite difficult to find traces of the other extreme – we have already seen that the *Epistle of Barnabas* utters sharp polemics against followers of Christ who claimed that the covenant between God and Israel remained intact. But perhaps one group of texts, which so far has been widely neglected for our understanding of the history of early Christianity/ies, can help us a bit more. In the year 1983 James H. Charlesworth edited a magisterial two-volume translation of so-called "Old Testament Pseudepigrapha"[83] – pseudepigraphical texts from the Hellenistic and Roman eras which are usually labelled as "Jewish", but have been transmitted primarily within Christian, monastic circles. However, some of these texts contain passages which cannot be interpreted in any way but "Christian" – if we want to use the classical labels. Some of the most well-known examples are books like the *Apocalypse of Elijah*, the *Life of Adam and Eve*, the *Ascension of Isaiah*, etc. Recent research has shown that

---

[82] H. RÄISÄNEN, Marcion, in: *A Companion to Second-Century Christian 'Heretics'* (ed. by A. Marjanen & P. Luomanen; VigChr.S 76; Leiden – Boston: Brill, 2005) 100–24, esp. 101.

[83] J.H. CHARLESWORTH, *The Old Testament Pseudepigrapha. 2 vols.* (ABRL; New York et al: Doubleday, 1983). See also the German series *Jüdische Schriften aus hellenistisch-römischer Zeit* published by Gütersloher publishing house.

in many cases it is extremely difficult to distinguish between "Jewish" *Grundschriften* and "Christian" redactions, and in the case of the *Ascension of Isaiah*, the text as a whole is now usually interpreted to be a Christian apocalypse of the first decades of the second century CE. One of the most exciting examples one could mention is the *Testaments of the XII Patriarchs*: in the year 1242 Robert Grosseteste, the bishop of Lincoln, translated the *Testaments* from the Greek into Latin, and thus introduced this text for the first time to a Western, learned audience. For several hundred years the *Testaments* had been considered a Christian writing, until in the late 19th century Friedrich Schnapp's dissertation *Die Testamente der Zwölf Patriarchen untersucht* (1884) argued for a Jewish origin of the text.[84] Scholars like R. H. Charles took over Schnapp's main thesis (with deep modifications)[85] which meant that up until the 1950s a consensus about the Jewish origin of the *Testaments* grew. Starting around the same time with the work of Marinus de Jonge, an influential school of scholars from Leiden was able to show that the situation was even more complex.[86] It is not possible

---

[84] F. SCHNAPP, *Die Testamente der Zwölf Patriarchen untersucht* (Halle: Alex Niemeyer, 1884). Schnapp's ideas became mainly influential via his article: Die Testamente der 12 Patriarchen, der Söhne Jakobs, in: *Die Apokryphen und Pseudepigraphen des Alten Testaments* (ed. by E. Kautzsch; Tübingen: Mohr, § 1921) 458–502.

[85] R.H. CHARLES, *The Testaments of the Twelve Patriarchs* (London: SPCK, 1917).

[86] See M. DE JONGE, *The Testaments of the Twelve Patriarchs: A Study in their Text, Composition and Origin* (Assen: Van Gorcum, § 1975 [1953]); IDEM (ed.), *Studies in the Testaments of the Twelve Patriarchs: Text and Interpretation* (Studia in Veteris Testamenti Pseudepigrapha 3; Leiden: Brill, 1975), H. W. HOLLANDER & H.J.

to go into more details here, but after several decades of controversial debates the following points in a consensus have crystallized:

(1) Even if it is possible that the *Testaments of the Twelve Patriarchs* go back to something that could be called a "non-Christian" Jewish writing, it is not possible to reconstruct a "purely Jewish" source or *Grundschrift* behind the extant text. (2) That's why it makes sense to interpret the final text as a writing read and used by a second-century group of "Christ-believers". To avoid misunderstandings – this does not mean that most parts of the text are very "Jewish" in character and that a "non-Christian" version of the *Testaments* perhaps existed at a certain time. The character of the text – parts without any sign of typical "Christian" beliefs connected to clearly "Christian" passages in ways that cannot be resolved further – has to do with the fact that – again – categories like "Jewish", "Christian" or even "Jewish Christian" do not work very well when we want to describe the group of people reading and using this text and their ideas. What does this text tell us about the God of Israel?

DE JONGE, *The Testaments of the Twelve Patriarchs: A Commentary* (Studia in Veteris Testamenti Pseudepigrapha 8; Leiden: Brill, 1985), and M. DE JONGE, *Pseudepigrapha of the Old Testament as Part of Christian Literature: The Case of the Testaments of the Twelve Patriarchs and the Greek Life of Adam and Eve* (Studia in Veteris Testamenti Pseudepigrapha 18; Leiden – Boston: Brill, 2003). - For an overview of research see now also T. DE BRUIN, *The Great Controversy: The Individual's Struggle Between Good and Evil in the Testaments of the Twelve Patriarchs and their Jewish and Christian Contexts* (diss. Leiden 2013; forthcoming in Studia in Veteris Testamenti Pseudepigrapha; Leiden – Boston: Brill, 2014).

Three points are of special interest:[87]

(1) At several places the *Testaments* speak about the future coming of God ὡς ἄνθρωπος, that is, "like a human being" or in the form of a human being (*TestSim* 6.5; *TestLev* 2.11; *TestSeb* 9.8; *TestBen* 10.7), he will come in humbleness (*TestIss* 7.7; *TestDan* 5.13), will dwell among the people (*TestLev* 5.2; *TestNaph* 8.2–3), eat and drink with them (*TestSim* 6.7 and *TestAss* 7.3). A typical example is *TestSim* 6.5, 7 where we read:

> "Then Shem will be glorified; because God the Lord, the Great One in Israel, will be manifest upon earth [as a man] ... Then I shall arise in gladness and I shall bless the Most High for his marvels, [because God has taken a body, eats with human beings and saves human beings]." (translation Charlesworth, 787).

While Charlesworth, the translator of the passage, tries to put into brackets what he understands as "Christian interpolations" within a purely Jewish *Grundschrift*, later authors showed that it is virtually impossible to distinguish "Jewish" and "Christian" parts of this text. This is the reason why Philip Kurowski for example pleads for a "Jewish *and* Christian" reading of the extant text,[88] and argues that the group "behind" our text – at least its 2ⁿᵈ century final version – should be understood as a kind of "Christianity" which feels "Jewish" or, in other words, a kind of "Judaism" which follows Christ. In the context of

---

[87] The following points are a resumé of main ideas of the dissertation by P. Kurowski, *Der menschliche Gott aus Levi und Juda: Die »Testamente der zwölf Patriarchen« als Quelle judenchristlicher Theologie* (TANZ 52; Tübingen: Narr Francke, 2010).

[88] P. Kurowski, *Gott*, 46.

this "Judaism" / "Christianity", Jesus Christ is understood as the God of Israel who came to the world "as" or "like a man".

(2) In its ideas of God's dwelling among his people the text pursues Old Testament and early Jewish ideas of God's *Schekhina* among his people, and at the same time wants to express an extreme closeness between God and his People. For the *Testaments* this *Schekhina* is not bound to the earthly building of the Jerusalem temple, which had been destroyed already by the Roman army in 70 CE (see *TestLev* 10.3; 15.1; *TestJud* 23.3; *TestBen* 9.2–4 as passages which support this view). The group behind the *Testaments* hopes for a heavenly sanctuary (*TestLev* 5.1; 18.6), where God, who forever is understood as the "most Holy *of Israel*" will reign.[89] For the group behind this text the answer to the question of whether the Covenant between God and his People is still intact, the answer is obviously 'yes!'

(3) Many other points could be mentioned and discussed: Marinus de Jonge has shown that certain passages in the *Testaments* can be understood as an interpretation of Paul's thoughts about Israel according to Rom 11.25–26,[90] while Philipp Kurowski insists on the impact of

---

[89] P. KUROWSKI, *Gott*, 54, writes: "Die neue Zuwendung Gottes in der Endzeit ist zwar an Israel als ein Land, Jerusalem als Sadt und den Tempel als Heiligtum gebunden, aber sie bleibt nicht dort. Der Vorhang reißt, der Tempel wird zerstört, das Volk zerstreut, und die Hoffnung richtet sich auf ein neues Jerusalem, in dessen Mitte Gott, der Heilige Israels, in Demut und Armut regiert."

[90] See M. DE JONGE, Light on Paul from the Testaments of the Twelve Patriarchs? The Testaments and the New Testament, in his: *Pseudepigrapha of the Old Testament as Part of Christian Litera-*

John 4.22 – "Salvation is from the Jews" – for the theology of the *Testaments*. A lot more work needs to be done. Authors of texts like the *Testaments of the XII Patriarchs* 'speak' in new ways and present possibilities of "Jewish" and at the same time "Christian" identities which we cannot even dream of when we only concentrate on texts from the representatives of so-called "proto-orthodoxy".

6. Conclusion

The *Testaments of the XII Patriarchs* are only one (still disputed) example of a writing somewhere "between" what we usually would call "Judaism" and "Christianity". Many more, like the *Ascension of Isaiah*, the *Life of Adam and Eve* and others could be discussed.[91] I do not want to be misunderstood: nobody wants to take away this wonderful Jewish literature from Judaism. They are, of course, "Jewish", but they are "Jewish" *and* "Christian" at the same time. They can thus be understood as witness for possibilities of Jewish-Christian relations and theologies which have been buried for centuries because what we would call "main lines" of thought dominated our images of history.

---

ture: The Case of the Testaments of the Twelve Patriarchs and the Greek Life of Adam and Eve (Studia in Veteris Testamenti Pseudepigrapha 18; Leiden – Boston: Brill, 2003) 160–77, esp. 171–2.

[91] And many more sources still wait for their becoming part of scholarly discussion. This will, for example, be made easier by the publication of R. BAUCKHAM – J. DAVILA – A PANAYOTOV (ed.s), *Old Testament Pseudepigrapha: More Noncanonical Scriptures* 1 (Grand Rapids: Eerdmans, 2013).

A few more points, can be added:

1. We discovered a line of thought going from authors like Aristides to Marcion and the Gnostics: several authors, among them Aristides (and the *Kerygma Petri*), distinguished between points where they more or less accepted "Jewish" worship and points which they ascribed to an incorrect understanding of God or, even more, understood it as worship of angels. The step that takes one from this idea to the 'Gnostic' thought, suggesting the Jewish God *is* an evil angel, is not too far.[92] Even if we should not be too quick in discovering and establishing direct lines of mutual dependence between writings and the thoughts expressed in them, there is a clear relation between these "proto-orthodox" writings on the one hand and Gnostic thoughts on the other.

2. Ideas of God's rejection of Israel are often connected with the motif of Israel's rejection of Jesus who, according to many second-century "Christian" writers, was increasingly seen as a divine figure. Interestingly, although the relation of Christology to "Theo-logy" (i. e., the challenges it presents to the ideas of monotheism) probably played an important role on the Jewish side of the discourse, at least the texts we discussed only indirectly touch this problem: where, however, Christ and God the

---

[92] Perhaps a kind of link could even be constructed if one looks into writers like Heracleon, a student of Valentinus, teaching in the 2nd half of the second century, who according to Origen, *comm. in Joh.* 13.17, quoted the *Kerygma Petri* and wrote: "Auch sollte man nicht das Göttliche in der Weise der Juden verehren, da ja sie, die glauben, Gott allein zu kennen, ihn vielmehr nicht kennen und Engel, Monat und Mond verehren."

Father are seen as belonging together very closely the argument is at hand that with the rejection of Christ, Israel also rejected its God – and thus following, God has rejected Israel.

3. In these polemics, many "Christian" authors wanted to take over important parts of Israel's heritage – the "Scriptures": when God dissolved his Covenant with Israel, the Scriptures are now in "Christian" hands – we will discuss this process more closely in the next chapter. Some of them, however, left Israel's Scriptures behind: while Marcion's and the Gnostics' negative treatment of Scripture will be discussed in the next chapter, *Ad Diognetum* provides us with a very singular example of a "Christian" writing dealing with "Jewish" worship, but from a distance so far from Judaism, that "Christianity" can be defined as a "new race" and allusions to the Scriptures are not used in its argument any more.

4. A final question can be asked. Interestingly, the range of thoughts even within the movement we would call "proto-orthodox" Christianity today, is very wide. However, there was a very clear limit of tolerance for Marcion and his followers (and later, against, other, mainly "Gnostic" movements as well). Both Marcionites and Sethian Gnostics cut all positive connections between their idea of "Christianity" and Israel. Is it possible that part of the "proto-orthodox" Church's claims to be the true heir of God's covenant with Israel has to do with these limits?[93] At least a few texts – like *3 Corinthians*

---

[93] This question has also been asked by H. BRENNECKE, Kirche, who concludes (68): "Die Formel von der Kirche als dem »wahren Israel« ist also – so will es mir jedenfalls im Moment erscheinen –

shortly introduced above – show motifs which could be understood in this way. In many other cases, however, I think I was able to show that the ancient texts try to provide answers in two different directions: on the one hand, answer to problems on the border between "Christian" communities and "synagogue(s)" and on the other hand, on the border from pagan polemics against a "Christian" superstition. That's why a definitive answer to the question must remain open for the moment – but perhaps more can be said after the next chapter dealing with "Christian claims" for Israel's Scriptures.

---

das Ergebnis einer innerchristlichen Debatte um die Kontinuität von Israel und Kirche und gehört eigentlich nicht (jedenfalls nicht in erster Linie) in eine jüdisch-christliche Debatte."

Chapter 3:

The Chosen People and its Scriptures: A New Hermeneutical Perspective[1]

Today, many Christians understand the fact that both Jews and Christians share parts of their Holy Scriptures – the "Hebrew Bible" or "the Old Testament"[2] – as a matter that connects both groups deeply. Certainly, this is not wrong. At the same time, in the history of Jewish-Christian relations this fact caused (and in part still

---

[1] Parts of the following text rework material from two previous articles of mine: T. NICKLAS, Frühchristliche Ansprüche auf die Schriften Israels, in: *Scriptural Authority in Ancient Judaism* (ed. by I. Kalimi, T. Nicklas & G. G. Xeravits; DCL.S 16; Berlin – New York: de Gruyter, 2013) 347–68, and T. NICKLAS, The Influence of Jewish Scriptures on Early Christian Apocrypha, in: *Oxford Handbook on Early Christian Apocrypha* (ed. by A. Gregory & C.M. Tuckett in collaboration with T. Nicklas and J. Verheyden; Oxford: Oxford University Press, 2014).

[2] For a discussion of the different names "Hebrew Bible", "Septuagint", "Old Testament", "First Testament", or "Scriptures of Israel" see for example C. DOHMEN – G. STEMBERGER, *Hermeneutik der Jüdischen Bibel und des Alten Testaments* (Studienbücher Theologie; Stuttgart: Kohlhammer, 1996), E. ZENGER, Heilige Schrift der Juden und der Christen, in his: *Einleitung in das Alte Testament* (Studienbücher Theologie; Stuttgart: Kohlhammer, ³1998) 9–36, and now the different contributions in K. FINSTERBUSCH – A. LANGE (ed.s), *What is Bible?* (Contributions to Biblical Exegesis and Theology 67; Leuven – Paris – Walpole, Mass.: Peeters, 2012).

causes) some severe difficulties. How is it possible that two different groups use the same collection of writings, but read and understand them in very different ways? From a "Christian" point of view, another question is closely related: how do the Scriptures of Israel relate to the Christ event and – later – how do they relate to the early Christian writings telling about the Christ event, that is, the texts which came to be the Christian "New Testament" today?

The answers provided by the Christian side could be quite various – some of them more, some of them less radical – and all of them providing information on how different "Christian" groups saw their relation to what they understood as "Judaism". The roots of the problem can already be seen in some of the earliest "Christian writings", like the letters of Paul.[3] Let me just mention one example: when Paul in 1 Corinthians argues for his belief in the resurrection of the dead, he bases his ideas on what we know as perhaps the oldest "Christian" confession, 1 Cor 15.3b-5. The text reads:

[3]For what I received I passed on to you as of first importance:

(1) that Christ died for our sins *according to the Scriptures*,
(2) [4]that he was buried,
(3) that he was raised on the third day *according to the Scriptures*,
(4) [5]and that he appeared to Cephas, and then to the Twelve.

---

[3] For a brilliant broader introduction see M.M. MITCHELL, *Paul, the Corinthians and the Birth of Christian Hermeneutics* (Cambridge: Cambridge University Press, 2010).

The kernel of this text consists of four statements: Christ died, he was buried, risen from dead and appeared to Cephas, that is, Peter, and the Twelve. The confession thus remembers the main aspects of the Christ-event. To understand the text, it is, however, necessary to understand that Christian belief connects memories about events in the past – one could say "historical" aspects – like Jesus death and burial (and if one wants to go so far, his appearances to his disciples and other witnesses) with interpretations of these events.[4] These interpretations are made from the perspective of the Christian believer (and are usually not comprehensible for the non-believer): line 1, for example, assumes that Jesus is understood as "Christ", and line 3 wants to tell us that God has raised Jesus from the dead.[5] The text, however, is going even further: the elements 1 and 3 – death and resurrection, are interpreted with the words *kata tas graphas* ("according to the Scriptures"). When Paul, the Jew believing in Christ, speaks about "Scripture" (or "the Scriptures"),[6] he means the Scriptures of Israel, more or less the same texts Christians would call the "Old Testament" today, and he usually read them in their Greek translation called the Septuagint today. The connection between special

---

[4] Of course, memories are never "objective" and always interpreted from a certain perspective.

[5] The question of whether the original confession already mentioned the "Twelve" is disputed, but not relevant for our question here. For more details of the discussion see for example D. ZELLER, *Der erste Brief an die Korinther* (KeK 5; Göttingen: Vandenhoeck & Ruprecht, 2010) 461–9 [Lit.].

[6] His use of the plural here is quite unusual and often used as an argument that we have to do it with traditional material here.

Scriptural passages with elements of what is understood as the "Christ event" allows it to give an even deeper sense to its single elements: the *historical* event of *Jesus'* death is interpreted as *Christ's* death *for our sins* (ὑπὲρ τῶν ἁμαρτίων ἡμῶν). For the earliest followers of Jesus his crucifixion must have been not only a shock, but a great riddle and "crucial" problem. If they did not want to give up their faith in Jesus they had to solve this problem and make "sense" of it. Of course, their Easter experiences – and I am sure one does not have to be a "Christian" to believe that they had experiences[7] – made an important impression, but surely these did not immediately answer all of their questions. As the earliest followers of Jesus exclusively were "Jews", they had to use their system of making sense of the world and history to make sense of what had happened to them. If one takes these points into account, it is surely no surprise that they found dimensions of this sense through their readings of the Scriptures, readings of (mysterious?) passages which could be applied to the elements of the Christ event. Even if it is by no way certain which passage lies behind the words "*for our sins*" in 1 Cor 15.3b (that is, our line 1), the text probably alludes to Isa 52.13–53.12, the fourth song of the suffering servant, and more precisely to Isa 53.5–6, 10–12.[8] It

---

[7] Even Celsus, one of the most important ancient critics of Christianity, did not doubt that the earliest followers of Jesus had experiences with Jesus after his death. He, however, did not believe that these experiences meant that God had raised Jesus from the dead.

[8] For a critical discussion of this solution see D. ZELLER, *1 Kor*, 463–4.

is quite difficult to prove this allusion here, but Isa 52–53 plays such an important role for early Christian understandings of Jesus' life, ministry and passion[9] that it is at least a very viable option.[10]

It is important to understand what this means. At least in the eyes of many Christ-followers, Isa 52–53 was now no longer (or at least not only) thought to be speaking about Moses, Israel's role among the nations or the role of the deported parts of Israel for the whole of the people, but about Jesus Christ and his suffering. Thus, from the perspective of the Christ event a new reading of an ancient text emerged.[11] This is only one of more than a hundred examples which could be given.

Here are a few other examples: to enroll the Jesus story into the history of Israel, the Gospel of Matthew starts with a long genealogy arguing that Jesus is the "Son of David and Son of Abraham" (Matt 1.1).[12] In many ways

---

[9] For an overview see K. Zamfir, Isa 52:13–53:12 in the Early Church, *Sacra Scripta* 11 (2013).

[10] The same can be said about element 3: while this passage is clearly alluding to Hos 6.2, it could be debated what was first: experiences on the third day or the biblical text speaking about God's salvific act on the third day.

[11] Regarding the new impact of the book of Isaiah as a whole for early Christians see J. F. A. Sawyer, *The Fifth Gospel: Isaiah in the History of Christianity* (Cambridge et al.: Cambridge University Press, 1996).

[12] Much more could be said about Matt 1.1 which is also important from a canon-critical perspective and for the question of relations between New and Old Testament as a whole. Highly interesting in this contexts are the provocative thoughts of T. Hieke, Biblos Geneseos: Mt 1,1 vom Buch Genesis her gelesen, in: *The Biblical Canons* (ed. by J.-M. Auwers & H. J. De Jonge; BETL 163; Leuven: Peeters, 2003) 635–49.

Matthew also interprets events of Jesus' life as fulfilments of prophecies: the story of Jesus' "virgin birth" (Matt 1.18–25), for example is interpreted as *fulfilment* of Isa 7.14 quoted in the LXX version, the Egyptian episode (Matt 2.13–15) as *fulfilment* of Hos 11.1 and Jesus' move from Nazareth to Capernaum (Matt 4.12–13) – both cities where nobody would have expected the Messiah to have come from – are seen as a *fulfilment* of Isa 8.23–9.1.[13] These are just a few examples. But at least two major steps can be seen from them:

(1) Even beyond what we have seen in 1 Cor 15.3–5, Matthew extends his use of Scriptural passages to events in the life of Jesus besides his death and resurrection. For him, the whole life and ministry of Jesus, starting with his birth and ancestry, must be understood in the light of Israel's Scriptures. This is only one step – we will hear of Christian authors who went even further and tried to understand the situation of the Church in comparable ways – in light of Israel's Scriptures who more and more were understood as the Church's Scriptures.

(2) At the same time this means the beginning of a new hermeneutics – a reading of Israel's Scriptures (or at least important parts of them) as related to the Christ event, Jesus' life and the mission of the Church. This hermeneutics has two aspects: first, the Scriptures are being read in

---

[13] For a broader discussion of Matthew's fulfilment quotations see U. Luz, *Das Evangelium nach Matthäus (Mt 1–7)* (EKK I/1; Zürich – Neukirchen-Vluyn: Benziger – Neukirchener, 1985) 134–40; regarding concrete quotations, their function and the textforms used see M.J.J. MENKEN, *Matthew's Bible: The Old Testament Text of the Evangelist* (BETL 173; Leuven; Peeters, 2004).

the light of the Christ event, and second, the Christ event is interpreted as a fulfilment of Scriptures – it is not always absolutely clear which of the two aspects comes first! In this way, very often allegorical, and in addition to this, typological interpretations of Scriptural passages are necessary. By allegorical exegesis I mean that important aspects of a Scriptural passage which *per se* does not speak about Christ or the Church are transferred into and thus made fitting to the situation and/or event they should make understandable. By "typological interpretation" I understand an exegesis of Scriptures which interprets a certain figure or event of the Old Testament as "prefiguration" of a New Testament figure or an event from early Church history. It is quite clear that hermeneutics like this can only convince people who already believe that they are true, but cannot be shared by non-believers.

The Gospel of Matthew is, of course, not the only example of an early Christian text sharing such a reading of Scripture – the techniques used by different ancient "Christian" authors can differ, the main lines of hermeneutics, however, are at least comparable. Let me just give a few more examples: the Gospel accounts of Jesus' crucifixion are full of allusions to Psalms of Lament (mainly Ps 22 and 69) and thus want to show that Jesus is the righteous sufferer.[14] In his letter to the Galatians Paul

---

[14] For a broader discussion of the use of Ps 22 in early Christian accounts of Jesus' passion see T. NICKLAS, Die Gottverlassenheit des Gottessohns: Funktionen von Psam 22/21 LXX in frühchristlichen Auseinandersetzungen mit der Passion Jesu, in: *Aneignung durch Transformation: Beiträge zur Analyse von Überlieferungs-*

tries to understand the relation between old and new covenant with the help of a bold allegorical exegesis in the relationship of Sara to Hagar (Gal 4.21–31),[15] in Rom 11.26–27 he uses a combination of Isa 59.20–21; Jer 31.33–34 and Isa 27.9 LXX as a prophecy for Israel's future salvation.[16] Although the Book of Revelation in turn does not give a single marked quotation of Scripture, its text can be compared to a tapestry woven out of intertextual allusions to almost the whole of Scripture, but with a focus on a few prophetic and apocalyptic writings like Daniel and Ezekiel.[17]

---

prozessen im frühen Christentum. Festschrift für Michael Theobald (ed. by W. Eisele; C. Schäfer & H.-U. Weidemann; HBS 74; Freiburg et al.: Herder, 2013) 395–415.

[15] For more details see for example B. KOLLMANN, Die Geschichte von Hagar und Sara, in: *Die Verheißung des Neuen Bundes: Wie alttestamentliche Texte im Neuen Testament fortwirken* (ed. by B. Kollmann; Biblisch-Theologische Schwerpunkte 35; Göttingen: Vandenhoeck & Ruprecht, 2010) 64–77, and A.L.A. HOGETERP, Hagar and Paul's Covenant Thought, in: *Abraham, the Nations, and the Hagarites. Jewish, Christian, and Islamic Perspectives on Kinship with Abraham* (ed. by M. Goodman, G.H. Van Kooten & J. Van Ruiten; TBN 13; Leiden – Boston: Brill, 2010) 345–59.

[16] For a detailed discussion of this text see T. NICKLAS, Paulus und die Errettung Israels. Röm 11,25–36 in der exegetischen Diskussion und im jüdisch-christlichen Dialog, *Early Christianity* 2 (2011) 173–97.

[17] It is almost impossible to overlook all the relevant literature on this topic. For a recent overview see Th. HIEKE, Das Alte Testament in der Offenbarung des Johannes, in: *Poetik und Intertextualität in der Johannesapokalypse* (ed. by S. Alkier, Th. Hieke & T. Nicklas; WUNT; Tübingen: Mohr, 2014); for a discussion of Revelation's hermeneutics of Scripture see M. LABAHN, 'Das Buch dieser Prophetie' – Die Schriften Israels und die Schrift des Sehers:

In any case: in their attempts to make "sense" of the Christ event, early Christians started to read the Scriptures of Israel – or at least part of them – differently, they developed a new "Christian" hermeneutics: because of questions developed out of the Christ event, the Scriptures of Israel were (at least partly) read as speaking about the Christ event, or even as prophecies of the Christ event. The Christ event, Jesus' life and important events in the life of the Church, in turn, came to be understood as fulfilment.

The exegetical discussions around these new readings can, at least in their earlier stages, be understood as inner-Jewish debates around the meaning(s) of Scripture. Different "Christian" texts, however, again show different stages of this exegetical debate and from a certain point mirror "Christian"-"Jewish" relations in differing concrete contexts. Again, I will discuss a few examples:

1. Ignatius of Antioch

As we have already seen in Chapter 1, at least some of Ignatius of Antioch's extant letters mirror a conflict with believers in Christ who followed Jewish practices. "Jewish practices", however, usually have to do with an interpretation of Torah – be it written or oral Torah. We do not know in detail what the specifics of *halakhic* practices of

Überlegungen zur Schrifthermeneutik der Johannesoffenbarung, in: *The Scriptures of Israel in Jewish and Christian Tradition. Essays in Honour of Maarten J. J. Menken* (ed. by B. J. Koet, S. Moyise & J. Verheyden; NovT.S 148; Leiden – Boston: Brill, 2013) 265–84.

the Jews of Magnesia and Philadelphia looked like. The only concrete point Ignatius addresses is Sabbath observance (*Magn.* 9.1), but we can be sure that other practices must have played a role as well.[18] In any case, they were so attractive for at least some followers of Christ that Ignatius interpreted this as a danger. Ignatius, however, was not so much interested in the discussion of particular practices, but in the underlying hermeneutics of Scripture,[19] which, according to him, does not lead to Christ, but to "Judaism". He writes:

"[I]f anyone expounds Judaism to you, do not listen to him. For it is better to hear about Christianity from a man who is circumcised than about Judaism from one who is not. But if either of them fails to speak about Jesus Christ, I look on them as tombstones and graves of the dead, upon which only the names of people are inscribed" (*Philad.* 6.1, translation Holmes 118–9).

Ignatius thus is already a witness of what we described before: at least for him there are two different ways of reading Scripture, and these two ways exclude each other.

---

[18] For a more detailed discussion see J. M. LIEU, *Image and Reality: The Jews in the World of the Christians in the Second Century* (Edinburgh: T & T Clark, 1996) 33–4; M. MURRAY, *Playing a Jewish Game: Gentile Christian Judaizing in the First and Second Centuries CE* (Studies in Christianity and Judaism 13; Waterloo, Ont.: Wilfried Laurier University Press, 2004) 84–91; W. R. SCHOEDEL, *Ignatius of Antioch* (Hermeneia; Philadelphia: Fortress, 1985) 123.

[19] W. UEBELE, »*Viele Verführer sind in die Welt ausgegangen*«. *Die Gegner in den Briefen des Ignatius von Antiochien und in den Johannesbriefen* (BWANT 151; Stuttgart: Kohlhammer, 2001) 66 and 82, even goes so far to say that matters of "practice" did not play a decisive role while the dispute focussed on interpretation of Scripture.

For him, any reading of the Scriptures which does not lead (directly and solely) to Christ, is absolutely worthless – in his view, Christ has become the *only* principle for an adequate understanding of the Scriptures. While we do not know whether the Christ-followers he addresses were possibly open to both ways of understanding, this principle was, of course, unacceptable for Jews not following Christ.

Other passages can be added: several times Ignatius claims the "prophets" for "Christianity". According to him, the prophets had not lived in agreement with Judaism (*Magn.* 8.1), but in accordance with Christ Jesus. That is the reason he calls them disciples of Christ who had enunciated Christ (*Philad.* 5.2; 9.2) and waited for him as teacher (*Magn.* 9.2). He goes even so far as to say that "they also believed in him [= Christ], they were saved, since they belong to the unity centred in Jesus Christ, saints worthy of love and admiration, approved by Jesus Christ and included in the gospel of our shared hope" (*Philad.* 5.2; see also 9.2; translation Holmes, 118). And a bit later he calls Jesus "the door of the Father, through which Abraham and Isaac and Jacob and the prophets and the apostles and the church enter in" (*Philad.* 9.1; translation Holmes, 120). Ignatius thus does not simply defend a *new* reading of Scripture in addition to old ones: if we take these ideas serious, then Judaism *never* had understood its Bible adequately.

However, what about Moses? Does Ignatius understand Moses as a prophet? And what about the passages which cannot be attributed to the Christ-event? Ignatius' extant writings do not give us a clear answer. A few observations, however, are interesting: Ignatius' letters do not offer a single marked quotation of Scripture nor even clear allusions to it. The texts show some more or less vague, possible parallels to passages from the Psalter, the Proverbs, Isaiah and Zechariah – and nothing from the Torah! There is, however, no case where one has the impression that a reader needs to know these texts to understand what Ignatius wants to say.[20] This cannot be explained as having to do with Ignatius' situation as a captive, after all he more than once alludes to Pauline writings and the Gospel of Matthew.[21] The Scriptures of Israel do not play a decisive, positive role for the development of Ignatius' theology any more. Does this mean that Ignatius rejects the Torah? After all, *Magn.* 8.1 speaks about "strange doctrines and antiquated myths" which are "worthless" (translation Holmes, 105).[22] It seems at least that Ignatius means the Torah here. But does he speak about written Torah, i.e., the books from Genesis to Deuteronomy, or about oral Torah, i.e., halakhic and haggadic interpretations of these texts? In *Philad.* 8.2 we read: "I heard some people say: 'If I do not find it in the

---

[20] See for example the indices in A. LINDEMANN – H. PAULSEN (ed.s), *Die Apostolischen Väter* (Tübingen: Mohr, 1991) 566–7.

[21] For a detailed discussion see P. FOSTER, The Epistles of Ignatius of Antioch and the writings that later formed the New Testament, in: *The Reception of the New Testament in the Apostolic Fathers* (ed. by A. Gregory & C.M. Tuckett; Oxford et al.: Oxford University Press, 2005) 159–86.

[22] J.M. LIEU, *Image*, 28 interestingly puts this kind of argument in the world of "the rhetoric of polemic in the pagan but also in the Jewish world. Depending on myths or fables was probably a common accusation against Judaism."

ἀρχεῖα, I do not believe it in the gospel" (translation adapted from Holmes, 119). The translation of the Greek term ἀρχεῖα is somewhat difficult. Does Ignatius speak about "the archives" here as Michael Holmes' translation would suggest? But which "archives" could he mean? I think it is better to translate it as "the documents" or "the records", which then seems to be a paraphrase for Torah (or Scriptures).[23] In any case, for Ignatius these "documents" *per se* are, again, worthless. He answers: "But for me, the ἀρχεῖα are Jesus Christ, the unalterable ἀρχεῖα are his cross and death and his resurrection and the faith that comes through him; by these things I want, through your prayers, to be justified" (*Philad.* 8.2; translation Holmes, 119).

One single positive statement about the Torah remains: In his letter to the Smyrneans Ignatius seems to face somewhat different problems. Questions of Jewish and Christian ways of life thus only play a minor role here[24] – perhaps this allows him a somewhat more relaxed attitude regarding this problem. *Smyrn.* 5.1, however, reminds us, at least partly, of what we have found in *Magn.* and *Philad.*:

"Certain people ignorantly deny him [= Jesus Christ; TN], or rather have been denied by him, for they are advocates of death

---

[23] According to W.R. SCHOEDEL, *Ignatius*, 208, who quotes Josephus, *Contra Apionem* 1.29 as a parallel, there can be no doubt that the term ἀρχεῖα must mean the Scriptures. For a comparable view see H. PAULSEN, *Die Briefe des Ignatius von Antiochia und der Brief des Polykarp von Smyrna* (HNT 18; Tübingen: Mohr, 1985) 86.

[24] Regarding the situation in Smyrna see for example W. UEBE-LE, *Verführer*, 82–92.

rather than that of the truth. Neither the prophecies nor the law of Moses have persuaded them, nor, thus far, the gospel nor our own individual suffering ..." (translation Holmes, 122).

Interestingly, Ignatius distinguishes between "the prophecies" and the law of Moses (νόμος Μωϋσέως) here. Anyway, the law comes to stand in a series together with "the prophecies", the gospel and Ignatius' own suffering. All these elements, however, do not have worth on their own – for Ignatius their worth consists in the fact that they are pointing to the Christ event. For Ignatius the Torah thus remains part of his Scriptures, it is however not God's guidance for leading a proper life any more. In his thinking which is on the one hand totally Christ-centred, but on the other hand not interested in the historical Jesus, the Jew, questions of *halakha* do not play a role any more. Ignatius thus develops a "Christian way of life" where the Torah as God's order for a proper life is more or less forgotten, but only serves as a part of Scriptures prophesying the "Christ-event".

2. The Gospel of John and the *Unknown Gospel* on Papyrus Egerton 2

Ignatius' writings already give us an example of a *meta-discussion*, that is, not only a discussion on concrete interpretations of Scriptural passages, but a discussion on proper ways of interpretation. Traces of comparable disputes can be found in some narrative texts as well: two closely related examples can be found in the New Testament Gospel of John and the somewhat later *unknown*

Gospel on Papyrus Egerton 2. While the Gospel of John can probably be dated to the turn of the first to the second century CE, the *unknown Gospel* is only a bit younger. Let me first give some introductory information on this text:[25] when in the year 1935 Papyrus Egerton 2 was edited for the first time this caused a little sensation. According to H.I. Bell and T.C. Skeat, its first editors, the fragment was "unquestionably the earliest specifically Christian manuscript yet discovered in Egypt."[26] Although a few decades later the discovery of another piece of the same manuscript, Papyrus Cologne 255, caused some caution regarding the assignment of dates that were too early, Papyrus Egerton 2 is still one of the oldest extant Christian manuscripts, dating to probably around 200 CE.[27]

The date of the manuscript, moreover, is not necessarily identical to the date of its text which of course can be (and usually is) much older: what we find on Papyrus Egerton 2 (+ Papyrus Cologne 255) are fragments of an

---

[25] For an introduction and full discussion of the fragments see T. Nicklas, The 'Unknown Gospel' on *Papyrus Egerton 2*, in: *Gospel Fragments* (ed. by T.J. Kraus, M.J. Kruger & T. Nicklas; Oxford Early Christian Gospel Texts; Oxford et al: Oxford University Press, 2009) 9–120, for a short overview see T. Nicklas, Papyrus Egerton 2, in: *The Non-Canonical Gospels* (ed. by P. Foster; London – New York: T & T Clark, 2008) 139–49.

[26] H.I. Bell – T.C. Skeat (ed.s), *Fragments of an Unknown Gospel and Other Early Christian Papyri* (London: British Museum, 1935) 1.

[27] Perhaps one has to be even more cautious now, as the article of P. Orsini – W. Clarysse, Early New Testament Manuscripts and their Date. A Critique of Theological Palaeography, *ETL* 88 (2012) 443–74 suggests.

otherwise lost early Christian apocryphal Gospel[28], that is, a dispute between Jesus and some "experts in Law", the end of a scene where Jesus withdraws himself from an attempt to arrest (or stone) him, a story about the healing of a leper, a very fragmentary miracle at the river Jordan and, finally, a discussion about the paying of taxes. Because it is not entirely clear at first sight whether the unknown Gospel is literarily dependent on the New Testament Gospels, there has been a controversy regarding the exact date of this apocryphal composition. It seems, however, the safest choice to understand it as a text which is at least in part dependent on an already written Gospel of John which also has some certain knowledge of the Synoptic Gospel accounts. That's why I would date it to the first decades, perhaps the middle of the second century CE.[29] While the text seems to be concerned with Jesus as a Torah-observant teacher, fragment 1 verso contains a highly interesting dispute between Jesus, the "experts in Law" and the "leaders of the people" – please be aware that we are dealing with a fragment!

"the experts in Law ... each, who transgresses ... the law and not me ... what he does, how he does it. Turned towards the leaders of the people, he said the following word: 'Search the Scriptures, in which you think you have life! These are the ones which bear witness about me. Do not think that I have come to accuse you before my Father. There is already someone who

---

[28] Of course, we cannot be absolutely sure whether these fragments were intended to be part of a full Gospel or put together only a few Jesus stories for whatever purposes.

[29] For a discussion of the Scriptural hermeneutics of this fragment see T. NICKLAS, Das 'unbekannte Evangelium' auf P.Egerton 2 und die 'Schrift', *SNTU.A* 33 (2008) 41–65, esp. 44–50.

accuses you; Moses, in whom you have hope.' But when they
said: 'We know that God has spoken to Moses, but of you we do
not know where you come from,' Jesus responded to them and
said: 'Now accusation will be made against your unbelief in relation to what he gave testimony of. For if you believed Moses,
you would also have believed me. Because he has written about
me to your forefathers ..." (translation Nicklas, 25).

The short passage above does certainly not contain memories about Jesus' actual life and his debates with authorities of his time. At least in part this text is combining
several very similar passages from the Gospel of John
(John 5.39, 46 and 9.29):

John 5.39
You search the Scriptures because you think that in them you
have eternal life; and it is they that bear witness about me,

John 5.46
For if you believed Moses, you would believe me; for he wrote
of me ...

John 9.29
We know that God has spoken to Moses, but as for this man, we
do not know where he comes from.

It seems, instead, that this text – like John 5 and 9 – mirrors much later conflicts between "Christian" communities and synagogue authorities[30] about adequate reading
of "the Scriptures" – in other words: the *unknown Gospel*
(and the Gospel of John), again, offer us insights in what

---

[30] The idea that conflicts between Jesus and "the Jews" in the
Gospel of John should be read as witnesses of conflicts between
Johannine community and synagogue has already been developed
by J.L. MARTYN, *History and Theology in the Fourth Gospel*
(Nashville: Abingdon, 1979).

could be called a kind of a meta-discussion. While in the Gospel of John the dispute is caused by a transgression of the Sabbath law by the Johannine Jesus, the fragmentary state of the *unknown Gospel* does not offer us any hint of a possible background any more. In both cases what is important is the following: according to both the Gospel of John and the *unknown Gospel*, the leaders of the people *only think* to have life in the Scriptures. According to both writings, the Scriptures bear witness to Jesus; and somewhat later they say that Moses wrote about Jesus. That's why, even if the "leaders of the people" know that God himself spoke to Moses, they should, in addition to this, know that what Moses wrote down, is about Jesus. If they, then, do not believe in Jesus, they indeed have the Scriptures, but do not properly understand them. In other words, this text uses early Christian Christological hermeneutics of the Scriptures to claim that only the "we"-group of Christ-followers, but not the authorities of the synagogue, understand the Scriptures adequately. There are thus two slight differences to what we found in Ignatius:

(1) While both John, the *unknown Gospel* and Ignatius claim that a Christological reading of the Scriptures is absolutely necessary for an adequate understanding, John and the *unknown Gospel* do not say that the Scriptures do not speak about anything else but Christ. This seems, at least for the *unknown Gospel* which in some scenes depicts Jesus as a Torah-observant teacher,[31] of significance.

---

[31] See, for example, the *unknown Gospel*'s version of the healing of the leper. See T. NICKLAS, 'Werde rein ... und sündige nicht mehr!' (Heilung eines Aussätzigen) – P.Egerton 2, in: *Kompendium*

(2) While Ignatius seems to almost totally neglect the practical and ethical dimensions of the Torah for his theology, both John and the unknown Gospel explicitly claim Moses as a witness to Christ. This, again, certainly has to do with the fact that both the communities of John, and (if we can say anything about it) of the *unknown Gospel* still attach impact to their Jewish heritage.

In addition to this, both John and the *unknown Gospel* use a different technique than Ignatius: while Ignatius bases his argument on his authority as a bishop (and even more, as a bishop on his way to martyrdom, i. e. bearing witness to Christ), John and the *unknown Gospel* base their claims in Jesus' alleged words themselves.

3. Justin Martyr

The writings of Justin Martyr (ca. 100/110–165 CE) offer even more insights[32] – I will mention a few points of interest.

3.1 Our short look into Justin's *first apology* in Chapter 2 showed us how Justin used Scripture not only to interpret the Christ event but also the present situation. While we have seen how *apol. 1.49* used Isa 65.1–3 to describe

---

der frühchristlichen Wundererzählungen 1: Die Wunder Jesu (ed. by R. Zimmermann et al.; Gütersloh: Gütersloher, 2013) 869–72, esp. 871.

[32] For a broader recent discussion of Justin's hermeneutics of Scripture see B. CHILTON, Justin and Israelite Prophecy, in: *Justin and His Worlds* (ed. by S. Parvis & P. Foster; Minneapolis: Fortress, 2007) 77–87.

the relation of what he understands as "Judaism" and "Christianity" as fulfilment of Scripture, *apol.* 1.47 puts together a combination of Scriptural passages to interpret the historical situation after the Bar-Kohkba War (132–135 CE) from Justin's perspective:

"That the land of the Jews, then, was to be laid waste, hear what was said by the Spirit of prophecy. And the words were spoken as if from the person of the people wondering at what had happened. They are these: "Sion is a wilderness, Jerusalem a desolation. The house of our sanctuary has become a curse, and the glory which our fathers blessed is burned up with fire, and all its glorious things are laid waste: and Thou refrainest Thyself at these things, and hast held Thy peace, and hast humbled us very sore." And ye are convinced that Jerusalem has been laid waste, as was predicted. And concerning its desolation, and that no one should be permitted to inhabit it, there was the following prophecy by Isaiah: "Their land is desolate, their enemies consume it before them, and none of them shall dwell therein." And that it is guarded by you lest any one dwell in it, and that death is decreed against a Jew apprehended entering it, you know very well" (translation adapted from *Ante-Nicene Fathers*).

Two long quotes from Scripture serve Justin for his argument – he uses Isa 64.10–12 and a combination of Isa 1.7 and Jer 2.15 to show that the situation after 135 CE, when Jerusalem was not only destroyed but Jews were not allowed any longer to enter the remnants of the Holy City, was not just an accidental event, but – in his (and probably many pagan Christians') eyes – a fate fulfilling prophecies from Israel's Scriptures. Justin's example – and many more could be added – is thus a witness to a few developments:

(1) While the first examples of "Christian" interpretation of Scripture we mentioned were still developed out of the experiences and crises connected to the Christ event, Justin's exegesis shows us that the "new" hermeneutics is now more and more expanded to other matters of interest for ancient "Christian" communities. The developing scheme was quite easy – the Scriptures of Israel were more and more understood as "Old Testament" – an expression for the first time used by Melito of Sardis (according to Eusebius, *h.e.* 4.24) – containing promise and prophecy; the present situation, however, was understood in terms of "fulfilment". Many "Christian" scholars are only now just beginning to understand that this kind of reading is far from adequate for Israel's Scriptures – even if seen from a "Christian" perspective.[33]

(2) In this development Israel's Scripture could now be used more and more *against* Judaism. What we read in Justin is by no means an isolated example – it is quite clear that Justin did not develop his example on his own, but utilized collections of *Testimonia* which were used by other writers as well. Other second-century writers (and writings), like the *Epistle of Barnabas*, *the Gospel of Peter*, Melito of Sardis etc. used Scripture in similar ways.

(3) The examples quoted above also show that many authors' main interest was not to *understand* what the Scriptures wanted to say, but that they wanted to make the Scriptures fit their interests. In this process they sometimes went so far as to "correct", that is, change

---

[33] See, for example, the discussion in F.-L. HOSSFELD (ed.), *Wieviel Systematik erlaubt die Schrift? Auf der Suche nach einer gesamtbiblischen Theologie* (QD 185; Freiburg et al.: Herder, 2001).

Scripture for their purposes. These changes were made on different levels: putting Scriptural passages out of their context, putting together passages from different contexts to form a new "text", and, at least in some cases, changing their Scriptural *Vorlage*. The next example will show us that this must have happened more than once – and surely on both "Jewish" and "Christian" sides of the debate.

3.2 Shortly after the middle of the second century CE (ca 160 CE?) Justin also wrote an extensive *Dialogue with Trypho the Jew*, a text even more interesting for our question than his apologies.[34] Like Ignatius did somewhat earlier, Justin's *Dialogue* works with the contrast of two different categories – "Christianity" and "Judaism". In a certain sense, however, Justin goes much deeper than Ignatius: in his *Dialogue with Trypho* he brings the two categories *into debate with each other*. It has, for a long time, been discussed whether or not Justin's *Dialogue* with the Jew Trypho (or Tarfon) really took place (and how it took place). The whole scene is located shortly after the end of the Bar-Kohkba war, i. e., around 135 CE, in Ephesus. However, a somewhat closer look into this writing reveals that what we find in the extant work is surely not an account which mirrors a *real dispute* between two *real* people of flesh and blood. It is rather a

---

[34] For a broader discussion of Justin's image of Jews developed in the *dialogue* see also T. Rajak, Talking at Trypho. Christian Apologetics as Anti-Judaism in Justin's Dialogue with Trypho the Jew, in: *Apologetics in the Roman Empire: Pagans, Jews, and Christians* (ed. by M. Edwards; Oxford: Oxford University Press, 1999) 59–80.

highly stylized account of a dialogue between two representatives of two categories: "Christianity" and "Judaism". Even more, this dialogue is largely written from the perspective of only one side – Justin's "Christian" one – that for pages we only read a monologue, with a Jew Trypho who only now and then is allowed to ask his critical questions. We should thus know that (at least the literary) Trypho is nothing more than Justin's "sparring-partner" allowing Justin to unfold all his arguments.

As discussions of proper readings of Scripture form a central theme of the *Dialogue*, this text is of highest interest for our question: while most of the examples we have seen so far, centre on the question whether a certain perspective on the Scriptures of Israel is allowed or not, Justin's work is also a witness to debates *on the correct textual form* of important scriptural passages.

Dial. 66 is part of a longer passage where Justin argues that Isa 7.10–17 can only be understood in its relation to Christ. Trypho objects (*dial.* 67.1) – according to him, Justin's interpretation of Isa 7.14 is only possible because he uses an incorrect textual form of this passage. This is, by the way, a problem discussed until today – while the Hebrew text of Isa 7.14 mentions an *almah*, that is, a young woman, bearing a child, the LXX translates the Greek παρθένος which can (even if this is no "must") well be translated as "virgin".[35] According to Trypho, the correct text of Isa 7.14 does not speak about a virgin, but about a young woman; that's why he relates the prophecy

---

[35] See, for example, M.J.J. MENKEN, The Textual Form of the Quotation from Isaiah 7:14 in Matthew 1:23, *NovT* 43 (2001) 144–60.

to the times of king Hezekiah, the king of Judah between ca. 725 and 697 BCE, in whose life it already had been fulfilled. Justin's answer is interesting: for him the Septuagint is certainly a trustworthy basis for any scriptural argument. However, some "Jewish" teachers had consciously tried to change its text (cf. *dial.* 68.7; 71.1; see also Eusebius, *h.e.* 4.18.8) and only these changes allowed the Jewish interpretation. He writes:

"If therefore, I shall show that this prophecy of Isaiah (= Isa 7.14; TN) refers to our Christ, and not to Hezekiah, as you say, shall I not in this matter, too, compel you not to believe your teachers, who venture to assert that the explanation which your seventy elders that were with Ptolemy the king of the Egyptians gave, is untrue in certain respects? For some statements in the Scriptures, which appear explicitly to convict them of a foolish and vain opinion, these they venture to assert have not been so written. But other statements, which they fancy they can distort and harmonize with human actions, these, they say, refer not to this Jesus Christ of ours, but to him of whom they are pleased to explain them. Thus, for instance, they have taught you that this Scripture which we are now discussing refers to Hezekiah, in which, as I promised, I shall show they are wrong" (*dial.* 68.7–8; translation adapted from *Ante-Nicene Fathers*).

A bit later we read:

"But I am far from putting reliance in your teachers, who refuse to admit that the interpretation made by the seventy elders (i.e., the translators of the LXX; TN) who were with Ptolemy [king] of the Egyptians is a correct one; and they attempt to frame another. And I wish you to observe, that they (i.e., Jewish teachers; TN) have altogether taken away many Scriptures from the translations effected by those seventy elders who were with Ptolemy, and by which this very man who was crucified is proved to have been set forth expressly as God, and man, and as being crucified, and as dying; but since I am aware that this is denied by all of your nation, I do not address myself to these points, but I proceed to carry on my discussions by means of those passages which are still admitted by you. For you assent to those which I have brought before your attention, except that you contradict the statement, 'Behold, the virgin shall conceive, 'and say it ought to be read, 'Behold, the young woman shall conceive.' And I promised to prove that the prophecy referred, not, as you were taught, to Hezekiah, but to this Christ of mine: and now I shall go to the proof." (*dial.* 71.1; adapted from *Ante-Nicene Fathers*)

According to Justin, Isa 7.14 is not the only passage where this had been the case: a bit later he mentions a passage from the book of Ezra which otherwise is only known via Lactantius, *inst.* 4.18.22 (*dial.* 72.1), Jer 11.19 (*dial.* 72.2–3), for the followers of Christ an important parallel to Isa 53.7, and others. In any case: Justin's *Dialogue* is not just a witness of different hermeneutics of Scripture, but also of disputes for the correct form of its text.

3.3 Justin, however, also offers us some of the first examples of an exegesis reading whole passages of Scripture as allegories on Jesus' life – one could, for example talk about his allegorical interpretation of Psalm 22[36] or his interpretation of Isa 7.10–17 combined with Isa 8.4 in *dial.* 77–78 – here he changes the text flow of Isaiah to make his argument fitting. This is necessary because Isa 8.4 becomes a key for his argument – the matter of the dispute, again is on the question whether Isa 7 can relate to Hezekiah or Jesus Christ. I can quote only a part of

---

[36] For a broader discussion of Justin's exegesis of Psalm 22 see my article T. NICKLAS, Gottverlassenheit, 410–4.

the whole argument. After having shown that Trypho's interpretation must be incorrect, Justin interprets Jesus' adoration through the magi coming from the east as fulfilment of Isa 8.4, something which cannot be said about the Israelite king Hezekiah. While Isaiah's "King of the Assyrians" is identified with Herod (*dial.* 77.4), the magi who according to Justin came from *Arabia* (*dial.* 77.4; 78.1,2,7) fulfil the Isaianic Damascus prophecy (*dial.* 78.9). Several aspects of Justin's argument are highly interesting: while we argued that the roots of "Christian" Christological hermeneutics of Scripture can be found in the Christ event of Jesus, death and resurrection, Justin – in a certain sense developing the Gospel of Matthew's fulfilment quotations – is now interested in understanding many details of Jesus' life as fulfilment of scripture. Or better, if we look into his story of Jesus' life, we get the impression that he often makes this story fitting to the scriptural passage he uses. Even if we do not know exactly what the "gospels" Justin used looked like,[37] for the Jesus story he tells here he must have created or at least used a harmony of different Gospel accounts: *Dial.* 77–78 offers an infancy story harmonizing Matt 2.1–14, 16 with elements from Luke 2.1–5 and adding some apocryphal elements like the idea of the magis' alleged origins in Arabia (*dial.* 77.4; 78.1,2,7) or Jesus' birth in a cave

---

[37] For a discussion of the "Christian" writings Justin used see C. D. ALLERT, *Revelation, Truth, Canon and Interpretation. Studies in Justin Martyr's Dialogue with Trypho* (VigChr.S 64; Leiden – Boston: Brill, 2002) 188–220, and O. SKARSAUNE, Justin and his Bible, in: *Justin Martyr and His Worlds* (ed. by S. Parvis & P. Foster; Minneapolis: Fortress 2007) 53–76.

(*dial.* 78.6; see the parallels in the apocryphal *Protevangelium of James* 18.1). In any case: Justin's *Dialogue with Trypho* creates the impression that Justin and Trypho already represent two different groups, and even two different thought worlds already quite distant from each other – two groups who because of textual differences are using *almost* the same scriptures, and who differ extremely in their hermeneutics.

4. Marcion, "Gnostics", and Others

4.1 Neglect of Israel's Scriptures in "proto-orthodox" Writings

While the writings of Justin Martyr – mainly the *Dialogue with Trypho* – lead us into the heart of a "Christian" theology built on an allegorical interpretation of Israel's Scriptures in the prophecy – fulfilment scheme, there are also second-century Christian writings where Israel's Scriptures play almost no role at all. At least in some cases this has to do with matters of genre and intended audience: when Tatian's *Oratio ad Graecos*, a kind of a *logos protreptikos* written around 165 CE and "advertising" for Christian belief, is full of quotations from pagan literature but does not even mention the Scriptures at all, this has to do with the intended audience and the function of the writing[38] – the remaining fragments of Ta-

---

[38] For more information on Tatian see W. L. Peterson, Tatian the Assyrian, in: *A Companion to Second Century Christian 'Heretics'* (ed. by A. Marjanen & P. Luomanen; VigChr.S 76; Leiden –

tian's *Diatessaron*, a Gospel harmony, speak another language.[39] The same is the case with Athenagoras of Athens' *Apology for the Christians* where we find only a few (and open) allusions to the Scriptures while Homer's *Iliad*, at least sometimes, plays an important role.[40] In the case of the apocryphal pseudo-Pauline *Letter to the Laodiceans* the lack of allusions and quotations to Israel's Scriptures has been interpreted as a sign of the Marcionite origin of the text.[41] Although this thesis cannot be held any longer,[42] the text seems to represents a kind of "Christian" theological argument where Israel's Scriptures do not play a role.

Boston: Brill, 2005) 125–58; for his use of pagan authors see S. FREUND, 'Und wunderbar sind eure Dichter, die da lügen ..." (Tat., orat. 22,7). Beobachtungen zu Gestalt, Auswahl und Funktion von Dichterzitaten in der griechischen Apologetik am Beispiel Tatians, in: *Ad veram religionem reformare: Frühchristliche Apologetik zwischen Anspruch und Wirklichkeit* (ed. by C. Schubert &. A. von Stockhausen; Erlanger Forschungen Reihe A. Geisteswissenschaften 109; Erlangen: Universität Erlangen – Nürnberg, 2006) 97–121.

[39] See, for example, R.F. SHEDINGER, *Tatian and the Jewish Scriptures: A Textual and Philological Analysis of the Old Testament Citations in Tatian's Diatessaron* (CSCO 591; Subsidia 109; Leuven: Peeters, 2001).

[40] For text and introduction to this piece see W.R. SCHOEDEL, *Athenagoras: Legatio and De Resurrectione* (Oxford: Clarendon, 1972).

[41] See, for example, G. QUISPEL, The Epistle to the Laodiceans: A Marcionite Forgery, in his: *Gnostica, Judaica, Catholica. Collected Essays of Gilles Quispel* (NHMS 55; Leiden – Boston: Brill, 2008) 689–93.

[42] See Ph.L. TITE, *The Apocryphal Epistle to the Laodiceans: An Epistolary and Rhetorical Analysis* (TENT 7; Leiden – Boston: Brill, 2012) 6–8. 129–32.

A comparable argument could also be made with some *Acts of Christian Martyrs*: while a text like the *Martyrdom of Polycarp* in its attempt to depict Polycarp's martyrdom in the light of Jesus' passion, at least every now and then, alludes to Scripture, a writing like the *Acts of the Scillitan Martyrs* concentrates on the legal procedures against a group of Christians in Carthage in the year 180 CE. Thus, the text is mainly interested in the interrogation and confession of the Christians as Christians. To state this another way, it is focused on the relation of Christians to the representatives of the Roman Empire, but is not interested in matters of relation to Judaism. Christian books, however, play at least a small role. When the proconsul asks the accused Christians: "What have you in your case," they answer "Books and letters of a just man named Paul" (*Act. Scil.* 12) – in a context, where "Christian" identity counts, the text focuses on distinctive features – only Christians would have Paul's letters in their case.

The unknown author of the writing *Ad Diognetum*, a text which, as we saw in chapter 2, was perhaps written in Alexandria around the end of the second century CE, surely goes a decisive step further: in his attempt to make "Christianity" attractive for an educated pagan elité in a city with a long history of pagan anti-Judaism he develops an image of Christianity as a "new race" which has almost nothing to do with Judaism. Looking out for quotes of or allusions to Scripture in this text is a useless task.

4.2 Marcion of Sinope

The above examples, however, have to be distinguished from another group of texts which consciously developed a still different attitude to Israel's Scriptures. For Marcion of Sinope, whom we already introduced in chapter 2, the Scriptures of Israel were inspired by a Deity different from the God worshipped by the Christians. Contrary to Justin, Melito or the author of the *Epistle of Barnabas*, Marcion did not read the Scriptures allegorically,[43] but was interested in their literal meaning. H. Räisänen writes:

"For mainstream expositors, the Old Testament was, for the most part, important as a collection of alleged predictions and promises about Jesus, which were 'discovered' in the Old Testament through the use of allegorical and typological devices. Allegorising also helped one to side-step various difficulties caused by many biblical passages, if they were to be understood literally. By contrast, Marcion read the Old Testament in a literal way, and abstained from explaining away the difficulties. His suspicion of allegory was indeed 'a mark of uniqueness in that age.'"[44]

If we want to understand Marcion's critique of Israel's Scriptures we first have to make clear that Marcion did

---

[43] See for example Origen, *Comm. in Matt.* 15.3 who writes: "Marcion says, that the Scripture must not be interpreted allegorically."

[44] H. Räisänen, Marcion, in: *A Companion to Second Century Christian 'Heretics'* (ed. by A. Marjanen & P. Luomanen; VigChr.S 76; Leiden – Boston: Brill, 2005) 100–24, esp. 107–8; see also S. Moll, *The Arch-Heretic Marcion* (WUNT 250; Tübingen: Mohr, 2010) 78–83.

not understand these texts as fake or as corrupt,[45] but as
inspired – and that he wanted to understand the nature of
the Deity who had inspired these texts. Unfortunately
Marcion's works are lost, and we can reconstruct his ideas only via the writings of his opponents – one of the most
important sources being Tertullian's *Adversus Marcionem*.[46] In his wish to refute Marcion's argument Tertullian sometimes has to quote his opponent's ideas. Tertullian living in Carthage, North Africa, at the turn of
the second to the third century CE was surely one of the
first really important Christian authors writing in Latin
(rarely in Greek). Tertullian was highly educated (some
assume that he had been a lawyer)[47], but even a person like
him sometimes had problems with Marcion's arguments.
At least a few aspects of Marcion's exegesis, however, can
be reconstructed. The following points are of special in-

---

[45] If, for Marcion, any part of what we would call Scripture was
corrupt, then it was the writings of the New Testament, which he
wanted to free from influences of Judaism. The question of Marcion's redactional activity, however, is still a matter of debate. For a
recent very critical voice see J.D. BeDuhn, The Myth of Marcion
as Redactor: The Evidence of Marcion's Gospel against an Assumed Marcionite Redaction, *ASE* 29 (2012) 21–48.

[46] Regarding Tertullian as an anti-Marcionite writer see C. Moreschini, Polemica antimarcionita e speculazione teologica in Ter-
tulliano, in: *Marcion und seine kirchengeschichtliche Wirkung.
Marcion and His Impact on Church History* (ed. by G. May, K.
Greschat & M. Meiser; TU 150; Berlin – New York: de Gruyter,
2002) 11–28.

[47] For a very good overview on Tertullian, his life and his teachings see T. Barnes, *Tertullian: A Historical and Literary Study*
(Oxford et al.: Oxford University Press, 1985).

terest[48] – one must admit that his observations are by no means silly:

(1) Marcion highlighted oppositions and disagreements between the "Old Testament" and Jesus' ideas. A very nice example for a typical "Marcionite" argument that the teachings of Christ are very different from the Creator, is reflected in Tertullian, *Marc.* 4.23. Tertullian's first obvious quote of Marcion:

"But, behold, Christ takes infants, and teaches how all ought to be like them, if they ever wish to be greater. The Creator, on the contrary, let loose bears against children, in order to avenge His prophet Elisha, who had been mocked by them" (translation adapted from *Ante-Nicene Fathers*).

In other words, Marcion compares an Old Testament story with a New Testament counterpart here. According to 2 Kings 2.23–24, a few infants mocked the prophet Elisha for his baldness. In response, Elisha cursed the boys who were immediately killed by two bears coming from the forest. According to Mark 10.13–16 (par. Matt 19.13–15; Luke 18.15–17), however, Jesus did not only bless children, but saw them as examples for people who wanted to be part of God's Kingdom. Tertullian tries his best to show that Marcion's argument is wrong:

"This antithesis is impudent enough, since it throws together things so different as infants and children, – an age still innocent, and one already capable of discretion-able to mock, if not to blaspheme. As therefore God is a just God, He spared not impious children, exacting as He does honour for every time of life, and especially, of course, from youth. And as God is good,

---

[48] For a more complete overview and many more examples see H. Räisänen, Marcion, 108–9.

He so loves infants as to have blessed the midwives in Egypt, when they protected the infants of the Hebrews which were in peril from Pharaoh's command. Christ therefore shares this kindness with the Creator" (adapted from *Ante-Nicene Fathers*).

(2) In addition, Marcion was also interested in contradictions within the Scriptures. Let us, again, have a look into Tertullian's *Adversus Marcionem*:

"Similarly on other points also, you reproach Him with fickleness and instability for contradictions in His commandments, such as that He forbade work to be done on Sabbath-days, and yet at the siege of Jericho ordered the ark to be carried round the walls during eight days; in other words, of course, actually on a Sabbath. You do not, however, consider the law of the Sabbath: they are human works, not divine, which it prohibits. For it says, "Six days shalt thou labour, and do all thy work; but the seventh day is the Sabbath of the Lord thy God: in it thou shalt not do any work." What work? Of course your own. The conclusion is, that from the Sabbath-day He removes those works which He had before enjoined for the six days, that is, your own works; in other words, human works of daily life. Now, the carrying around of the ark is evidently not an ordinary daily duty, nor yet a human one; but a rare and a sacred work, and, as being then ordered by the direct precept of God, a divine one. And it might fully explain what this signified, were it not a tedious process to open out the forms of all the Creator's proofs, which you would, moreover, probably refuse to allow. It is more to the point, if you be confuted on plain matters by the simplicity of truth rather than curious reasoning. Thus, in the present instance, there is a clear distinction respecting the Sabbath's prohibition of human labours, not divine ones. Accordingly, the man who went and gathered sticks on the Sabbath-day was punished with death. For it was his own work which he did; and this the law forbade. They, however, who on the Sabbath carried the ark round Jericho, did it with impunity. For it was not their own work, but God's, which they executed, and that too, from His express commandment" (*Adv. Marc.* 2.21; translation adapted from *Ante-Nicene Fathers*).

Marcion's argument is, again, based on an interesting observation. When according to the Ten Commandments, working on the Sabbath is forbidden, the Creator contradicts himself when in the book of Joshua he orders the people to carry the ark of the Covenant around the walls of Jericho for eight days, that is, including at least one Sabbath. For Marcion, the conclusion is clear – the Creator cannot be perfect. Tertullian, again, tries to show that we are dealing with two different cases – "human works of daily life" in the case of the Ten Commandments, and "a rare and sacred work" in the case of the siege of Jericho. Interestingly, in his argument against Marcion at least in the cases quoted above Tertullian moves to Marcion's level of argument: where we nowadays would argue with developments in the Jewish religion or different layers of Scripture, he sees, like Marcion, Scripture as a unity without contradictions. In addition – and perhaps more interesting – he does not answer with an allegorical interpretation to Marcion's literal understanding of Scripture, but where he tries to show that already Marcion's observations on the level of literal interpretation are incorrect.

4.3 Apelles

Marcion was not alone in his understanding of Scripture – as we have seen in Chapter 2 his movement went on for

centuries.[49] One of his most influential students was
Apelles whose school in Carthage seems to have been important enough to force Tertullian to write his (now lost)
treatise *Adversus Apelleiacos*.[50] It is not completely clear
in how far a break between Apelles and his teacher occurred: in any case, at least in a few points Apelles' teaching differed from Marcion's. This is also the case with
Apelles' understanding of the Scriptures of Israel. A very
nice example is quoted in Origen's *hom. in Gen.* 2.2 –
Apelles is concerned with the question of whether Noah's Ark could contain all the animals which are mentioned in the book of Genesis:[51]

"In no way could it have been accomplished that in so short a
time so many kinds of animals and their foods, which were to
last for a whole year, should be taken aboard. For when two by
two unclean animals, that is two male and two female of each –

---

[49] For more information see H. Räisänen, Marcion. For later
traces of Marcionite theology see W. Hage, Marcion bei Eznik von
Kolb, and M. Frenschkowski, Marcion in arabischen Quellen,
both in: *Marcion und seine kirchengeschichtliche Wirkung. Marcion
and His Impact on Church History* (ed. by G. May, K. Greschat &
M. Meiser; TU 150; Berlin – New York: de Gruyter, 2002) 29–38
and 39–63.

[50] For Apelles' teaching see G. May, Apelles und die Entwicklung einer Markionitischen Theologie, in his: *Markion: Gesammelte Aufsätze* (Veröffentlichungen des Instituts für Europäische
Geschichte Mainz; Abteilung für Abendländische Religionsgeschichte 68; Mainz: Philipp von Zabern, 2005) 93–110, esp. 94–9.

[51] For an interpretation of this passage see K. Greschat, *Apelles
und Hermogenes: Zwei theologische Lehrer des zweiten Jahrhunderts* (VigChr.S 48; Leiden – Boston: Brill, 2000) 67–8, who specu-
lates whether Apelles' criticism of the passage could have been influenced by contemporary critics of Homer who asked how a whole
army could have found place in the Trojan horse.

this is what the repeated word means – and seven by seven clean animals, that is, seven pairs, are described as led into the ark, how could the space described be made big enough to take even four elephants alone? It is clear that the story is false; but if this is so, it is clear that this writing is not from God" (translation Grant).

Per se Apelles' argument is quite clear: no ship can be big enough to cover all the animals and their food which according to Gen 7.2–3 entered Noah's Ark.[52] The main difference to Marcion's teaching can be discovered in the last sentence: "It is clear that the story is false; but if this is so, it is clear that this writing is not from God". While for Marcion Israel's Scriptures as a whole were inspired, but inspired by an evil God who cannot be perfect, it seems that Apelles distinguished between different layers of Scripture: some of them inspired and some simply false.[53]

4.3 *"Gnostic" Teachers*

Marcion and his followers were not the only believers in Christ who wanted to cut off their movement as much as possible from its Jewish roots. In Irenaeus of Lyon's treatise *Against all Heresies* written at the end of the second century CE, we read about several early "Christian" authors who understood the Torah as not given by God.

---

[52] On the whole, Marcion's and Apelles' critics seem to be at least partly in line with pagan critics of the Old Testament. For an overview, however, concentrating on mostly later authors, see J. G. COOK, *The Interpretation of the Old Testament in Greco-Roman Paganism* (STAC 23; Tübingen: Mohr, 2004).

[53] For a more differentiated approach see G. MAY, Apelles, 98.

Interestingly, this doctrine seems to have been developed in a few steps: if we believe Irenaeus, then Simon Magus – according to Christian tradition often seen as "the" founder of all heresy[54] – taught that the world was created by angels who also inspired the prophets in their writings (*haer.* 1.23.3). A little bit later, Irenaeus writes that Simon's successor Menander also believed that the world was created by angels (*haer.* 1.23.5) while the Syrian teacher Saturninus identified the God of Israel and giver of the law with one of them (*haer.* 1.24.2):

"The God of the Jews is one of the angels. When the Father wanted to destroy all the archons, the Christ came for the destruction of the God of the Jews and the salvation of those who believed him and have the spark of his life" (translation Grant).

Basilides of Alexandria,[55] one of the most important early "Gnostic" teachers, went even further (*haer.* 1.24.4):

"The angels who occupy the lower heaven seen by us made everything that the world contains and shared among themselves the earth and the nations on it. The chief of the angels is the one regarded as the God of the Jews. When he wanted to subject the other nations to his own people, the Jews, the other archons rose up against him and fought him, and therefore the other peoples rose against his people" (translation Grant).

---

[54] For an overview of Simon Magus' fascinating *Nachgeschichte* see A. FERREIRO, *Simon Magus in Patristic, Medieval and Early Modern Traditions* (Studies in the History of Christian Traditions 125; Leiden – Boston: Brill, 2005).

[55] On Basilides see B. A. PEARSON, Basilides the Gnostic, in: *A Companion to Second-Century Christian 'Heretics'* (ed. by A. Marjanen & P. Luomanen; VigChr.S76; Leiden – Boston: Brill, 2005) 1–31.

Ideas like these must, of course, have had decisive influence on the interpretation of the Torah. While we, however, have only very few fragments of the teachings of the above authors, the 1945 discovery of the Nag Hammadi library provided us with some first-hand knowledge of other "Gnostic" groups – let me focus on one of them: in chapter 2, we have already heard about the Sethian "Gnostics" who, in a certain sense comparable to Marcion, distinguished between two Deities – an evil (or sometimes only silly) Creator of the (bad) material world and a heavenly Deity far away from this world. In many cases, the Sethians retold Biblical stories – with a focus on the creation of world and man, paradise, sin and the story of the great flood[56] – and thereby changed perspectives. In this process, some of Scripture's good guys were seen as negative because they were elected by and adhered to the wrong deity, that is, the bad demiurge – one could speak about a "protest exegesis"[57]. In his important monograph "Gnostic Revisions of Genesis Stories and Early Jesus Traditions" Gerard P. Luttikhuizen offers a series of highly interesting examples showing how some "Sethian Gnostic" writings re-interpreted the Biblical stories of Creation to make them fitting to their own thought-

---

[56] See J. LAHE, *Gnosis und Judentum. Alttestamentliche und jüdische Motive in der gnostischen Literatur und das Ursprungsproblem der Gnosis* (NHMS 75; Leiden – Boston: Brill, 2012) 388. – On the basic principles of their "creation"-mythology see E. E. POPKES, The Gnostic Myth: Protology, *Revísta Catalana de Teología* 37 (2012) 55–66.

[57] J. LAHE, *Gnosis und Judentum*, 390, who, however, makes clear that we do not find this kind of exegesis throughout in "Gnostic" writings.

worlds.[58] Perhaps the most well-known writing is the *Apocryphon of John*, a text preserved in four manuscripts and also reflected in Irenaeus' *haer.* 1.29. According to Michael Waldstein, the second part of the text can be called a "critical midrash on Gen 1–7"[59] interpreting Israel's God as the diabolic creator of the material world, called Jaldabaoth or Samael. This, of course, drastically changes the perspective of the storyline. Christ, the "Savior", who according to our text, reveals the hidden truth to his disciples, more than once uses the words *"not* like Moses said" or *"not* like he wrote" (see mainly NHC II,1 13,20; 22,22; 23,2; 29,6 and parallels). Let us have a closer look into at least one passage: the text relates how after the demiurgical creator had imprisoned Adam's original divine element in a physical body he did everything to move his power away – one of these attempts was the creation of Eve (*ApJohn* NHC II,1 22–23):[60]

"The first ruler (= the demiurge; TN) knew Adam was disobedient to him because of enlightened Insight within Adam (= the divine element within Adam; TN), which made Adam stronger

---

[58] G.P. LUTTIKHUIZEN, *Gnostic Revisions of Genesis Stories and Early Jesus Traditions* (NHMS 58; Leiden – Boston: Brill, 2006). See also J. LAHE, *Gnosis und Judentum*, 191–392.

[59] M. WALDSTEIN, Das Apokryphon des Johannes (NHC II,2 ; III,1 ; IV,1 und BG 2), in: *Nag Hammadi Deutsch 1: NHC I,1-V,1* (ed. by H.-M. Schenke et al.; GCS Neue Folge 8. Koptisch-Gnostische Schriften II; Berlin – New York: de Gruyter, 2001) 95–150, esp. 96.

[60] For a more detailed interpretation of the passage see G.P. LUTTIKHUIZEN, The Demonic Demiurge in Gnostic Mythology, in: *The Fall of the Angels* (ed. by C. Auffarth & L.T. Stuckenbruck; TBN 6; Leiden – Boston, Brill, 2004) 148–61, esp. 155–8.

of mind than he. He wanted to recover power that he had himself had passed on Adam. So he brought deep sleep upon Adam.

I (= John) said to the Savior (= Christ): 'What is this deep
sleep?'

The Savior said, It is not as Moses wrote and you heard. He
said in his first book, 'He put Adam to sleep' (Gen 2.21). Rather,
this deep sleep was a loss of sense. Thus the first ruler said
through the prophet, 'I shall make their minds sluggish, that
they may neither understand nor discern.' (Isa 6.10). Enlightened Insight had herself within Adam. The first ruler wanted to
take her from Adam's side, but enlightened Insight cannot be
apprehended. Although darkness pursued her, it did not appre-
hend her. The first ruler removed part of Adam's power and
created another figure in the form of a female, like the mage of
Insight that had appeared to him. He put the part he had taken
from the power of the human being into the female creature. It
did not happen, however, the way Moses said: 'Adam's rib' (Gen
2.21–22).

Adam saw the woman beside him. At once enlightened Insight appeared and removed the veil that covered his mind. He
sobered up from the drunkenness of darkness. He recognized
his counterpart and said, 'This is now bone from my bones and
flesh from my flesh" (Gen 2.23) (translation M. Meyer).

The storyline thus follows quite closely what is told in
Gen. 2.21–23 which is also quoted now and then. The
Apocryphon of John, however, is trying to narrate what it
regards to be the real version of the events: the creation of
Eve was an attempt of the demiurgical creator to move
away (parts of) Adam's "enlightened Insight". This attempt, however, failed, and, finally two "human beings"
having a divine element inside were created.

Even if these patterns of interpretation seems extremely strange to us today, Gerard Luttikhuizen finds an in-

teresting parallel to ways of interpreting Scripture that
we just discussed. He writes:

"Just like other early Christians, *ApJohn*'s mythopoets were
convinced that the true significance of the Jewish Scriptures
was disclosed when they were read in the light of the Christian
revelation. However, the agreement is purely formal because
early Christians had very divergent ideas about the actual con-
tent and meaning of the revelation brought by Christ. A basic
element in the demiurgical Gnostic, the Marcionite, and Ptolemy's Valentinian understanding of the Christian message was
the conviction that Christ revealed another God than the Old
Testament creator and ruler of the world."[61]

5. Pseudepigraphical Writings: "Jewish" or "Christian"?

The picture of second-century "Christian" interpretation of Scripture would, however, not be complete if we
did not mention another use of Scripture which binds at
least some strands of early Christianity very close to early Jewish attempts of "expanding" and/or "rewriting
Scriptures" and make them fitting to new situations while
preserving main lines of their message and impact.[62] During the last decades, many of the newly discovered and
edited writings of Qumran have been attributed as "re-

---

[61] G. P. LUTTIKHUIZEN, *Gnostic Revisions*, 27.
[62] On the current discussion on the (somewhat problematic)
term "Rewritten Bible" or "Rewritten Scripture" see, for example,
M. M. ZAHN, Rewritten Scripture, in: *The Oxford Handbook of the
Dead Sea Scrolls* (ed. by T. H. Lim; Oxford et al.: Oxford University Press, 2010) 323–36.

written Scripture"; others, like the book of Jubilees, *Joseph and Aseneth* or Pseudo-Philo's *Liber Antiquitatum Biblicarum* have already been known for longer. While I am well-aware of the fact that the term "rewritten Scripture" creates some problems and is used in very different ways,[63] I would like to use it in a very broad sense and talk about ancient texts which are composed by using and expanding Old Testament stories and writings, filling their gaps and telling more about their protagonists. One could already start in the New Testament where the Book of Revelation could be called a tapestry woven out of Scriptural allusions, motifs and images. Revelation's relation to the text of Ezekiel, for example, goes so deep that the author of Revelation has been called a "new Ezekiel."[64]

In addition, there are also at least a few highly interesting apocryphal texts working in comparable ways. Perhaps the best example is *5 Ezra*, an apocalypse probably dating from the turn of the second to the third century CE, which has been transmitted in some manuscripts of the Latin Vulgate as chapters 1–2 of *4 Ezra*. While the text, comparable to Revelation, does not contain any ex-

---

[63] For the discussion see: M.M. ZAHN, Genre and Rewritten Scripture: A Reassessment, *JBL* 131 (2012) 271–88, or EADEM, Talking about Rewritten Texts. Some Reflections on Terminology, in: *Changes in Scripture: Rewriting and Interpreting Authoritative Traditions in the Second Temple Period* (ed. by H. von Weissenberg, J. Pakkala & M. Marttila; BZAW 419; Berlin – New York: de Gruyter, 2011) 93–119.

[64] T. HIEKE, Der Seher Johannes als neuer Ezechiel: Die Offenbarung des Johannes vom Ezechielbuch her gelesen, in: *Das Ezechielbuch in der Johannesoffenbarung* (ed. by D. Sänger; BThSt 76; Neukirchen-Vluyn: Neukirchener, 2004) 1–30.

plicit quotations of Scripture, it is full of allusions to
mainly prophetic literature.[65] Interestingly, one of the
most important intertexts is the *Book of Baruch*, in today's Christian circles counted among the deuterocanonical resp. apocryphal writings of the Old Testament.

5 Ezra 2.2–5 is, for example, a close parallel to *Baruch*
4.8–23 – parallels are underlined:[66]

"The mother who bore them [= Israel; TN] *says to them: 'Go,
children, because I am a widow and forsaken. I brought you up
with gladness, I will send you away with mourning and sadness,
because you sinned before the Lord God* and did iniquity in his
presence. *But now*, what will I do for you? for *I am a widow and
forsaken* by my children. *Go children, seek mercy from the
Lord*, for *I am desolate*." (translation Bergren).

What does this mean for our overall question? *5 Ezra* can
be understood as a *relecture* of motifs, images and texts
we also find in the Scriptures of Israel; it claims to be a
very ancient prophecy, but at the same time has to deal
with "actual" matters. For *5 Ezra* the deuterocanonical /
apocryphal *1 Baruch* is especially interesting because this
book describes Israel in a desperate situation; while *Baruch*, however, ends with the promise of future hope for
Israel and (especially) Jerusalem, *5 Ezra* uses the material
to write a prophecy of Israel's ultimate rejection and the
election of a new people of God, that is, "the Christians".

5 Ezra, however, tells us even more: if bound to *4 Ezra*,
as is usually the case in the extant Latin manuscripts, the

---

[65] A full analysis of this text's intertextual network is currently
undertaken by my doctoral student Veronika STRÖHER.

[66] For more details see T. BERGREN, *Fifth Ezra: The Text, Origin
and Early History* (SBL.SCS 25; Atlanta: Scholars, 1990) 257–8.

text adds a new "Christian" perspective to *4 Ezra*'s ideas concerning the destruction of the Temple, the role of the Holy People and the end of times, or even better: it frames *4 Ezra*'s eschatological ideas with a "Christian" perspective.[67]

5 Ezra (together with *6 Ezra*) is, however, also an example of a "Christian" (non-typological) re-use of famous figures from the Scriptures of Israel. While some important Old Testament characters like David and Aaron seem to have not led to the creation of new writings, we know of even more apocalypses using the figure of Ezra (e.g. the Greek *Revelation of Ezra* and the Latin *Visio Esdrae*), several (very different) texts using and developing parts of Solomon's image (e.g., the *Odes of Solomon*[68] or the *Testament of Solomon*), (Christian) literature on *Adam and Eve* or even a (fabulous) *History of the Rechabites*, also called the *Vision of Zosimos*.

As we have already seen in chapter 2, the *Ascension of Isaiah*, an apocalypse going back to the first decades of the second century CE,[69] today is more or less universally acknowledged as a writing coming from a late-first or

---

[67] See also P. GEOLTRAIN, Remarques sur la diversité des pratiques discursives apocryphes: l' exemple de 5 Esdras, in : *Pierre Geoltrain : ou comment 'faire l'histoire' des Religions* (ed. by: S. C. Mimouni & I. Ullern Weité ; Bibliothèque de l'école des hautes études. Sciences Religieuses 128 ; Turnhout: Brepols, 2006) 35–44.

[68] Regarding the impact of the figure of Solomon and its reception history for the *Odes of Solomon* see T. NICKLAS, Salomo, Christus und die *Oden Salomos*, in: *The Figure of Solomon in Jewish, Christian and Islamic Tradition: King, Sage and Architect* (ed. by J. Verheyden; TBN 16; Leiden – Boston: Brill, 2012) 165–82.

[69] Regarding introductory issues see E. NORELLI, Ascension d'Isaïe, in: *Écrits apocryphes chrétiens* I (ed. by F. Bovon & P. Geol-

early second-century group of prophets who understood themselves as followers of Christ whom they characterized as God's "Beloved". The extant text offers not only a new Isaiah story using figures like king Hezekiah and his son Manasseh, the prophet Isaiah, Ahab, Michah ben Jimla, but also tells about the influence of satanic powers like Beliar and Sammael. Let us have a short look into at least one passage to get an impression of this writing – it starts in the following manner:

> "In the twenty-sixth year of his reign Hezekiah king of Judah summoned Manasseh his son, for he was his only son. He summoned him in the presence of Isaiah, the son of Amoz, the prophet, and in the presence of Josab the son of Isaiah, in order to hand over to him the words of righteousness which the king himself had seen, and (the words concerning) the eternal judgments, and the torments of Gehenna, and the prince of this world, and his angels, and his authorities, and his powers, and the words concerning faith in the Beloved which he himself had seen in the fifteenth year of his reign during his sickness. ..." (translation Knibb, OTP).

Already these few lines use lots of information we otherwise know from the Scriptures: such as the fact that Hezekiah's reign lasted twenty-nine years (see 2 Kings 18.2; 21.1), that his son Manasseh took over his reign, or that Isaiah's father had the name Amoz (Isa 1.1) whom *AscIsa* 4.22 identifies with the Biblical prophet Amos. Josab, in addition, is mentioned aleady in Isa 7.3, and the king's sickness is narrated in 2 Kgs 20; Isa 38 and 2 Chron 32.24. Within this passage, we also hear about "faith in

---

train; Éditions de la Pléiade; Paris: Gallimard, 1997) 501–45, esp. 501–7.

the Beloved" who at this very moment is still unknown and whom the readers will learn to identify with Jesus Christ.

In addition to this, the *Ascension of Isaiah*, at least in several places, explicitly relates itself to the Scriptures. This is, for example, the case in *AscIsa* 2.6 where we read "And the rest of the acts, behold, they are written in the book of the kings of Judah and Israel" – the books of 1–2 Kings and/or Chronicles are meant! In *AscIsa* 4.19 (related to Isa 13) we read: "And the rest of the words of the vision are written in the vision of Babylon." If one does not want to use the term "rewritten Scripture", one could call this a "narrative interpretation" of Scripture. Perhaps one could go even further – is the *Ascension of Isaiah* something like a narrative elaboration of an idea that we have already heard: the idea that the prophets had already enunciated Christ (*Philad.* 5.2; 9.2) and awaited him as a teacher (*Magn.* 9.2) as we have read in the writings of Ignatius of Antioch, an idea underlying many of the ancient Christian interpretations as we have heard now. But even if this is the case, the *Ascension of Isaiah* uses another approach to Scripture – it does not read it allegorically, but on the one hand retells and expands important passages about one prophet, Isaiah, and on the other, creates a new Isaianic vision about the future coming of Christ:

"And I heard the voice of the Most High, the Father of my Lord, as he said to my Lord Christ, who will be called Jesus. Go out and descend through all the heavens. You shall descend through the firmament and through that world as far as the angel who (is) in Sheol, but you shall not go as far as Perdition. And you shall make your likeness like that of all who (are) in the five heavens, and you shall take care to make your form like that of the angels of the firmament and also (like that) of the angels who (are) in Sheol. ..." (*AscIsa* 10.7–10; translation Knibb).

Even if the text sounds like a witness of early "Judaism" and even if its manner of using Scripture is very near to what we find in texts like *Jubilees, Joseph and Aseneth* and others, it marks some very clear boundaries to "Judaism" – in its story about Jesus' life and death it even recalls stereotypes we have already discussed in chapter 1:

"And I saw (that) in Nazareth he sucked the breast like an infant, as was customary, that he might not be recognized. And when he had grown up, he performed great signs and miracles in the land of Israel and (in) Jerusalem.

And after this the adversary envied him and roused the children of Israel who did not know who he was, against him. And they handed him to the ruler, and crucified him, and he descended to the angel who (is) in Sheol. In Jerusalem, indeed, I saw how they crucified him on a tree, and likewise (how) after the third day he rose and remained (many) days" (*AscIsa* 11.17–21; translation Knibb).

6. Conclusion

If one adds an additional point to an already existing system of thoughts it is possible that this point does not change the system at all. As we have seen, the Christ-event of Jesus' death and resurrection for many believers meant much more than just an idea added to an already existing system of beliefs, thoughts and ideas. Starting at least with Paul, the Christ-event became a focal point of thought for many believers which began to change perspectives on other parts of the system in some cases quite radically. As we have seen this has been particularly the case with "Christian" hermeneutics of Scripture: where the Scriptures of Israel should furthermore play a role within a system of belief now centred around an idea that God has raised the crucified Jesus from the dead and they must be related to this event. This could be done in different ways: in many cases already existing traditions of allegorical or typological exegesis helped in interpreting Israel's Scriptures differently. As early as Paul, many believers in Christ were interpreting the Scriptures in the light of the "Christ-event", that is, as prophecies making sense of Christ's death and resurrection, but also of important events of his life and the life of the Church. It did not take a very long time until authors like the author of the Fourth Gospel, Ignatius of Antioch, the author of the *Epistle of Barnabas* or Justin Martyr began to claim that their reading of Scriptures was the only adequate one.

This was, however, not the only possibility of dealing with the Scriptures of Israel – we know of many less radical voices reusing famous figures from the Scriptures and writing and rewriting new texts in ways which remind us of what we found in the examples of a "rewritten Bible" in Qumran. Others were even more radical: they changed their system of belief so radically that even the God of Israel was not understood as a positive factor in it any more. In the case of Marcion and his disciples, this allowed them to go on reading the Scriptures of Israel literally, and criticize them for their alleged inconsistencies and errors. In this case, they were no longer connected positively to the Christ event any more. Finally, the

Sethian Gnostics went so far as to re-write some key-texts of Israel's Scriptures in ways that were fitting to their system of belief in which the God of Israel only played the role of an evil (or at least imperfect, incompetent) demiurge.

Again, we see fragments of a highly diverse picture – at least some patterns can be recognized, but all of them have to do with the question of how far the Scriptures of Israel can be related to the Christ event. One important factor, however, is still lacking in our image: to what degree were aspects of "Jewish" interpretation of the Torah, *halakha*, abandoned in this new system, or to what degree did they move to the foreground in different "Christian" groups' struggles for identity. We will address this question in chapter 4.

Chapter 4:

Matters of *Halakha*

One important point is still missing in this essay concerning "Christian" readings of Israel's Scriptures. Chapter 3 was dominated by a perspective which wanted to relate Israel's Scriptures with matters of Christology (and which more or less excluded the use of Scripture for a better understanding of God's will pertaining to how one might live righteously). We have seen that (and how) this perspective with the related hermeneutics was also applied to the Torah, the "heart" of the TaNaK.[1] Of course, this does not mean that questions relating to how one might lead a proper life did not play any role for "Christians" any more. The same Gospel of Matthew where we found the explicit fulfilment quotations mentioned in chapter 3 also offers us the Sermon on the Mount (Matt 5–7) where Jesus is presented as a Moses-like authoritative teacher of the Torah[2] who presents a

---

[1] Regarding both terms see L.H. SCHIFFMAN, The Term and Concept of Torah, and T. ILAN, The Term and Concept of TaNaKh, both in: *What is Bible?* (ed. by K. Finsterbusch & A. Lange; Contributions to Biblical Theology & Exegesis 67; Leuven – Walpole, Mass.: Peeters, 2012) 173–91 and 219–34.

[2] R. DEINES, *Die Gerechtigkeit der Tora im Reich des Messias: Mt 5,13–20 als Schlüsseltext matthäischer Theologie* (WUNT 177; Tübingen: Mohr, 2004) has described the impact of Matt 5.13–20 as a key text for the Matthean hermeneutics of the Torah. For a recent

halakha which relates itself (critically) to contemporary Pharisaic *halakha*.[3] And in addition, at the end of the same Gospel of Matthew the risen Christ asks his disciples to teach the nations "to obey everything what I have *commanded* you" (Matt 28.20a). As far as I understand, this can mean nothing else than followers of Jesus, according to Matthew, should obey the Torah, but in the form of a special Jesus *halakha*.[4] This does not mean to neglect the many conflicts between followers of Jesus and Pharisees and Scribes mirrored in the Gospel of Matthew,[5] but even the infamous speech against Scribes and

---

treatment of the historical Jesus' *halakha* see Th. KAZEN, *Scripture, Interpretation of Authority? Motives and Arguments in Jesus' Halakhic Conflicts* (WUNT 320; Tübingen: Mohr, 2013).

[3] Of course, it is highly difficult to know exactly how Pharisaic *halakha* of Jesus' times looked like – we can just draw conclusions from the Sermon on the Mount itself and from later Rabbinic writings.

[4] For more information regarding the type of this *halakha* and its relation to other early Jewish ideas see H. VAN DE SANDT, Law and Ethics in Matthew's Antitheses and James's Letter: A Reorientation of Halakah in Line with Jewish Two Ways 3:1–6, in: *Matthew, James, and Didache: Three Related Documents in Their Jewish and Christian Settings* (SBL.SS 47; Atlanta: Scholars, 2008) 315–38, esp. 323–30.

[5] For a deeper discussion see, for example A.-J. LEVINE, Matthew's Portrayal of the Synagogue and its Leaders, in: *The Gospel of Matthew at the Crossroads of Early Christianity* (ed. by D. Senior; BETL 243; Leuven – Paris – Walpole, Mass.: Peeters, 2011) 177–93, and K. LÖNING, Die Auseinandersetzung mit dem Pharisäismus in den Weherufen bei Matthäus (Mt 23) und Lukas (Lk 11,37–53), in: *»Dies ist das Buch ...« Das Matthäusevangelium. Interpretation – Rezeption – Rezeptionsgeschichte. Für Hubert Frankemölle* (ed. by R. Kampling; Paderborn et al.: Schöningh, 2004) 217–34; regarding the (problematic) reception history of Matthew's depiction of Jew-

Pharisees in Matt 23 seems to hold fast to the idea of Pharisaic authority in teaching. After all, it starts with the words that everybody should *do* what Pharisees and Scribes are saying (Matt 23.3). In any case, it means that Matthean "Christianity" developed a kind of ethics which understood itself as trying to observe God's will as expressed in the Torah, in which not even a single letter may be changed (see Matt 5.17–19), and as it is interpreted by Jesus of Nazareth.[6]

The situation may have been quite different in Pauline communities: as we know, Paul and some of his fellows like Barnabas, Timothy and Titus started a new kind of "mission" – or better "preaching the Good news about Jesus" – directed mainly to "the nations", that is, "pagans"[7] all over the world. It is very probable that in many

---

ish leaders see U. Luz, Anti-Judaism in the Gospel of Matthew as a Historical and Theological Problem: An Outline, in his: *Studies in Matthew* (Grand Rapids – Cambridge, Eerdmans, 2005) 243–61.

[6] Of course, much more could be said about Matthean ethics. See for example U. Luz, The Fulfilment of the Law in Matthew (Matt 5:17–20), in his: *Studies in Matthew* (Grand Rapids – Cambridge, Eerdmans, 2005) 185–218; H.J. Bernard COMBRINK, The challenge of overflowing righteousness: to learn to live the story of the Gospel of Matthew, in: *Identity, Ethics, and Ethos in the New Testament* (ed. by J.G. Van der Watt; BZNW 141; Berlin – New York, de Gruyter, 2006) 23–48 [lit!] or D. MARGUERAT, Indicatif du salut et imperative éthique chez Matthieu: Une alternative? in: *Matthew at the Crossroads of Early Christianity* (ed. by D. Senior; BETL 234; Leuven – Paris – Walpole, Mass.: Peeters, 2011) 241–61.

[7] The use of the term "pagan" is an anachronism. For an interesting overview of the development of this term in late antiquity see P. BROWN, *Through the Eye of a Needle. Wealth, the Fall of Rome, and the Making of Christianity in the West, 350–550 AD* (Princeton, NJ: Princeton University Press, 2012) 102.

cases they focused on "God-Fearers", that is, pagans who believed in the God of Israel, attended services at the local synagogue and perhaps even observed some of the Laws of Israel, but did not formally convert to Judaism.[8] In other cases, however, it seems that Paul and his companions also convinced pagans without this background to become "followers of Christ". In today's perspectives, this may seem not to be a major step. In our terms "Christians" tried to convert pagans: the main point, however, was that Paul and his fellows did not expect the new pagan followers of Christ to be circumcised.[9] In this way, communities of *pagan* followers of the *Jewish* Messiah Jesus of Nazareth were founded whose members were not formally part of Israel. We do not have time and space here to reconstruct Paul's argument for this major move. As far as I understand, he understood the believers' relation to Christ as responsible for salvation – and not the *erga nomou* any more (see for example Gal 2.16). It has been debated for a long time what this term *erga nomou*, which is usually translated as "works of the Law", denotes. Does it mean the "works which are according to the Law" or does it denote "boundary markers" between Jewish and non-Jewish groups (like circumcision, dietary

---

[8] For more information on this group see B. WANDER, *Gottesfürchtige und Sympathisanten: Studien zum heidnischen Umfeld von Diasporasynagogen* (WUNT 104; Tübingen: Mohr, 1998).

[9] Regarding the impact of circumcision in different groups and contexts of early Judaism see S. C. MIMOUNI, *La circoncision dans le monde judéen aux époques grecques et romaine. Histoire d'un conflict interne aux judaïsme* (Collection de la Revue des Études Juives 42; Leuven: Peeters, 2007).

laws etc.)?[10] Does it describe concrete commandments of the Torah, but not human acts of fulfilment[11] or do we have to understand them as cultic acts in distinction of ethical deeds?[12]

In any case, Paul's focus on the believers' appropriate relation to Christ, their being "in Christ", believing "in Christ", being baptised "into Christ", being part of the "body of Christ" etc. does not mean that the Torah did not play any positive role in his idea of the history of salvation any more. One could perhaps use the metaphor of

---

[10] Regarding the idea of "boundary markers" which at least in Gal 2.16 seems quite plausible see J. D. G. DUNN, *The New Perspective on Paul* (WUNT 185; Tübingen: Mohr 2005).

[11] See mainly M. BACHMANN, Rechtfertigung und Gesetzeswerke bei Paulus, in his: *Antijudaismus im Galaterbrief?* (NTOA 40; Freiburg, CH – Göttingen: Vandenhoeck & Ruprecht, 1999) 1–32; IDEM, Keil oder Mikroskop? Zur jüngeren Diskussion um die ‚Werke des Gesetzes', in: *Lutherische und neue Paulusperspektive* (ed. by M. Bachmann; WUNT 182; Tübingen: Mohr, 2005) 69–134; IDEM, Zur Rezeptions- und Traditionsgeschichte des paulinischen Ausdrucks ἔργα νόμου: Notizen im Blick auf Verhaltensregeln im Christentum als einer ‚Gruppenreligion', in: *Gruppenreligionen im römischen Reich. Sozialformen, Grenzziehungen und Leistungen* (ed. by J. Rüpke; STAC 43; Tübingen: Mohr, 2007) 69–86, and, finally, IDEM, Bemerkungen zur Auslegungen zweier Genetivverbindungen des Galaterbriefs: ‚Werke des Gesetzes' (Gal 2,16 u. ö.) und ‚Israel Gottes' (Gal 6,16), in: *Umstrittener Galaterbrief: Studien zur Situierung der Theologie des Paulus-Schreibens* (ed. by M. Bachmann & B. Kollmann; BThSt 106; Neukirchen-Vluyn: Neukirchener, 2010) 95–118.

[12] See K. HAACKER, Verdienste und Grenzen der 'neuen Perspektive' der Paulus-Auslegung, in: *Lutherische und neue Paulusperspektive* (ed. by M. Bachmann; WUNT 182; Tübingen: Mohr, 2005) 1–16, esp. 13–4.

"diagnosis" and "therapy"[13] – in Paul's thought, the Torah functioned as a diagnosis showing humanity's sinful
and destructive relation to God leading into death, while
the relation to the crucified and risen Christ was seen as
the "therapy" leading to salvation. In addition, I would
add that nowhere in his extant writings does Paul declare
the Law *per se* as obsolete. To the contrary, there are at
least a few passages like Gal 5.14 and Rom 13.8–10 where
he understands fulfilment of the love command of Lev
19.18 as fulfilment of the Torah.[14] He writes:

[8] Let no debt remain outstanding, except the continuing debt to
love one another, for whoever loves others has fulfilled the law.
9 The commandments, "You shall not commit adultery," "You
shall not murder," "You shall not steal," "You shall not covet,"
and whatever other command there may be, are summed up in
this one command: "Love your neighbour as yourself." [10] Love

---

[13] I have expressed these ideas in the article T. NICKLAS, Die ver-
borgene Herrlichkeit des Paulusdienstes: Überlegungen zu 2Kor
3,1–4,6, in: *Der zweite Korintherbrief. Literarische Gestalt – historische Situation – theologische Argumentation. Festschrift zum
70. Geburtstag von Dietrich-Alex Koch* (ed. by D. Sänger; FR-
LANT 250; Göttingen: Vandenhoeck & Ruprecht, 2012) 240–56,
with a reference to the ideas of N. BAUMERT, *Mit dem Rücken zur
Wand: Übersetzung und Auslegung des 2. Korintherbriefes* (Paulus
neu gelesen; Würzburg: Echter, 2008). – For a much more differentiated view on Paul's relation to the Torah see the relevant articles in
F. AVEMARIE, *Neues Testament und frührabbinisches Judentum.
Gesammelte Aufsätze* (ed. by. J. Frey & A. Standhartinger; WUNT
316; Tübingen: Mohr, 2013) 493–699.

[14] Interestingly, the love command plays an important role for
many early "Christian" groups – for more information see M. KON-
RADT, The Love Command in Matthew, James, and the Didache, in:
*Matthew, James, and Didache. Three Related Documents in Their
Jewish and Christian Settings* (ed. by H. van de Sandt & J. Zangen-
berg; SBL.SS 45; Atlanta: Scholars, 2008) 271–88.

does no harm to a neighbour. Therefore love is the fulfilment of the law. (Rom 13.8–10).

This is, of course, a very rudimentary *halakha* developed for pagan converts to the new movement, but in a certain sense this is still an ethical criterion developed by means of Torah-interpretation.[15]

I mention this as an introduction because we will discover (at least) two main lines of early "Christian" attitudes towards the Torah – one of them more or less developed along the lines we found in the Gospel of Matthew, and the other moving a decisive step forward from what we read in Paul. Again, a look into the writings of Ignatius of Antioch makes sense. We have already learned that in Ignatius' "Christian way of life" the Torah as God's order for a proper life did not play a major role any more. At least in his extant letters Ignatius never justifies an ethical commandment with the fact that it is found in or developed from the Torah. Comparable to Paul, Ignatius shows a strong focus on the relation "love" and "belief /

---

[15] One could, however, argue that Paul in other instances developed a real *halakha* for pagan converts to the "Christian" movement. The best examples can perhaps be found in his 1 Corinthians. For a deeper discussion of the matter see P. J. TOMSON, *Paul and the Jewish Law: Halakha in the Letters of the Apostle to the Gentiles* (CRINT III/1; Assen – Maastricht – Minneapolis: Van Gorcum – Fortress, 1990); for overviews of the whole of New Testament writings see F. AVEMARIE, *Tora und Leben: Untersuchungen zur Heilsbedeutung der Tora in der frühen rabbinischen Literatur* (TSAJ 55; Tübingen: Mohr, 1996) 584–96 and the articles in B.S. JACKSON (ed.), *Essays on Halakhah in the New Testament* (Jewish and Christian Perspectives 16; Leiden – Boston: Brill, 2008).

faith", but he never describes mutual love as fulfilment of the Torah. Instead, we find sentences like the following:

"None of these things escapes your notice, if you have perfect faith and love toward Jesus Christ. For these are the beginning and the end of life: faith is the beginning and love is the end, and the two, when they exist in unity, are God. Everything else that contributes to excellence follows from them. No one professing faith sins, nor does anyone possessing love hate" (*Eph.* 14.1–2a; translation Holmes).

In another passage, Ignatius says that believers in Christ should accept an attitude which relates them to God and "respect one another, and let no one regard his neighbour in merely human terms, but in Jesus Christ love one another always" (*Magn.* 6.2; translation adapted from Holmes). This is not far from the love command we find in Lev 19.18, the reason of believers' mutual love, however, for Ignatius is their common "being in Jesus Christ", not the fulfilment of the Torah any more.

Ignatius is surely an extreme case, and, of course, his letters with their emphasis on living "Christian" instead of "Jewish" should not be understood as dogmatic treatises. Above all, however, we know of many ancient Christian writers who argued differently.

1. Christ as the Law:
the Shepherd of Hermas

As we have seen, the relation of belief in Christ and following the Law has been, starting with Paul's times, a crucial problem for the earliest communities of Christ believers. The relation of "Christ" and the "Law" indeed bothered later authors as well:

One of the strangest ancient Christian writings is the so-called *Pastor Hermae* or *Shepherd of Hermas*, an apocalypse written in Rome probably in the middle of the second century CE.[16] At least in some circles, this text was surprisingly popular and at least in parts of the Roman Empire – e. g., in Egypt – it achieved a quasi-canonical status. The third main part of the text presents a series of visions which contain allegorical elements and that's why they are called "Parables".

In *Parable* 8 Hermas sees a big willow tree under which all members of the people are sitting, "who are called by the name of the Lord" (*Par.* 8.1.1). A magnificent angel of the Lord cuts off sticks from the tree and gives them to the people; at the same time the tree remains whole. After a while the angels asks everybody to give back their sticks which are now looking very differently: some of them withered, some of them at least partly green, others green, and, finally, some of them with buds or even fruit. After

---

[16] Actually, it is very difficult to establish the text's exact date – an author like H. KOESTER, *Einführung in das Neue Testament im Rahmen der Religionsgeschichte und Kulturgeschichte der hellenistischen und römischen Zeit* (Berlin – New York: de Gruyter, 1980) 694 argues that any time between 60 and 160 CE would be possible. For a more detailed discussion see now A. GREGORY, Disturbing Trajectories: 1 Clement, the Shepherd of Hermas and the Development of Early Roman Christianity, in: *Rome in the Bible and the Early Church* (ed. by P. Oakes; Carlisle: Paternoster, 2002) 142–66, esp. 151–3. – Regarding overall introductory issues see D. HELLHOLM, Der Hirt des Hermas, in: *Die Apostolischen Väter: Eine Einleitung* (ed. by W. Pratscher; UTB; Göttingen: Vandenhoeck & Ruprecht, 2009) 226–53.

that, everybody who brought a stick bearing fruit receives a crown of palm leaves and is, together with the ones whose branches were at least green, allowed to enter a big tower which for Hermas symbolized the Church as the community of the believers made pure by expiation.[17] Meanwhile the withered and partly-green branches are planted into the earth to see which of them at least have the chance to come back to life (*Par.* 8.8.2).

After this, Hermas wants to know the meaning of the tree – and receives the following answer:

"This great tree, which overshadows plains and mountains and all the earth, is the law of God, which is given to the whole world, and this law is the Son of God, who has been proclaimed to the ends of the earth. And the people who are under the shadow are those who have heard the preaching and believed in him. And the great and glorious angel is Michael, who has authority over this people and guides them, for he is the one who puts the law into the hearts of those who believe. He, therefore, examines those whom he gave it, to see if they have kept it. Now observe the sticks of each one, for the sticks are the law. When you see that many sticks have been made useless, you still know that they are all those who have not kept the law, and you will see each one's dwelling. ... All those ... who transgressed the law that they received from him he left under my authority for repentance; but all those who have already satisfied the law and kept it he retains under his own authority. ... Those who are crowned are the ones who wrestled with the devil and conquered him. These are the ones who have suffered for the law. And all the others who also returned their sticks green and with buds, though not with fruit, are those who were persecuted for the law, but did not suffer, nor did they deny the law. Those who

---

[17] For a closer discussion see N. BROX, *Der Hirt des Hermas* (KAV 7; Göttingen: Vandenhoeck & Ruprecht, 1991) 118–20, and D. HELLHOLM, Hermas, 238–9.

returned them green, just as they received them, are reverent and righteous people who have walked with an extraordinary clean heart and have kept the Lord's commandments. But the rest you will learn when these sticks have been planted and watered" (*Par.* 8.8.3; translation Holmes).

Of course, the *Shepherd of Hermas* with its focus on the question of a second expiation after baptism (see *Mand.* 4.1.8 *Vis.* 2.2.4–5 et al.);[18] is highly interested in questions of correct ethical behaviour; he connects ideas of sin and purification, and even speaks about the "Law" here several times (see, for example, *Sim.* 5.6.3). His "law", which is brought and fulfilled by Christ in exemplary manner, however, is not connected to Israel, but given to the "whole world", and even identified with Christ.[19] While it is never absolutely made clear whether and how "the law of God given to the whole world" relates to the Torah of Israel (one gets the impression that there is no relation between both of them[20]), the role of the "law" in the life of the believer is nonetheless interesting. According to *Hermas*, it is not "doing of the law" *per se* that brings salvation, but belief followed by purification through

---

[18] For a short overview on relevant passages see D. HELLHOLM, Hermas, 236–7.

[19] For a detailed discussion of the secondary literature on the topic see M. GRUNDEKEN, *Community Building in the Shepherd of Hermas. A Critical Study of Some Key Aspects* (unpublished diss. Leuven 2013) 73–5.

[20] M. GRUNDEKEN, *Community*, 76 writes: "Hermas does not contend with or reject the Jewish law, but his silence on circumcision (and similarly on Jewish dietary laws, Sabbath observance and other aspects of the Jewish law), is probably more than just a matter of coincidence. All these issues seem to be out of question."

baptism (*Vis.* 3.7.3 and *Sim.* 9.16).[21] Doing the "law",
however, is necessary to remain in an adequate relationship with God. In a striking manner this resembles what
an author like E.P. Sanders wrote in regard to the relationship of Covenant to Torah in what he calls Second
Temple "Common Judaism".[22] In this case, the relation
established between God and Israel through the Covenant is decisive for salvation; doing the Torah, however, is
necessary to *remain* in this relation. Even though *Hermas*
is obviously not interested in discussing details of
halakha, the text defends a combination of a salvific "relation between God and believer" and doing "God's will"
which is closely comparable to what we find at least in
many Jewish groups of late Second Temple times (and
surely afterwards as well).

Hermas is only one example of a second-century text
connecting or even identifying "Christ" and "Law" –
others like the fragmentary *Kerygma of Peter*, passages in

---

[21] See U. KÜHNEWEG, Christus als Gesetzgeber und Gesetz in
den Schriften der sog. Apostolischen Väter II: Der Hirt des Hermas, in his: *Das Neue Gesetz. Christus als Gesetzgeber und Gesetz*
(MThSt 36; Marburg: Elwert, 1993), 53–75, esp. 65: "Die Taufe ist
das Fundament der Kirche und geht dem Gesetz voran. ... Das
Halten der Gebote erwirbt ihm [d. h. dem Getauften; TN] nicht das
Heil, sondern sichert es nur." – See also D. HELLHOLM, Hermas,
240–1.
[22] See his well-known E.P. SANDERS, *Paul and Palestinian Judaism* (London: SCM, 1977), and his *Paul, the Law and the Jewish
People* (London, SCM, § 1985). – Sanders' ideas have, of course,
been debated controversially. For a good overview of critical voices
see the two volumes by D.A. CARSON – P.T. O'BRIEN & M. SEI-
FRIED (ed.s), *Justification and Variegated Nomism* (WUNT 140
and 181; Tübingen: Mohr, 2001 and 2004).

Clement of Alexandria's writings or pseudo-Hippolytus' *Peri Pascha* could be discussed as well.[23] For our purposes, it is, however, more interesting to have a look into some texts for which at least aspects of *halakha* still mattered or seemed to matter.

2. The Doctrine of the "Two Ways": the *Epistle of Barnabas* and the *Didache*

2.1 The Epistle of Barnabas

While we have seen that for the foundation of Ignatius of Antioch's ethics the Torah did not play an explicit role any more,[24] this simply cannot be said about other authors of the so-called *Apostolic Fathers*.

We have already seen that the *Epistle of Barnabas* with its attempt to create a "Christian" identity against "Judaism" is an indirect witness that there must have been an opposing group of believers in Christ for whom matters of Torah-observance seemed to have played an important role – a role which the author and his group did not want to accept. An interesting passage is chapter 10 where *Barn.* gives his interpretation of the Mosaic Food Laws:

---

[23] For a discussion of the motif in these writers see M. CAMBE, *Kerygma Petri: Textus et Commentarius* (CC. Series Apocryphorum 15; Turnhout: Brepols, 2003) 283–313; for even more examples and details see U. KÜHNEWEG, *Das Neue Gesetz: Christus als Gesetzgeber und Gesetz* (MThSt 36; Marburg: Elwert, 1993).

[24] The same is the case for a text like *Ad Diognetum* mentioned in chapter 2.

"Now when Moses said, 'You shall not eat a pig, or an eagle or a hawk or a crow, or any fish that has no scales,' he received, according to the correct understanding three precepts. Furthermore, he says to them in Deuteronomy, 'I will set forth as a covenant to this people my righteous requirements.' Therefore it is not God's commandment that they should not eat; rather Moses spoke spiritually. Accordingly he mentioned the pig for this reason: you must not associate, he means, with such people, who are like pigs. That is, when they are well off, they forget the Lord, but when they are in need, they acknowledge the Lord, just as the pig ignores its owner when it is feeding, but when it is hungry it starts to squeal and falls silent only after being fed again" (*Barn.* 10.1–3; translation Holmes).

The logic of *Barn.*'s argument is simple: he starts with a combination of different dietary laws from Lev 11 and Deut 14 put in the form of a quote and connects them to an independent quotation from Deut 4.1,5. According to *Barn.*, the key to understanding God's commandments is understanding how they have to do with righteousness. With this hermeneutical key, dietary laws may not be understood literally, but spiritually – believers should not associate with people who are like pigs, that is, according to *Barn.*, people who are not really faithful in the "Lord."

While it is not clear from this argument to what degree questions of dietary laws played a role for *Barn.*'s opponents, at least in a few instances the text is clear. Very similar to the famous Pauline triads, *Barn.* stresses the combination of "faith", "love" and "hope" (see *Barn.* 1.4,6) and understands "love" as a "testimony of works of righteousness" (ἔργα δικαιοσύνης instead of the Pauline ἔργα νόμου!) which are later contrasted with "works of lawlessness" (ἔργα ἀνομίας; *Barn.* 4.1). In another passage, he speaks about "the new law of our Lord Jesus Christ" (*Barn.* 2.6) which he characterizes as being "free of a yoke of compulsion", an interesting implicit contrast to the Law of Israel!

As we have seen, the author of *Barn.* does not write much about the opposing group of Christ-believers. However, the following hints are important:

While *Barn.* 4.6 quite clearly opposes groups of Christ-followers who regard God's covenant with Israel as "remaining valid" (and that's why they obviously have to follow the Torah), *Barn.* 3.6 states:

"So for this reason, brothers and sisters, the one who is very patient, when he foresaw how the people whom he had prepared in his beloved would believe in all purity, revealed everything to us in advance, in order that we might not shipwreck ourselves as proselytes to their law" (translation Holmes).

Even if the Greek word used here for "proselytes" is not transmitted unambiguously, it is clear the people believing "in all purity" are by no means Israel, but the "Christians", to whom everything has been revealed through Scriptures. In other words: (pagan) followers of Christ should not become proselytes following the Torah. As we should not regard *Barn.*'s polemics too one-dimensionally as a mirror of the ideas of the people the text opposes, we should avoid any reconstruction of a *halakha* of *Barn.*'s opponents – it seems, however, as if at least questions of Sabbath observance, fasting, dietary laws and perhaps even circumcision played a role for them.

On the other hand, it would be wrong to conclude from *Barn.* 10.1–3, that *Barn.* did not allow literal under-

standings of any commandment coming from the Torah:
like all other groups of Christ-followers, *Barn.*'s community needed at least a pattern of ethical doctrines which
allowed them to survive as a group with a distinct identity. The main aspects of this ethical teaching can be found
in *Barn.* 18–20, a so-called "doctrine of the two ways"
comparing a "way of light" to a "way of darkness" (*Barn.*
18.1).

If we look into the ethical commands that make up the
"way of light" we find astonishingly few which could be
characterized as distinctively "Christian" (in opposition
to "Jewish"). Let me quote a few lines:

"2 You shall love the one who made you; you shall fear the one
who created you; you shall glorify the one who redeemed you
from death. You shall be sincere in heart and rich in spirit. You
shall not associate with those who walk along the way of death;
you shall hate everything that is not pleasing to God; you shall
hate all hypocrisy; you must not forsake the Lord's commandments. 3 You shall not exalt yourself, but shall be humble-mind-
ed in every respect. You shall not claim glory for yourself. You
shall not hatch evil plots against your neighbour. You shall not
permit your soul to become arrogant. 4 You shall not be sexual-
ly promiscuous; you shall not commit adultery; you shall not
corrupt children. ... 5 You shall not take the Lord's name in
vain. You shall love your neighbour more than your own life.
You shall not abort a child, nor, again, commit infanticide"
(*Barn.* 19.2–5; translation Holmes).

What we find here is a combination of different ethical
commands that we also have in the Mosaic books (similar
in form to early Jewish interpretations of them).[25] The

---

[25] For more details see F.R. PROSTMEIER, *Der Barnabasbrief*
(KAV 8; Vandenhoeck & Ruprecht: Göttingen, 1999) 536–43.

tripartite command to love, fear and praise God finds its counterpart in Deut 6.5 (see also Sir 7.30–31), the main difference being that for *Barn.* Jesus and God are understood as very closely connected – the same problem arises when we read about "the Lord's commandments". While nothing in the additional commands of *Barn.* 19.2 are distinctively "Christian" or "Jewish", they do have parallels to Lev 18.30; 22.3 and Deut 4.2. Also, 19.3 is reminiscent of Prov 29.23 and Ps 27/28.3; 19.4 quotes Exod 20.13 par. Deut 5.17; while parts of verse 5 can be interpreted as an interpretation of Lev 19.18. From all of this, the most distinctively "Christian" command is the prohibition of abortion and infanticide.[26] One could go on in this way. The following points are remarkable: while *Barn.* several times sharply condemns a literal understanding of the Torah, in the "Two-Ways-Teaching" he offers a collection of ethical commands coming directly from the Torah, but never marks them as quotations from the Torah. Parallels in other writings like the so-called *Didache*, a text we will look at later, make it clear that *Barn.* used (and probably slightly reworked) an older source here. As far as we can reconstruct this oldest "Two-Ways"-source, this text must have come very close to what we find in parts of 1QS, the "Manual of Discipline" from the Qumran

---

[26] There is a discussion about ancient "Jewish" stances regarding both abortion and infanticide. See D. R. SCHWARTZ, Did the Jews practice infant exposure and infanticide in Antiquity? *Studia Philonica Annual* 16 (2004) 61–95. – Interestingly, the *Apocalypse of Peter*, perhaps coming from Alexandria at about the same time as *Barnabas* shows comparable attitudes. See P. GRAY, Abortion, infanticide, and the social rhetoric of the *Apocalypse of Peter*, *JECS* 9 (2001) 313–37.

movement.[27] The background of ancient "Christian" "Two-Ways-Doctrines" thus leads us very close to the "Jewish" origins of the Jesus-movement.

In his attempt to create a form of "Christianity" as sharply distinguished from Israel and its history, *Barn.* thus uses two principles of taking over Israel's Scriptures: as we have already seen, parts (like laws concerning food and Sabbath observance) are interpreted "spiritually" now, while others are simply taken over (and in sections show a practice very near to what we find in early "Jewish" circles), but from the perspective of the author of *Barn.*, they are interpreted as distinctively "Christian". As far as I see, the text never develops a criterion in which case which principle has to be applied.

2.2 *The Didache*

Another early example of a "Two-Ways-Doctrine" can be found in the so-called *Didache*. *Did.* 1–6 and *Barn.* 18–20 exhibit so many parallels to each other that for many years now, scholars have suspected various forms of literary dependency between the texts.[28] The situation behind the *Didache* appears to be very different from what we find in *Barn.* While *Barn.*'s stress on "faith, love

---

[27] For a detailed discussion see J.-P. AUDET, Literary and Doctrinal Relationships of the 'Manual of Discipline', in: *The Didache in Modern Research* (ed. by J.A. Draper; AGJU 37; Leiden et al. Brill, 1996) 129–47.

[28] See, for example, the discussion of the history of research given by J. DRAPER, The Didache, in: *The Writings of the Apostolic Fathers* (ed. by P. Foster; London – New York: Continuum, 2007) 13–20, esp. 14–7.

and hope" on the one hand can be seen as continuation of (one) Pauline line of thought and its "two-ways doctrine" offers an ethics very closely related to what one could call an early Jewish *halakha*, the so-called *Didache* is a text closely related to the Gospel of Matthew.[29] During the last twenty years the *Didache* has developed into one of the most disputed writings of early Christianity:[30] while many scholars regard it as a text dependent on at least some Gospel writings and thus having its origins in the first decades of the second century CE, others have argued for its independence and proposed a very early date.[31] The answer to this question is, again, closely relat-

---

[29] For a very detailed discussion see for example C. M. TUCKETT, The *Didache* and the Writings that later formed the New Testament, in: *The Reception of the New Testament in the Apostolic Fathers* (ed. by A. Gregory & C. M. Tuckett; The New Testament and the Apostolic Fathers; Oxford et al.: Oxford University Press, 2005) 83–127, esp. 95–127 who writes (127): "Certainly, he or she [= the author of the *Didache*; TN] did not have Matthew's gospel open in front of him or her as he or she wrote. Any 'dependence' here is likely to be somewhat indirect, perhaps mediated through a process of oral tradition and/or memory." – In addition, H. VAN DE SANDT (ed.), *Matthew and the Didache. Two Documents from the Same Jewish-Christian Milieu?* (Assen – Minneapolis: Van Gorcum – Fortress, 2005) offers a collection of essays dealing with aspects of this question.

[30] For an already somewhat older overview see J. A. DRAPER, The *Didache* in Modern Research: An Overview, in: *The Didache in Modern Research* (ed. by J. A. Draper; AGJU 37; Leiden et al: Brill, 1996) 1–42.

[31] For the first position see for example the commentary by K. NIEDERWIMMER, *Die Didache* (KAV 1; Göttingen: Vandenhoeck & Ruprecht, § 1993), for the second see A. MILAVEC, *The Didache: Faith, Hope, and Life of the Earliest Christian Communities, 50–70 C. E.* (New York – Mahwah, N. J.: Newman, 2003).

ed to another problem, that is, the question in how far the extant text of the *Didache* can be seen as a literary unity or was developed in several stages. The answer lies probably somewhere in between – the *Didache* seems to use some very old sources, but has been reworked several times according to the community's changing situation. In any case, we are dealing with a very old manual of discipline[32] from a community of "Jewish" Christ believers which, according to its superscription, can be understood as a kind of instruction for "pagan" converts. If one wants to be a bit speculative – if the Gospel of Matthew closes with the risen Jesus' command to the Apostles to teach (διδάσκω) the nations what he has commanded, then the *Didache*, that is in full, *The Lord's Teaching to the Nations by the Twelve Apostles*, can be read as an extension to this command.[33] The text's many parallels to material from Matthew – especially the Sermon on the Mount (or

---

[32] In fact, the description of the genre of the *Didache* is quite complicated because of the text's different stages of development. For a broader discussion see the recent monograph of N. PARDEE, *The Genre and Development of the* Didache: *A Text-Linguistic Analysis* (WUNT II.339; Tübingen: Mohr, 2012) 5–63.

[33] Regarding the discussion of the relation between Matthew and the *Didache* see recently H. VAN DE SANDT, Matthew and the Didache, in: *Matthew and his Christian Contemporaries* (ed. by D.C. Sim & B. Repschinski; LNTS; London – New York: T & T Clark, 2008) 123–38, and J. VERHEYDEN, Jewish Christianity, a state of affairs: affinities and differences with respect to Matthew, James, and the Didache, in: *Matthew, James, and the Didache: Three related documents in their Jewish and Christian Settings* (ed. by H. van de Sandt & J. Zangenberg; SBL.SS 45; Atlanta: Scholars, 2008) 128–35.

at least Matthew's source) – make this an even more meaningful reading.

In its first six chapters the text offers a doctrine of the "two ways" giving ethical commands for the believer to choose the way of life (instead of the way of death; *Did.* 1.1). While the material in the *Didache* from chapter 7 and beyond is primarily concerned with questions of ritual and church order (plus questions related to the end of time), chapters 1–6 (which have sometimes been read as a kind of a book all to its own) show almost no traces of typical "Christian" beliefs or ideas. This means it is possible that they could, with very few exceptions, be understood as a purely "Jewish" source for ethical instruction. The degree to which *halakha* was important for the *Didache*-community has been discussed several times. I will offer only a few examples coming from both the first and the second parts of the *Didache*:

(1) Compared to *Barn.* 18–20, the "Two-Ways Manual" of the *Didache* shows an even closer focus on the Decalogue.[34] While *Did.* 1.2, "the head of the document,"[35] gives a prominent place to a combination of the com-

---

[34] On the wider question of the impact of the Decalogue for early Christianity see H. Löhr, Der Dekalog im frühesten Christentum und seiner jüdischen Umwelt, in: *Judentum und Christentum zwischen Konfrontation und Faszination. Ansätze zu einer neuen Beschreibung der jüdisch-christlichen Beziehungen* (Judentum und Christentum 11; Stuttgart: Kohlhammer, 2002) 29–43, esp. 37–8.

[35] J. Kloppenborg, *Didache* 1.1–6.1, James, Matthew and the Torah, in: *Trajectories through the New Testament and the Apostolic Fathers* (ed. by A. Gregory & C. M. Tuckett; The New Testament and the Apostolic Fathers; Oxford et al.: Oxford University Press, 2005) 193–221, esp. 207.

mands to love God and your neighbour (Deut 6.5 and
Lev 19.18) and adds the well-known "Golden Rule", *Did.*
2.2 could be called a "decalogue adapted for Gentiles".[36]
Using a syntax resembling closely to what we find in the
LXX versions of the decalogue,[37] it consists of ten commandments four of which correspond to the decalogue.
A comparison to the Exodus version of the decalogue
shows the following – I quote the overview of A. Milavec:[38]

"A1 = seventh commandment (Ex 20:13)
A2 = sixth commandment (Ex 20:14)
A3 = unlisted (pederasty)
A4 = unlisted (illicit sex)
A5 = eighth commandment (Ex 20:15)
A6 = unlisted (magic)
A7 = unlisted (sorcery)
A8 = unlisted (abortion)
A9 = unlisted (infanticide)
A10 = tenth commandment (Ex 20:17)."

In addition, *Did.* 1.2 (plus 3.4 and 6.3) is closely related to
commandment 1, while *Did.* 2.3 resembles the third and
ninth commandments (swearing and false witness).
Commandments 2 (about the use of images), 4 (regarding
the Sabbath rest) and 5 (honouring the parents), may perhaps have been omitted because of the situation of the
text's intended audience. A. Milavec writes:[39]

---

[36] A. MILAVEC, *Didache*, 117.
[37] For details see J. KLOPPENBORG, *Didache*, 208.
[38] A. MILAVEC, *Didache*, 118.
[39] A. MILAVEC, *Didache*, 124 & 128.

"The second commandment prohibits making or using a 'graven image' (Exod 20:4). For a gentile whose public buildings, private homes, and even the money used in the marketplace were routinely decorated with such images, it would have been entirely unworkable to imagine that all of this could somehow be discarded, effaced, or replaced. For gentiles, the second commandment would have been nearly impossible to maintain unless they entirely abandoned their homes and cities. ...

For gentiles, the Sabbath rest (Ex 20:8f.) would have imposed an unworkable expectation, since the Roman lunar calendar governing public life made absolutely no provisions for a cessation of work every seventh day. ...

The fifth commandment requires children to honor their parents. Gentiles could hardly be trained to honor their parents (Ex 20:12) when that 'filial piety' so highly prized by Romans would have made the desertion of ancestral gods and the abandonment of their parental upbringing unthinkable save in those instances where a whole patriarchal household converted to the Lord as a group."

The omission of commandments 2, 4 and 5, thus, not only makes very good sense in the situation of the *Didache* community, but *Did.* 2.2–3 can also be understood as a kind of introductory *halakha* for Gentiles becoming part of the *Didache* community.

(2) Other parts of *Did.* 1–6 can be discussed in the context of early Jewish *halakha* as well: Kurt Niederwimmer, for example, understands the early rabbinic school as a *Sitz im Leben* of the five admonitions of *Did.* 3.1–6 and relates the texts to Jewish sapiential traditions,[40] while already in the year 1958 Gedaliah Alon discussed dozens of parallels between commands of the *Didache* about abortion (*Did.* 2.2), astrology and sorcery (*Did.*

---

[40] K. Niederwimmer, *Didache*, 126–7.

3.4) or the treatment of slaves (*Did.* 4.10) and Rabbinic literature.[41]

But even in the later parts of the *Didache* many elements can be found which show a close relation to what we find in more or less contemporary Jewish discussions of *halakhic* matters.[42] I would like to concentrate on the discussion of the use of water for baptism we find in *Did.* 7.1–3. The text states:

"Now concerning baptism, baptize as follows: after you have received all these things, baptize in the name of the Father and the Son and of the Holy Spirit in running water. But if you have no running water, then baptize in some other water; and if you are not able to baptize in cold water, then do so in warm. But if you have neither, then pour water on the head three times in the name of Father and Son and Holy Spirit" (translation Holmes).

The above passage is interesting because its focus on baptism "in the name of the Father and the Son and of the Holy Spirit" is clearly "Christian," while its discussion about the use of appropriate water shows how "Jewish"

---

[41] G. ALON, The Halacha in the Teaching of the Twelve Apostles [1958], in: *The Didache in Modern Research* (ed. by J.A. Draper; AGJU 27; Leiden et al.: Brill, 1996) 165–94, esp. 172–6.

[42] I can only discuss one small example. For more evidence see, for example, P.J. TOMSON, The Halakhic Evidence of Didache 8 and Matthew 6 and the Didache' Community's Relationship to Judaism, in: *Matthew and the Didache: Two Documents from the Same Jewish Milieu?* (ed. by H. van de Sandt; Assen – Minneapolis: Van Gorcum – Fortress, 2005) 131–41; M. DEL VERME, *Didache and Judaism: Jewish Roots of an Ancient Christian-Jewish Work* (London – New York: T & T Clark, 2004) 189–220, or H. VAN DE SANDT – D. FLUSSER, *The Didache: Its Jewish Sources and its Place in Early Judaism and Christianity* (CRINT III/5; Assen – Minneapolis: Van Gorcum – Fortress, 2002) 271–329.

the whole argument in fact is.[43] The text first shows that the primary concern of water baptism of pagan converts was to purify them from their uncleanness.[44] This is why the kind of water which serves best for this purpose is so important. Already in the Mosaic writings "living water" (i. e., water flowing from a fountain, a creek or a river) was held in high esteem as texts like Lev 14.5, 50–52 (about purification after leprosy) and Numb 19.17 (about purification after contact with a dead body) show. David Flusser and Huub van de Sandt suppose that the extant text of *Did.* 7.1–3 is already a relaxation of an originally stricter practice which expected the use of "living water" exclusively.[45] They even find a parallel to *Did.* 7 for this kind of concession in in Rabbinic literature. m.Mikw 1.1–8, for example, reads:

"There are six grades among pools of water, one more excellent than another. The water in ponds ... More excellent is the water

---

[43] The following material is taken from H. Van de Sandt – D. Flusser, *Didache*, 281–3.

[44] One should, however, be not too quick to connect *Did.* 7.1–3 with the "Jewish" practice of baptizing proselytes to Judaism in water. For a critical discussion of the relevant rabbinic sources see G. Rouwhorst, A Remarkable Case of Religious Interaction: Water Baptisms in Judaism and Christianity, in: *Interaction between Judaism and Christianity in History, Religion, Art and Literature* (ed. by M. Poorthuis, J. Schwartz & J. Turner; Jewish and Christian Perspectives 17; Leiden – Boston: Brill, 2009) 103–26, esp. 108–12.

[45] H. Van de Sandt – D. Flusser, *Didache*, 281–2: "At an earlier stage, it just might have been the 'living water' ... exclusively which was called for as necessary for the performance of Christian baptism – and possibly for the initiatory Jewish proselyte baptism as well. This kind of water was probably considered the best and most effective kind of water and was supposed to have the indispensable potential to ceremonially purify gentiles."

of a rain-pond before the rain-stream has stopped. ... More excellent is a pool of water containing forty seahs ... More excellent is a well whose own water is little in quantity and which is increased by a greater part of drawn water ... More excellent are smitten waters which render clean such time as they are flowing water. More excellent than they are living waters ..." (translation Danby).

Many more examples could be added – the *Didache* thus leads us into the world of a group of "Jewish" followers of Jesus who opened themselves for the inclusion of "pagans".[46] For this group aspects of proper behaviour according to an interpretation of the Torah influenced by early "Jewish" debates (in which, of course, the Matthean Jesus *halakha* played a decisive role) were still of greatest impact. If this text, as sometimes is assumed, was written in or near Antioch, that is, Ignatius' "diocese" (if we want to use this anachronistic term), it shows us again how different forms of "Christianity" were able to co-exist in the same place.

---

[46] The question regarding the degree to which the *Didache*-group saw itself part of the synagogue has been a matter of dispute. See for example J.A. Draper, Do the Didache and Matthew Reflect an 'Irrevocable Parting of the Ways' with Judaism? in: *Matthew and the Didache: Two Documents from the Same Jewish-Christian Milieu?* (ed. by H. van de Sandt; Assen – Minneapolis: Van Gorcum – Fortress, 2005) 217–42, and H. van de Sandt, Was the Didache Community a Group within Judaism? An Assessment on the Basis of Its Eucharistic Prayers, in: *A Holy People: Jewish and Christian Perspectives on Religious Communal Identity* (ed. by M. Poorthuis & J. Schwartz; Jewish and Christian Perspectives 12; Leiden – Boston: Brill, 2006) 85–108 who sees the growing number of gentiles in the *Didache* community as a reason that the community, at least in the last stage of the development of the *Didache*, had become a group separated from Judaism.

3. Matters of Purity:
The *Protevangelium of James*

As we have already seen, matters of purification seemingly played a role for the form of water baptism practised in
the *Didache* community; matters of purification, however, played a significant role in other communities as well.
In particular, I would like to examine the special field of
questions of sexual purity. Again, I would like to concentrate on one quite prominent example: an infancy Gospel
which today is usually called the *Protevangelium of
James*.[47] While we would expect that "marginal" writings

---

[47] Regarding matters of purity in the *Didache* mentioned above
see B. REPSCHINSKI, Purity in Matthew, James, and the Didache,
in: *Matthew, James, and the Didache. Three Related Documents in
Their Jewish and Christian Settings* (ed. by H. van de Sandt & J.
Zangenberg; SBL.SS 45; Atlanta: Scholars, 2008) 379–95, esp. 392–
4. – Another example could be Polycarp's *Letter to the Philippians*.
In this writing, the term ἁγνεία ("[sexual] purity") plays a surprisingly important role – we find it in *Phil.* 4.2; 5.3, while later parts of
the text which are not preserved in Greek offer the Latin synonym
castitas (12.3; see also 11.1 [*castus*]). Is this already a sign of a debate
concerning questions of Torah observance, as sometimes has been
stated? The relevant passages are too short to say much more – and
we should be careful not to find what we would like to find every-
where where we look for it. For more information see E. Leigh GIB-
SON, The Jews and Christians in the *Martyrdom of Polycarp*, in:
*The Ways That Never Parted: Jews and Christians in Late Antiqui-
ty and the Early Middle Ages* (ed. by A. H. Becker & A. Yoshiko
Reed; Minneapolis: Fortress, 2007) 145–58, esp. 157, and, more detailed, H. MAIER, Purity and Danger in Polycarp's Epistle to the
Philippians: The Sin of Valens in Social Perspective, *JECS* 1 (1993)
229–47. – For an introduction to this text see B. DEHANDSCHUT-
TER, Der Polykarpbrief, in: *Die Apostolischen Väter: Eine Einlei-*

going back to so-called "Jewish Christians"[48] might deal
with matters like sexual purity, there is at least one very
prominent example in the *Protevangelium of James*. This
text was transmitted under various titles [49] – perhaps the
original one being *Birth of Mary*. To further complicate
the discussion, the provenance of the text cannot be established with certainty, yet Syria seems to be a good
choice. Nevertheless, the extant text consists of three
main parts: the *Apocryphon of James* (= Birth of Mary,
chapters 1–17); *Apocryphon of Joseph* (chapters 18–21);
and *Apocryphon of Zacharias* (chapters 22–24). While the
text has been passed down as one book, its parts, the first
two of which probably date to the end of the second century CE, while the third part is later, were probably originally independent. The three parts seem to have been
connected before the turn of the third to the fourth century CE.[50] Even as a non-canonical text, the *Protevangelium* (and even more: parts of its imagery) became
highly popular in many ancient "Christian" circles. Today we know of around 150 manuscripts, partly witnessing ancient translations into languages like Syriac, Geor-

---

tung (ed. by W. Pratscher; UTB 3272; Göttingen: Vandenhoeck &
Ruprecht, 2009) 130–46.

[48] The term is, of course problematic. I will deal with it more
extensively a bit later.

[49] See the overview by S. PELLEGRINI, Das Protevangelium des
Jakobus, in: *Antike christliche Apokryphen in deutscher Überset-
zung I: Evangelien und Verwandtes* (ed. by C. Markschies & J.
Schröter; Tübingen: Mohr, 2012) 903–29, esp. 906. The title *Prote-
vangelium of James* goes back to the 16th century Jesuit author
Guillaume Postel who published a Latin translation of the text (see
PELLEGRINI, Protevangelium, 909–10).

[50] I follow closely S. PELLEGRINI, Protevangelium, 907–9.

gian, Latin, Armenian, Slavonic, Arabian, Coptic and even other languages.[51] In addition, later apocryphal infancy Gospels like the late ancient /early medieval *Gospel of Ps-Matthew* (7th century CE?) heavily use texts, ideas and images from the *Protevangelium*.

Interestingly, the text shows clear signs of interest in matters of both ritual and menstrual purity in its description of the childhood of Mary, the writings' protagonist.[52] Many of the actions of her mother Anna toward her show that Anna is extremely concerned with preserving Mary's ritual purity, and this is the reason she goes beyond what is required by Torah. For example, after Mary's birth Anna immediately cleans herself from the childbed flow of blood. Then she begins breast-feeding her daughter only after the days of post-birth impurity are complete (*ProtJas* 5 [2]; see Lev 12.5). In addition, Mary is not only provided with a typical sleeping room, but a "sanctuary" (ἁγίασμα), into which she does not allow anything "profane (κοινός) nor impure (ἀκάθαρτος)" to enter (*ProtJas* 6 [1]).[53] All this has to do with the idea

---

[51] Cf. S. Pellegrini, Protevangelium, 910.

[52] In the following argument I follow closely L. Vuong, "Let us Bring Her up to the Temple of the Lord." Exploring the Boundaries of Jewish and Christian Relations through the Presentation of Mary in the Protevangelium of James, in: *Infancy Gospels. Stories and Identities* (ed. by C. Clivaz, A. Dettwiler, L- Devillers & E. Norelli; WUNT 281; Tübingen: Mohr, 2011) 418–32, esp. 426–31 and eadem, *Gender and Purity in the Protevangelium of James* (WUNT II.358; Tübingen: Mohr, 2013).

[53] L. Vuong, Let Us Bring Her, 427 writes: "As a way to prevent al things profane/common ... or impure/unclean ... from making contact wither daughter (which include Mary's eating habits), Anna insures that the ritual impurities of everyday life – which, by

that Mary who, according to *ProtJas* 4 (1) has been promised by an angel, had to be dedicated as a (sacrificial) gift
(δῶρον) to God (see *ProtJas* 4 [1] and 7 [1]). Mary, however, has to leave the Temple at the age of Twelve because a
new stage in her life-cycle has begun where she is passing
over from late childhood to early womanhood, a stage
which is otherwise attested in the Mishnah (see *m.Nid-
dah* 5.4, 7–8).[54] According to Lily Vuong, the priests' decision to send Mary away from the Temple should not be
interpreted as a sign of their bad character, instead "the
Temple priests act appropriately" – the text wants to rein-
force "their legitimacy in the narrative and their power
vis-à-vis the other characters"[55].

In how far can motifs in a narrative, like we find them
in the *Protevangelium of James*, tell us something what
was of impact for real ancient circles of Christ-followers?
It is quite clear that questions like the ones asked above
did not play the same role for all the many pious readers
of the *Protevangelium* in late antiquity. The *Protevangelium*, however, does not stand alone: some of the most
interesting parallels to the examples mentioned above can
be found in the late third century Syrian *Didascalia Ap-
ostolorum*. While the *Didascalia* utters polemics against
"Jewish" practices of menstrual separation, it witnesses

definition, are unavoidable and acceptable for all others – are thus
averted for Mary."

[54] The different stages of Mary's life (0–3 // 3–12 // 12 onwards)
described in *ProtJas* show, as T. HORNER, Jewish Aspects of the
Protevangelium of James, *JECS* 12 (2004) 313–35, esp. 320–5, and
L. VUONG, Let Us bring Her, 429, clearly to the stages used in the
Mishnah.

[55] L. VUONG, Let Us bring Her, 430.

that some women in the community still insisted on these practices[56] – at least in some groups of even third-century Syria things like menstrual purity mattered.

4. "Jewish-Christian" Texts, Groups and Ideas

If we solely read authors like some of the "proto-ortho-dox" writers like Ignatius, apologists like Justin, Athena-goras or Aristides or "heretics" like Marcion and his fol-lowers, we get the impression of a deep cut between "Jew-ish" and "Christian" readings of Scripture. As we have already seen, this has not been the case with every group of ancient Christ-followers. The *Didache*-group men-tioned above was not the only example of a community of followers of Christ for whom burning questions of lead-ing a proper life were connected to interpretation of (at least aspects of) the Torah. In other words: when we talk about the relation of "Jews" and "Christians" according to second-century "Christian" sources we cannot ignore the remains of the so-called "Jewish-Christian" litera-ture. It should, however, already be quite clear that if the categories "Jewish" and "Christian" must be seen as at-tempts to construct realities rather than mirrors of reali-ty, terms like "Jewish Christian" or "Christian Jewish" must be highly problematic.[57] F. Stanley Jones, one of the

---

[56] For more details see A. Vööbus, *Celibacy: A Requirement to Baptism in the Early Syrian Church* (Papers of the Estonian Theo-logical Studies in Exile 1; Stockholm: Estonian Theologies in Exile, 1951) 223 also quoted by L. Vuong, *Gender.*

[57] See, for example the contributions of A. Gregory, Hindrance

most prolific experts on "Jewish Christianities" puts the problem in the following way:[58]

---

or Help: Does the Modern Category of 'Jewish-Christian Gospel' Distort our Understanding of Texts to which it Refers?', *JSNT* (2006) 387–413, and D. FRANKFURTER, Beyond 'Jewish Christianity': Continuing Religious Sub-Cultures of the Second and Third Centuries and their Documents, in: *The Ways That Never Parted: Jews and Christians in Late Antiquity and the Early Middle Ages* (ed. by A.H. Becker & A. Yoshiko Reed; Minneapolis: Fortress, 2007) 131–43.

[58] F. Stanley JONES, Jewish Christians, in his: *Pseudoclementina Elchesaiticaque inter Judaeochristiana: Collected Studies* (Orientalia Lovaniensia Analecta 203; Leuven et al: Peeters, 2012) 453–5, esp. 453. But see also the critical thoughts by D. BOYARIN, 'Rethinking Jewish Christianity: An Argument for Dismantling a Dubious Category (to which is Appended a Correction of my Border Lines)', *Jewish Quarterly Review* 99 (2009) 7–36. – For another, very helpful approach see P. LUOMANEN, *Recovering Jewish-Christian Sects and Gospels* (VigChr.S 110; Leiden – Boston: Brill, 2012) 11–2, who tries to develop profiles of different so-called Jewish-Christian groups. He thus does not use a fixed definition of the term, but develops a series of questions. The answers to these questions now can help to describe different patterns of ideas, thoughts, and behaviours in different groups. Luomanen's questions are: "1. Are characteristically Jewish practices such as (Jewish) circumcision, the Sabbath and purity laws observed? ...

2. Are characteristically Jewish ideas such as Yahweh as the only God, the temple as Yahweh's abode, or the Torah, maintained?

3. What is the pedigree of the group/person? Jewish or not? ...

4. What is the role of Jesus in worship and ideology of the community? Is Jesus considered as a Jewish prophet or is he more a divine being, worshipped as Kyrios ('Lord'), an equal to God? ...

5. Is baptism in the name of Jesus (or the triune God) an entrance rite to the community? ...

6. To what extent are these or other issues important for inter- or intra-group relations? What roles do they play in defining the borders or identity of the group in question?"

"Jewish Christians were the original core of a reform movement within Judaism that later emerged as a separate religion known as Christianity. Owing to the dynamics and changes within this process, scholarship has struggled to find a historically acceptable definition of Jewish Christianity. At one extreme, some have focused on all sorts of early Christian thought expressed in forms borrowed from Judaism (J. Daniélou). At the other extreme, some have preferred to use 'Jewish Christians' only for the movement's radical wing that refused to accept Gentile Christians (H. J. Schoeps). The following definition allows room for diversity and development:

'Earliest Jewish Christianity' is equivalent to the body of Jews who soon confessed Jesus as a venerable person or as the messiah and thus to all of earliest Christianity. Earliest Christianity contained various undeveloped points of view on the precise nature of Christianity.

'Early Jewish Christianity' stands for *one* development out of earliest Christianity. Its characteristics are: (1) confession of Christ, (2) Jewish observance (when relevant, to a degree that separated it from the evolving Great Church, particularly one or more of the following elements: [a] observance of the Sabbath, [b] observance of the Jewish calendar, [c] observance of the commands regarding sexual purity, [d] observance of circumcision, and [e] attendance at a synagogue), and (3) some sort of direct genetic relationship to earliest Jewish Christianity."

The question of identifying the ideas of Jones' second category, that is "early Jewish-Christian" groups, however, is made difficult through the fact that most of their writings are lost or only extant in fragments. In addition to this, most of these fragments are transmitted in quotations of "proto-orthodox" Christians who at least sometimes seem to have confused different groups and their sources.

4.1 Agrapha: Luke 6.5D

For a long time, the so-called "Agrapha" (or "words of the Lord" found outside the Gospels) belonged to the most neglected ancient Christian sources. This is surely due to the fact that they have only been examined as possible sources for the "historical" Jesus – with mainly negative results.[59] Only in recent decades it has become clear that many of them are of highest interest regarding the transmission of Jesus material and at least some of them witness later developments of "Christian" communities.[60] In an important article, William L. Petersen has shown that at least a few examples of these texts are also of impact for our question.[61]

---

[59] See, for example, O. Hofius, Versprengte Herrenworte, in: *Neutestamentliche Apokryphen I: Evangelien* (ed. by W. Schneemelcher; Tübingen: Mohr, ⁶1990) 76–9 who, finally lists only seven "agrapha", and only regards three as possibly authentic. Unfortunately, the situation remains more or less unchanged in the new edition. See O. Hofius, Außerkanonische Herrenworte, in: *Antike christliche Apokryphen in deutscher Übersetzung I: Evangelien und Verwandtes* (ed. by C. Markschies & J. Schröter; Tübingen: Mohr, 2012) 184–9.

[60] See T. Nicklas, Zur Problematik der so genannten "Agrapha" – eine Thesenreihe, *RB* 113 (2006) 78–93, or E. Norelli, Une collection de paroles de Jésus non comprises dans les évangiles canoniques, *Apocrypha* 17 (2006) 223–44, and E. Norelli, Gesù in frammenti. Test apocrifi di tipo evangelico conservati in modo frammentario, in: *Un altro Gesù? I vangeli apocrifi, il Gesù storico e il cristianesimo delle origini* (Trapani, 2009) 39–88. – At the same time an important collection of sayings has been put together by M. Pesce, *Le parole dimenticate di Gesù* (Scrittori greci e latini; Roma: Arnaldo Mondadori, 2004).

[61] W. L. Petersen, Constructing the Matrix of Judaic Christianity from Texts, in: *Patristic and Text-Critical Studies. The Col-*

One of the most interesting examples can be found in a short scene preserved only in the fifth-century Codex Bezae Cantabrigiensis. In this manuscript's version of the Gospel of Luke we find the following little scene after Luke 6.4 and instead of 6.5:

"On the same day, seeing someone working on the Sabbath, he [= Jesus; TN] said to him: 'Man, if indeed you know what you are doing, you are blessed; but if you do not know, you are cursed and a transgressor of the Law" (translation Petersen).

We cannot be absolutely sure when and in what context this little scene developed; in its present context in Codex Bezae it is part of a series of Lukan stories concerned with proper observation of the Sabbath.[62] In any case, the text seems to be concerned with correct behaviour according to the Torah, which is obviously understood as the basis of decisions on how to behave properly. The key to its interpretation must certainly be seen in the relation between its two "if-then" clauses: does the text mean that someone who knows what he is doing is allowed to break the Sabbath commandment of the Torah?[63] Or does it

---

lected Essays of William L. Petersen (New Testament Tools, Studies and Documents 40; Leiden – Boston, Brill, 2012) 362–79.

[62] For a discussion of the text in its present context see T. NICK-LAS, Das Agraphon vom 'Sabbatarbeiter' und sein Kontext: Lk. 6:1–11 in der Textform des Codex Bezae Cantabrigiensis, *NovT* 44 (2002) 160–75.

[63] As far as I understand W. L. PETERSEN, Matrix, 372 understands the logion in this way. He writes: "The Bezae logion consists of two finely balanced 'if – then' clauses: the first clause offers the option of breaking the Law, *provided* that you 'know what you are going'; otherwise, says the second clause, you are a 'transgressor of the Law.' The logion is not mindlessly 'pro-'nomian; the situation is

mean that if someone knows an appropriate reason why he does not follow the Sabbath commandment, he is blessed while the commandment *per se* remains valid? I would prefer the second interpretation even if one cannot be absolutely certain. In any case, the logion attests a background where matters of Sabbath observance were treated with a certain freedom but still mattered in a way which made it necessary to create a Jesus logion[64] around one's practice.

4.2 Hegesippus' Portrait of James the Just

While many of them rejected Paul and his mission, one of the "key" figures for many ancient "Jewish" believers in Christ was James the Brother of the Lord. Even until today the (probably) pseudepigraphical Epistle of James is often read as a canonical counter-balance or even corrective voice to some aspects of the *Pauline Corpus* (or at least misunderstandings that could be evoked from it).[65] Interestingly, interest in James (often called James the

---

much more complex than that. This suggests several possibilities: that Judaic Christianity itself made more subtle discrimination within the Law – regarding some parts of it as obsolete or corrupt, and other parts as still binding – than modern scholarship generally recognizes; that Judaic Christianity was not monolithic, but was divided ... into various sects, each of which had its own attitude towards the Law, with some groups perhaps being stricter, and others less so."

[64] I do not think that we have to do it with a logion going back to the historical Jesus.

[65] For a broader discussion of this matter (and other proposals for the possible relation) see D.C. ALLISON, Jr., Jas 2:14–26: Polemic for Paul, Apology for James, in: *Ancient Perspectives on Paul* (ed.

Just) grew in various second-century circles. For instance, while the original "Jewish-Christian" *Ascents of James* is lost, it can be partially reconstructed as one of the sources for the *Pseudo-Clementine Recognitions* (1.27–72). James is also the alleged author of the *Birth of Mary*, today better known as the *Protevangelium of James* (see above), and the hero of several Gnostic writings such as the *1ˢᵗ* and *2ⁿᵈ Apocalypses of James* or the *Letter of James* discovered in the famous library of Nag Hammadi.[66] On of the most interesting witnesses for our purpose is a fragment of the author Hegesippus' *Hypomnemata* (middle of the second-century).[67] The text as a whole is lost today, but a few fragments are preserved in Eusebius' *Ecclesastical History* (plus some other authors). While a few ancient Christian writings like the Epistle to the Hebrews (and in a certain sense, probably the Book of Revelation) present Christ as an ideal and eternal High Priest,[68] Hegesippus, probably writing in Syria, is interested in describing Jesus' brother James as the true High Priest. Although many details of Hegesippus' account are certainly not based on historical facts, it shows that al-

---

by T. Nicklas, A. Merkt & J. Verheyden; NTOA 102; Göttingen: Vandenhoeck & Ruprecht, 2013) 123–49.

[66] A second copy of the *First Apocalypse of James* is now also extant as the second writing of Codex Tchacos (CT 2) containing the *Gospel of Judas*.

[67] Regarding introductory issues see M. Durst, Hegesipp, in: *LACL* (1988) 278.

[68] While this is clear for Hebrews it is a matter of discussion for Revelation. See, however, F. Tóth, *Der himmlische Kult: Wirklichkeitskonstruktion und Sinnbildung in der Johannesoffenbarung* (Arbeiten zur Bibel und ihrer Geschichte 22; Leipzig: Evangelische Verlagsanstalt, 2006) 179–88.

most a century after the destruction of the Second Temple in some circles of Christ-believers matters of priestly *halakha* still played a role.[69]

The following passage is decisive:

"James the Lord's brother received the succession with the apostles in the church. He was called the Just by everyone from the Lord's times up to our own, since many were called James. But he was holy from his mother's womb; he did not drink wine or fermented drink, nor did he eat anything in which was life. No razor passed over his head, he never anointed himself with oil, and he did not use the bath. It was lawful for him alone to enter into the Holy of Holies, for he did not wear wool but linen. He entered the temple alone, and was found kneeling on his knees and seeking forgiveness for the people, so that his knees grew hard as a camel's … Because of the greatness of his righteousness he was called Just and Oblias[70] …, as the prophets foretold of him" (Hegesippus, in Eusebius, *h.e.* 2.23.6, translation Grant).

---

[69] Interestingly, another, certainly less clear witness of such an interest is the *Protevangelium of James* (already mentioned). For a discussion of the role of priestly matters in this text see L. VUONG, Let Us Bring Her, 424–6.

[70] The exact meaning of this name is still unclear. See the discussion in R. BAUCKHAM, James and the Jerusalem Church, in his: *The Book of Acts in Its First Century Setting IV: The Book of Acts in Its Palestinian Setting* (Grand Rapids – Carlisle: Eerdmans, 1995) 415–80, esp. 448–50; J. PAINTER, *Just James: The Brother of Jesus in History and Tradition* (Columbia, SC: University of South Carolina Presds, 1997) 127, and W. PRATSCHER, Der Herrenbruder Jakobus bei Hegesipp, in: *The Images of Judaeo-Christians in Ancient Jewish and Christian Literature* (ed. by P. J. Tomson & D. Lambers-Petry; WUNT 158; Tübingen: Mohr, 2003) 147–61, esp. 156–7.

A closer look into this description reveals that Hegesippus' James shows a whole series of characteristics which find their parallels in the Torah:[71]

"He never anointed himself with oil" (see Exod 29.7; Lev 8.12; Exod 30.30)
"He did not use the bath" (see Exod 29.4; Lev 8.6; 16.4b,24a)
"It was lawful for him to enter into the Holy of Holies" (Lev 16.17a)
"He did not wear wool but linen" (Lev 16.4a)
"He entered the Temple alone" (Lev 16.17a)
"He was found kneeling on his knees
and seeking forgiveness for the people" (Lev 16.17b,24b,30)
"so that his knees grew hard as a camel's
because he was always kneeling on them, worshipping God"
"and asking forgiveness for the people" (Lev 16.17b,24b,30)

Hegesippus thus depicts James as the only legitimate priest at the Jerusalem Temple of his time. In addition, the fact that James is described as the only person allowed to enter into the Holy of Holies (instead of the actual High Priest) means that James is even seen as fulfilling the role of a high priest. His priesthood, however, is not fulfilled in preparing and doing sacrifices, but in intense prayer, a prayer which concentrates on "seeking forgiveness for the

---

[71] See the overview of E. ZUCKSCHWERDT, Das Nasiräat des Herrenbruders Jakobus nach Hegesipp (Eusebius, h.e. II 23,5–6), *ZNW* 68 (1977) 276–87, esp. 281 who concludes (282): "Im Blick auf diese beiden, ursprünglich selbständigen Reihen … kann es … kaum zweifelhaft sein, daß hier der lebenslange Naziräer, nach dem vorliegenden Textzusammenhang Jakobus, in ursprünglich zwei »idealen Szenen« als Hoherpriester, auch wenn er als solcher nicht ausdrücklich bezeichnet wird, beim Vollzug seines »Amtes« dargestellt ist." For a thorough discussion see also W. PRATSCHER, Herrenbruder, 148–50.

people". In this way, James takes over a decisive role of the High Priest who via the liturgy of the Yom Kippur, the Day of Atonement, accomplished God's forgiveness for the people's sins.[72] According to the text, this special role is possible because of James' life as a Nazorean[73] who was "holy from his mother's womb" (see Judges 13.7 and 16.7 [LXX B]; cf. Luke 1.35), "did not drink wine or fermented drink" (Judges 13.4,7,14; 1 Sam 1.11 [LXX],15; cf. Luke 1.15), "nor did eat anything which was in life" (Judges 13.14a) while "no razor passed over his head" (Judges 13.5; 16.17; 1 Sam 1.11; translations Grant). Even decades after the end of Temple sacrifices, James is thus depicted as a combination of paradigmatic of Nazorean and high-priestly piety – a piety concentrated on intense prayer (perhaps developed via Isa 56.7 and Matt 21.13) and an extraordinary form of purity while not forgetting

---

[72] Regarding the theology and liturgy of the Day of Atonement see B. Janowski, *Das Geschenk der Versöhnung: Leviticus 16 als Schlussstein der priesterlichen Kulttheologie*; I. Kalimi, *The Day of Atonement in the Late Second Temple Period: Saducees' High Priests, Pharisees' Norms, and Qumranites' Calendars*, and G. Stemberger, *Yom Kippur in Mishnah Yoma*, all in: *The Day of Atonement: Its Interpretations in Early Jewish and Christian Traditions* (ed. by T. Hieke & T. Nicklas; TBN 15; Leiden – Boston: Brill, 2012) 3–32, 75–96 and 121–138. See also D. Stökl Ben Ezra, *The Impact of Yom Kippur on Early Christianity. The Day of Atonement from Second Temple Judaism to the Fifth Century* (WUNT 163; Tübingen: Mohr, 2003).

[73] For a discussion of this very motif, see E. Zuckschwerdt, *Nasiräat*; regarding the special intertexts used see esp. 277. – See also W. Pratscher, *Herrenbruder*, 150, who, in addition, accentuates the vegetarian aspect of this description.

traditions about a correct priestly (but not high-priestly) vesture.

4.3 The Ebionites

The term "Ebionites", that is, "the poor", is a self-designation for a group mentioned by "proto-orthodox" heresiologists like Irenaeus of Lyons, Origen, Eusebius, Jerome and Epiphanius of Salamis.[74] In addition to this, Epiphanius preserves some fragments from an otherwise lost *Gospel of the Ebionites* which was, as far as we can see today, a kind of harmony of synoptic Gospel accounts with a few redactional changes fitting to Ebionite life style and Christology. While it was likely written around the middle of the second century CE, the exact date of this Gospel is difficult to determine. Its place of origin was probably in the trans-Jordanian regions where, according to authors like Eusebius, *h.e.* 1.7.14; *onomast.* 14.15 and Jerome, *nom.hebr.*, most Ebionite communities were living. Although our few extant sources, all of them fragmentary and going back to non-Ebionites, do not allow us to draw a complete picture of Ebionite life and belief, the information provided by Irenaeus of Lyons, already shows some highly interesting features. Irenaeus writes (*haer.* 1.26.2):

---

[74] On the early history of the Ebionite movement see R. BAUCKHAM, The Origin of the Ebionites, in: *The Image of the Judaeo-Christians in Ancient Jewish and Christian Literature* (ed. by P.J. Tomson & D. Lambers-Petry; WUNT 158; Tübingen: Mohr, 2003) 162–81.

"Those who are called Ebionites, then, agree that the world was made by God; but their opinions with regard to the Lord are [not] similar to those of Cerinthus and Carpocrates. They use the Gospel according to Matthew only and repudiate the apostle Paul, saying that he was an apostate from the Law. As to the prophetical writings, they do their best to expound them diligently; they practise circumcision, persevere in the customs which are according to the Law and practice a Jewish way of life, even adoring Jerusalem as if it were the house of God" (Klijn/Reinink, 104f.).

A little bit later, Hippolytus of Rome gives a comparable piece of information (*haer.* 7.34.2; see also 10.22.1); he adds, however, an important piece helping to understand Ebionite Christology and soteriology somewhat better:

"[The Ebionites] live conformable to Jewish customs saying that they are justified according to the Law, and saying that Jesus was justified by practicing the law. Therefore it was that he was named both the Anointed of God and Jesus, since not one of the (rest) kept the Law. For if any had practiced the commandments of the Law he would have been the Anointed. And they themselves also, having done the same, are able to become Anointed Ones; for they say that he himself was a man like all" (Klijn/Reinink, 112f.).

If we put together the evidence given by these two texts, we can already see a few lines of interest to us. While the question of the relation between Ebionite thinking and the ideas of the above mentioned Cerinthus and Carpocrates[75] is not of major importance for our ques-

---

[75] Regarding Cerinthus see M. MYLLYKOSKI, Cerinthus, in: *A Companion to Second-Century Christian 'Heretics'* (ed. by A. Marjanen & P. Luomanen; VigChr.S 76; Leiden – Boston: Brill, 2005) 213–46; regarding Carpocrates see C. MARKSCHIES, Carpocrates, in: *LACL* (1998) 119.

tion, it is highly interesting that the Ebionites used the Gospel of Matthew which describes a Jesus (1) who in his Sermon on the Mount addresses the "poor in Spirit" (Matt 5.3) – perhaps a reason for Ebionite self-understanding –, (2) proclaims fulfilment of the Law and prophets (Matt 5.17), while also (3) not allowing for the changing of even a single Letter of the Tora (Matt 5.18). Irenaeus does not address to what degree the Ebionites used the special "Jesus Halakha" developed in the Sermon on the Mount, but he makes clear that observance of the Torah was of crucial importance for them. The motif of "adoring" Jerusalem seems to show that even matters of oral Torah played an important role. Hippolytus' witness perhaps can help us to add another interesting detail. In the Ebionite system of thinking, Christology and observance of the Torah were seen as deeply bound together. Obviously the crucial point in Ebionite Christology must have been that Jesus practiced the commandments of the Law in an ideal, complete way, and only this made him "the Anointed One". He thus was seen as a kind of an example for Ebionite ways of life. An example that had to be followed and could even be reached in one's own life.

This image fits well into what we know from the few remaining fragments of the *Gospel of the Ebionites*, which is, as far as we can see today, a slightly revised version of the canonical Gospel of Matthew. These fragments also witness to the fact that the Torah played a highly important role for the Ebionites who obviously developed a very peculiar, even rigid *halakha*. According to fragment 3, quoted by Epiphanius, *haer.* 30.14.4–5, the *Gospel of the Ebionites* offered a parallel Matt 3.4–6 describing John the Baptist and his way of life. Interestingly, the Ebionites replaced the information that John the Baptist ate wild locusts with the idea that he lived on honey cakes. In addition to this, according to fragment 7 (Epiphanius, *haer.* 30.22.4) even Jesus refuses to have meat at the celebration of the Passover. This evidence makes it very probable that the Ebionites, for whom Jesus was an example of an ideal life according to the Torah, practised vegetarianism. The reason for this seems to be clear: the Ebionites, who lived in a somewhat pagan environment, abstained from eating meat to avoid any possible contamination by impure food.[76]

4.4 The Elchesaites

One of the most mysterious groups going back to the second century CE are the followers of a certain Elchasai (or: according to several sources, Elxai), called Elchesait-

---

[76] J. Frey, Die Fragmente des Ebionäerevangeliums, in: *Antike christliche Apokryphen in deutscher Übersetzung 1: Evangelien und Verwandtes 1* (ed. by C. Markschies & J. Schröter; Tübingen: Mohr, 2012) 607–20, esp. 615–6, writes: "Die bei der Nahrung des Täufers erfolgte Ersetzung der Heuschrecken durch Kuchen (Frg. 3) und – noch mehr – die Jesus in den Mund gelegte Zurückweisung des Fleischgenusses beim letzten Passahmahl (Frg. 7) lassen auf eine rigide halachische Praxis schließen, die auf Fleischgenuß generell verzichtete, um so auch eine versehentliche Befleckung durch unreine, nicht korrekt geschächtete oder gar durch heidnische Kulthandlungen kontaminierte Nahrung zu vermeiden. In dem völligen Fleischverzicht spiegelt sich wohl das Bestreben, in einer nichtjüdisch geprägten Umwelt nach jüdischen Ordnungen zu leben."

es.[77] All our information concerning this group is going back to a few passages in the works of authors like Origen (according to Eusebius, *h.e.* 6.38), Hippolytus of Rome (*ref.* 9.13–17; 10.29), the much later Epiphanius of Salamis (*haer.* 19 & 30) or the *Cologne Mani Codex*.[78] According to the few fragments we have, Hippolytus received his information about a book authored by Elchasai via a certain Alcibiades, one of Elchasai's disciples.

While the few extant fragments of the *Book of Elchasai* do not allow for a reconstruction of the whole text (or even its main contents) and while it is still a matter of dispute whether the *Book of Elchasai* may have been some kind of an Apocalypse (putting together Elchasai's special revelations) or a very ancient community order of the Elkesaites, sometimes called *Sobiai*, i.e., the "Baptised Ones", at least a few traces of the community's ideas survive until today. According to Hippolytus, *ref.* 9.13.1–3, Elchasai came from the regions of Parthia. Epiphanius, in *haer.* 19.2.10–12 (see also 53.1) speaks about the regions in the East of the Jordan. Elchasai himself claimed to have received his book via a revelation by two gigantic angels, one of them being the Son of God, and the other being the

---

[77] For an overview of the state of research see, for example, S. C. MIMOUNI, Les elkasaïtes: états des questions et des recherches, in: *The Image of the Judaeo-Christians in Ancient Jewish and Christian Literature* (ed. by P. J. Tomson & D. Lambers-Petry; WUNT 158; Tübingen: Mohr, 2003) 209–29.

[78] For a presentation and discussion of the extant sources see G. P. LUTTIKHUIZEN, *The Revelation of Elchasai: Investigations into the Evidence for a Mesopotamian Jewish Apocalypse of the Second Century and its Reception of Judeo-Christian Propagandists* (TSAJ 8; Tübingen: Mohr, 1985).

Holy Spirit (see also Epiphanius, *haer.* 30.17.7; Eusebius, *h.e.* 6.38, quoting Origen). This revelation, according to Hippolytus, *ref.* 9.13.3–4, took place in the third year of the Emperor Trajan (98–117 CE). The fact that the book expects an eschatological war three years after Trajan's war against the Parthians (114–116 CE) means that it must have been finished around this time (Hippolytus, *ref.* 9.16.4). While the followers of Elchasai concentrated primarily in Palestinian and Syrian regions, the group also had some influence in Rome around 220 CE when the above mentioned Alcibiades from Apameia brought the book to Rome (Hippolytus, *ref.* 9.13.1–2). Even if we do not know how big and influential the groups of Elchasai's followers were, his teachings had an enormous influence on Mani, the founder of the later world religion of the Manichaeans, who until the age of 24 was a member of an Elkesaite community.

When we look into what remains from Elchasai's teaching we learn again how problematic our usual categories of "Christian", "Jewish" and "pagan" are: Elchasai's followers obviously believed not only in the God of Israel, but in Christ and the Holy Spirit who they understood as gigantic angels (Hippolytus, *ref.* 9.13.2–3; Epiphanius, *haer.* 19.4.1–2; 30.17.5–7). According to the Elchesaites, Christ transmigrated "in many bodies and now in Jesus. Similarly he has come into existence from God, at another time he has become a spirit, at one time from a virgin, and at another time not. And thereafter this one continually transmigrates in bodies and is made known in many at various points in time" (Hippolytus, *ref.* 10.29.2; translation F. Stanley Jones, 375; see also Epiphanius, *haer.* 30.3.3–5). In addition to this, they expected the end of the world to be coming soon and believed in the forgiveness of sins through a second baptism under invocation of seven elements (Hippolytus, *ref.* 9.15.1–6; Eusebius, *h.e.* 6.38 quoting Origen). They were obviously interested in matters of sexual purity (Epiphanius, *haer.* 30.2.3–5), but, at the same time, preferred marriage over virginity and sexual continence (Epiphanius, *haer.* 19.1.7).

They directed their prayers to Jerusalem, but (perhaps feeling to be in a line with the biblical prophets) Elchasai criticized priestly cult and sacrifices "as never at all having been offered to God by the fathers and the law and yet there he says it is necessary to pray toward Jerusalem, where there was the altar and the sacrifices" (Epiphanius, *haer.* 19.3.6; translation F. Stanley Jones, 376). Elchasai's argument is interesting: on the one hand he refers to the fathers and the law which seems to be important for him and his followers, on the other hand he, however, rejects the fire of the sacrifices because of his idea "that water is proper and fire is foreign" (Epiphanius, *haer.* 19.3.7). In addition to this, we know that Elchasai used the Hebrew Bible in his teachings on the question of whether or not worship of idols must be understood as a sin in every possible situation (and obviously early Jewish traditions; see Epiphanius, *haer.* 19.1.8; 19.2.1). And finally, the Elkesaites practised circumcision and observed the Sabbath, partly, however, because of astrological reasons (Hippolytus, *ref.* 9.16.2–4). The "mix" – if we want to call it a "mix" – of different religious elements important for the Elkasaites can perhaps be seen in the following fragment from Hippolytus, *ref.* 9.16.2–4:

"There are wicked stars of impiety. This has now been said to us, pious ones and disciples. Be on guard against the authorities of the days of their rule; do not undertake the commencement of works in their days; and do not baptize man or woman in the days of their authority, whensoever the moon passes out of them and conjoins with them. (3) Guard the day itself until it goes out away from them, and then baptize and engage in every commencement of your works. Now honor furthermore the day of the Sabbath, for it is one of those days. (4) But guard against commencing also on the third day of the week, for when three years of the Emperor Trajan are again completed – from the time when he subjected some of the (areas) of the Parthian's authority – when three years have been completed, the war will flame up between the angels of impiety of the north. All the kingdoms of impiety will be disturbed because of this" (translation F. Stanley Jones, 373–4).

In any case: even if the few remains of Elkesaite teachings make (at least) us (from our perspective) feel that this group developed a highly strange *halakha* and used (obviously) pagan ideas about astrology plus theories about the elements of the world to interpret the Law, the Torah seemed to have played a highly important role in this group's life. The questions whether we should call them "Christian" or "Jewish" and how far we should estimate the impact of so-called "pagan" ideas, however, still remain. We do not even know whether we are dealing with a group that was marginal from its very beginnings or one which, at least in some of the Eastern parts of the Roman Empire, played a certain role. It is, however, clear that their relation to "Judaism" and its Scriptures must be seen as very different from what we have learned from the so-called "proto-orthodox" writers.

Of course, the image developed above regarding "Jewish" followers of Christ is not complete. One should consider the testimonies in the discussions on matters of purity in the apocryphal *Acts of Thomas* (plus later Eastern writers like Aphraates the Persian Sage), the *Testaments of the Twelve Patriarchs* which developed an ethics centering on the combination of the commands to love God and your neighbour, or the *Ascension of Isaiah*, an apocalypse at the turn of the first to second centuries CE (see chapters 2 and 3) which was probably written by a community of Christ followers that understood themselves as "righteous", were grouped around a few prophets and tried to fulfil God's will in the end of times.[79] One could go on – but even if we add a few more examples – we still have to face the question of whether or not "Jewish Christianities" were only a marginal phenomenon among the communities of second- and third-century followers of Jesus Christ. If we look into the usual patristic sources, read the representatives of "proto-orthodoxy" and base our analysis only on their writings we must have the impression that all these groups must have been marginal from very early times. This was, at least in the post-Constantinian era (and in many cases surely before as well), probably the case. The fact, however, is that even later authors like Epiphanius of Salamis (315–403 CE) devoted many pages of his writings to marginal "Jewish Chris-

---

[79] For more details see M. HENNING – T. NICKLAS, Jewish, Christian – or What? Matters of Self-Designation in the *Ascension of Isaiah*, in: *The Ascension of Isaiah* (ed. by J.N. Bremmer & T. Nicklas, Studies on Early Christian Apocrypha; Leuven: Peeters, 2014).

tian" groups. Joseph Verheyden has recently offered a highly interesting argument. According to him, some "Jewish Christian" movements must have been quite small at the turn of the 4th to the 5th century, however the questions raised by their ways of life remained important. Verheyden writes:[80]

"[I]t is striking that he [Epiphanius; TN] still spends so many pages on refuting the Ebionites ... The reason may well be that he is fully aware of the importance of the issues that are addressed by the Ebionites and the likes. Yet in Epiphanius' opinion, their attempt at reconciling Christian faith with Jewish practice must necessarily fail. It is a failure not only because of the particularities and ambivalence of Ebionite teachings on Christ, but above all because it is simply made impossible through what Jesus did and said. Jesus did not come to abolish the Law, but to fulfil and transform it."

5. Conclusion

What does it mean to be a "pagan" believer in Christ in the first or second century CE? The answer seems quite simple: a person with a non-Jewish background who has come to belief that the crucified Jesus of Nazareth is the Anointed One, the Messiah of Israel. But what does this mean for everyday life? A pagan's conversion to "Christianity" did not automatically mean that he or she had to become "Jewish". This caused a myriad of practical ques-

---

[80] J. VERHEYDEN, Epiphanius on the Ebionites, in: *The Image of the Judaeo-Christians in Ancient Jewish and Christian Literature* (ed. by P.J. Tomson & D. Lambers-Petry; WUNT 158; Tübingen: Mohr, 2003) 182–208, esp. 205–6.

tions. How should the relation to the "world" (or other groups and realities in this world) be re-defined, when important "boundary-markers" of the Torah like circumcision, dietary laws, Sabbath observance, etc. were not followed any more? What would the ethical system of a community look like which thought that "works of the law" no longer had a decisive role in salvation? Already in the letters of Paul – perhaps most clearly in 1 Corinthians – we see how real questions regarding concrete behaviour as a group of pagan followers of Christ arose and created numerous problems.

As we have seen, the answers by different groups of Christ believers were of very different shape. While Paul himself (partly) defined Christian ethics around the idea of brotherly love which he understood as fulfilment of the Torah, others, like Ignatius, seem to have denied any possibility of using the Torah to answer questions regarding adequate behaviour. As we observed, however, aspects of *halakha* celebrated a come-back even in authors like *Barn.* who was obviously not able keep up his idea of an exclusively spiritual reading of the Scriptures. Consequently, that was the reason he integrated a "Two-Ways-Doctrine" into his Letter. Also, we found a similar case in parts of the *Didache* which were somewhat "Jewish", and we were able to explore how this genre of texts is very closely related to what we find, for example, in the Qumran "Rule of the Community".

Last, we have seen that for quite a long time groups typically called "Jewish Christians" must have existed. These groups saw themselves as part of Israel and, as far as we can still see today, developed forms of *halakha* partly different from what we read in later Rabbinic sources. Even if these groups became more and more marginalized, the questions they raised seem to have mattered to the degree that even a late author like Epiphanius, who collected all the possible dangerous errors and heresies among followers of Christ, could not totally neglect them.

Conclusion

Our journey through second-century "Christian" sources and ideas has led us into the highly diverse worlds of second-century "Christians". Even in contexts when the contours of "proto-orthodoxy" were becoming clearer we had to distinguish between the situations in different regions, cities, social, political and religious contexts and the thoughts of different groups. At the same time it would be an error to understand second-century Judaism as a single block of communities led by the emerging rabbinate.

If we, however, do not want to be lost in this diversity we have to look for common patterns of life-style and belief. I took several of them and tried to discuss them with a few examples – many more would have been possible. While we looked closer into images of the Chosen People, images of God, ideas of the Covenant and Scriptural hermeneutics, others fields could be added: the question of God's dwelling place, the organisation and understanding of liturgies, or questions of eschatological hope – just to mention a few. [1]

---

[1] Perhaps the most important point which could be added is the question of developing rituals and liturgies. See, for example, the questions raised by H. BUCHINGER, Jüdische Feste als Herausforderung christlicher Theologie und Liturgie: Eine Spurensuche

Even if we have to speak about a variety of Jewish groups (or even Judaism[s]) during the Second-Temple period (and surely afterwards as well) all these groups seem to have more or less shared the idea that there is one God who has chosen Israel as his people and given it His Covenant: The Torah as expression of God's will, God's dwelling among his People, celebrations of Israel's special relationship to God, questions of eschatological hope, etc., also belong to the different aspects that bind together different groups of Judaism. Different Jewish groups, however, defined and understood the relation between these (and other) aspects of "Judaism" in different ways – that is, they defined different patterns of living like a "Jew".

The first followers of Jesus – and many "Christians" of later generations – understood themselves as part of this "matrix" we call "Judaism". Jesus' life, his death, and the Easter experiences after his death which believers understood as showing that God raised him from the dead, however, had to be integrated into the already existing "pattern" or "matrix". While, as we have seen, for some groups of Christ-followers and in some situations the Christ event was obviously interpreted as an addition, which did not significantly change the system of lifestyles and beliefs, for others – like Paul and his followers – it became the new center and focus of the system that anything else was now re-interpreted in the light of the

---

in der Paschatheologie palästinischer Autoren, in: *Dialog oder Monolog? Zur liturgischen Beziehung zwischen Judentum und Christentum* (ed. by A. Gerhards & H.H. Henrix; QD 208; Freiburg: Herder, 2004) 184–207.

Christ-event. This re-interpretation had to be even more radical in contexts where the new movement opened itself to pagans.

In his Deichmann Lectures of 2004, Larry Hurtado asked the fascinating question: *How on Earth Did Jesus Become a God?*[2] The relation to God marks the inner center of Jewish (and Christian) life and belief – as soon, however, as at least some of his followers started to understand Jesus' relation to God in radically new ways, and they interpreted him as a "Divine Figure", as revealing God's very human face, as "Immanuel" – the God with Us –, their traditional pattern of thoughts had to be re-organized around this idea. In which cases are these re-organizations still within the limits of "Judaism" and when are they outside? In four chapters I have analysed four different aspects of the system and have seen that the re-organisations of the system took shape in very different manners: we have seen a whole spectrum of interpretations between extremes like some Jewish groups of Christ followers who changed only a few details and others like "Sethian Gnostics" or followers of Marcion who completely left the system.

But even if the picture we developed remains a fragment, a few additional conclusions seem to be allowed:

1. Where we speak about the relation of "Jewish" and "Christian" groups we should always be aware that the extant sources show us only a small section of realities of

---

[2] The 2004 Deichmann Lectures were published as L. W. HURTADO, *How on Earth Did Jesus Become a God? Historical Questions about Earliest Devotion to Jesus* (Grand Rapids: Eerdmans, 2005).

the past. This section is very often closely related to the *thinking* of upper class persons and only rarely to the *acts* and *lives* of lower class people. Only in rare cases – and sometimes through (dangerous) mirror-reading – we can catch glimpses of these aspects of ancient realities. This means that, even if we draw a complex picture, this will represent a very small part of the whole, in danger of over-emphasizing winners' perspectives and forgetting "common" people.

2. If, however, past realities were as complex as today's realities – and I think this is the case because all of us are human – our stories about the past should try to develop images of the past which are complex enough to at least understand better what we cannot grasp as a whole any more. To say this another way: we should not speak too quickly about borderlines between "Judaism" and "Christianity", but look closely where these borderlines were established, which concrete groups they divided (or wanted to divide), and for whom they worked in clearly defined situations.

3. Even more: even where we distinguish different groups of "Jews" and "Christians" and their group identities in different places and at different times, we have to be aware of the fact that individual members of a group could form their identity *in relation to* what a group ideally expected of them. If we come to see that real people in their real lives develop "an inner plurality of the individual" (Eric Rebillard)[3] and can act differently in differ-

---

[3] See his fascinating volume: E. REBILLARD, *Christians and their Many Identities in Late Antiquity, North Africa, 200–450 CE* (Ithaca, NY: Cornell University Press, 2012).

ent contexts and situations of their lives we start to understand the real difficulties of the problem. We have seen
a few glimpses in our description of Melito of Sardis who
could be on good terms with Jews when he wanted to get
to know more about the canon of the Hebrew Bible, but
also wrote a text like his *Peri Pascha*. We could add the
example of Clement of Alexandria whose texts were less
anti-Jewish than much of what we find in contemporary
writings, but who composed an anti-Jewish tractate for
the diocese of Jerusalem. Also, we could add the much
more well-known example of Simon Peter – Cephas –
who according to Galatians 2.11–12 ate with the pagan
members of the community when he was in Antioch of
Orontes, but ceased to do so when members of the group
around James the Just arrived.[4]

4. We have thus seen that the term "parting of the
ways" of "Jews" and "Christians" is in many ways mis-
leading. We should not simply speak about two uniform
and consistent groups of people who walked together
along the same path for a certain time and, from a certain
point in history, separated from each other. Even if it is
more dynamic I am also not so happy with the image of a
big tree with a long trunk and two main branches going

---

[4] Perhaps the fascinating example of the empress Poppaea Sabina
(30/32–65 CE) could be added who because of her intercession of
Jewish prisoners was called θεοσεβής (a proselyte? a sympathizer of
Judaism?) by Josephus (*Ant.* 20.195), but was well-known as a
femme fatale who did not abhor of any kind of cruelty. For a very
detailed discussion of her very complex religious "identity" see M.
WILLIAMS, θεοσεβὴς γὰρ ἦν – The Jewish Tendencies of Poppaea
Sabina, in her: *Jews in a Graeco-Roman Environment* (WUNT
312; Tübingen: Mohr, 2013) 81–94.

into different directions. Perhaps it is necessary to develop other ideas:

Quite recently, my colleague Andreas Merkt used the image of a party for group dances:[5] we see dancers being in continuous movement and finding new partners during different parts of the dance. If one looks at them from a certain distance, certain patterns emerge – certainly not everyone dances with everyone; some pairs remain together, some participants form groups among each other, even others stand more or less apart and avoid contact with others. Depending on one's perspective different patterns can be seen – if one is far away, the whole scene can, at least for moments, look like a complete chaos, and at other moments reveal a certain order. Perhaps our history of "Jewish-Christian" relations in antiquity can partly be compared to such an image – dancers of different groups attending a common complex celebration, having to share one room, trying to stay together, avoiding others (of not during the dance, perhaps at the bar), new groups coming and others going, some pairs falling in love and others hating each other.

Depending on his or her perspective a spectator of this dance can take different snapshots of different scenes of the dance – none of these scenes, however, can show the whole of the dance and its choreography, this can only be reconstructed in part by putting many of these snapshots

---

[5] He has used this image, however, for the description of another phenomenon – the phenomenon of the reception of New Testament passages by ancient Christian authors. See A. MERKT, Das Projekt Novum Testamentum Patristicum [unpublished paper at the 2013 conference on Intertextuality, Mainz Academy of Sciences].

together. If we speak about ancient history today, we have to reconstruct such a complex choreography – with but a few snapshots left, snapshots which often do not tell us exactly from which perspective they were taken, and snapshots which often focus on a few dancers who – at least when they were photographed – seemed most interesting.

As every image, the image of the dance, however, has its shortcomings as well: couldn't it be used of any aspect of (ancient) history? How can it show us the specifics of Jewish-Christian relations? How can it tell us that any kind of "Judaism" and "Christianity" belong together in a deeper sense than other religious movements?

That's why I would like to add another image – surely too peaceful, perhaps even naïve, and surely not dynamic enough.

Perhaps we could better use the image of a very robust bush without just one long trunk, but with a lot of bigger and smaller, stronger and weaker branches, who not only influence each others' growing in many ways, but partly blocking each other in their mutual way to catch as much as possible from the sun. Perhaps this bush is already very old, we see that parts of it suffered from fire, others from aridity, some have been cut out or died while other parts are green and growing. If we look at it from a certain distance we have the image that this bush is cut into two main parts, but as soon as we look closer we see that there are many more divisions, but there have always been veins connecting the different parts of this plant. Even, however, if some branches seem stronger than the others and even if some of them try to block the others in their way to the sun, all of them drink from the same source, and all of them want to reach the same light.

Ancient Authors and Sources

Modern Authors
(as mentioned in the main text)

Subjects